POLITICS, MONEY, AND PERSUASION

STUDIES IN CONTINENTAL THOUGHT

John Sallis, *editor*

Consulting Editors

Robert Bernasconi
John D. Caputo
David Carr
Edward S. Casey
David Farrell Krell
Lenore Langsdorf

James Risser
Dennis J. Schmidt
Calvin O. Schrag
Charles E. Scott
Daniela Vallega-Neu
David Wood

POLITICS, MONEY, AND PERSUASION

Democracy and Opinion in Plato's Republic

John Russon

INDIANA UNIVERSITY PRESS

This book is a publication of

Indiana University Press
Office of Scholarly Publishing
Herman B Wells Library 350
1320 East 10th Street
Bloomington, Indiana 47405 USA

iupress.org

© 2021 by John Russon

All rights reserved
No part of this book may be reproduced or utilized in any form or by any means, electronic or mechanical, including photocopying and recording, or by any information storage and retrieval system, without permission in writing from the publisher. The paper used in this publication meets the minimum requirements of the American National Standard for Information Sciences—Permanence of Paper for Printed Library Materials, ANSI Z39.48-1992.

Manufactured in the United States of America
First printing 2021

Cataloging information is available from the Library of Congress.
ISBN 978-0-253-05766-2 (hdbk.)
ISBN 978-0-253-05767-9 (pbk.)
ISBN 978-0-253-05769-3 (web PDF)

*This work is dedicated to John Sallis,
with my sincere thanks for
his friendship, his collegiality, and his teaching.*

According to the modern craze, especially in pedagogy, one is not so much to be instructed in the content of philosophy as to learn how to philosophize without any content. That amounts to saying that one is to travel endlessly without getting to know along the way any cities, rivers, countries, men, etc.

—1812 LETTER FROM HEGEL TO NIETHAMMER

Some are gold and silver in rank but their weapons are of iron or bronze; others are iron and bronze in rank but they use gold or silver in exchange

—SETH BENARDETE, *SOCRATES' SECOND SAILING*

CONTENTS

Acknowledgments xi

Note on Translations and Citations xiii

Introduction 1

    I. The Nature of Platonic Writing 3

    II. The Method of This Work 11

    III. The Argument 14

A. Politics, Money, and Persuasion

  1 The Problem of Abstraction 25

        I. The *Polis* and the Problem of the Guardians 27

        II. Expertise and Writing 37

        III. Money 44

        IV. *Technē*, Money, and the Commercial *Polis* 51

  2 The Currencies of Power 62

        I. Timocracy 63

        II. Oligarchy 70

        III. Democracy 79

B. The Vicissitudes of Opinion

   3 True Opinion   95

        I. Socrates and the New Intellectuals   96

        II. Knowledge and the "Divided Line"   103

        III. Sophistry   134

   4 Persuasion   145

        I. Persuasion   147

        II. Virtue   156

        III. Corruption   168

     Conclusion   189

Bibliography   193

Index of Subjects   203

Index of Passages   207

ACKNOWLEDGMENTS

For many years, I have benefited from having regular opportunities to discuss ancient Greek philosophy with a number of exceptionally gifted specialists, most notably Abraham Schoener, Bernard Freydberg, Ömer Aygün, Gregory Recco, Eric Sanday, Eve Rabinoff, Eli Diamond, Gregory Kirk, Patricia Fagan, James Crooks, Robert Metcalf, and Sean Kirkland. Each of these individuals brings together a rigorous commitment to the ancient texts and a very open and original interpretive perspective, and they all make ancient Greek philosophy a matter of pressing contemporary concern. Being able to think along with these people has been one of the most rewarding dimensions of my life, and I especially want to express my gratitude to them for the role they have played in allowing me to develop my own relationship with ancient Greek philosophy in general and with the *Republic* in particular (and to Patricia Fagan I owe special thanks for tutoring me in Homeric Greek). My work in this book is also deeply indebted to quite a number of other passionate and insightful interlocutors, most notably Kirsten Jacobson, Whitney Howell, Laura McMahon, Bruce Gilbert, Don Beith, Joe Arel, Nate Andersen, Pete Costello, David Ciavatta, Kym Maclaren, Jeff Morrisey, Susan Bredlau, Brian Rogers, Peter Simpson, Luis Jacob, and Shannon Hoff. These people have been a kind of family to me, and without them I doubt that I could have endured a career in academia. I also benefited immensely from the friendly guidance of Gregory Nagy, when I spent two years in the Department of the Classics at Harvard University as a postdoctoral fellow, and, before that, from the always insightful work of Francis Sparshott, Joseph Owens, and John Rist, who were my teachers during my doctoral studies at the University of Toronto. Finally, I am most especially grateful to John Sallis, with whom I worked at Penn State University for eight years, and who was always very generous with me in ways that had a tremendous impact on my personal and professional life and on my understanding of philosophy. I hope that these individuals at least will find value in this book I have written.

NOTE ON TRANSLATIONS AND CITATIONS

References to the *Republic* will be included in the text, identifying book and Stephanus pagination (e.g., I.343b); for quotations from the *Republic*, I have used Bloom's translation throughout. For other works of Plato, the Stephanus pagination will be preceded by the title of the work. For the *Laws*, I quote Pangle's translation; for the *Phaedo*, I quote the translation by Brann, Kalkavage, and Salem; and for the *Phaedrus*, I quote Scully's translation. Unless otherwise indicated, all other translations of Plato are from *Collected Works*.

For the works of Aristotle, I have used the translations in *The Complete Works of Aristotle*, except for the *Nicomachean Ethics*, for which I have used the translation by Bartlett and Collins.

POLITICS, MONEY, AND PERSUASION

INTRODUCTION

Like other great works, Plato's *Republic* can sustain and reward inquiry at many different levels and from many different angles. In the same way that Shakespeare's *Macbeth*, Paul's *Epistle to the Romans*, or Kant's *Critique of Pure Reason* can be read and reread, each time offering fresh inspiration—whether by giving new insights into old topics or by raising formerly unanticipated themes—the *Republic* is inexhaustible in its ability always to speak provocatively to whatever perspective one brings to it. Indeed, the *Republic* seems to grow as one's thinking matures. I began to read it for the first time in August 1981, and in the now forty years since then, it has been a work that I have regularly studied, consulted, taught, and, in general, thought about. Much like a good friend with whom one grows more and more intimate over time, the *Republic* has been a constant companion for me, shaping my perception of the world even as my deepening knowledge of the world allowed me ever more insight into the meaning and importance of this work of ancient writing.

The *Republic* is about justice, but this book that I have written cannot "do justice" to my developed history with the *Republic*, and it certainly cannot do justice to the richness and depth of the *Republic* as such. My book is not intended, therefore, as a comprehensive commentary on the *Republic* as a whole nor even as an exhaustive statement of my own sense of its meaning. It is, instead, a study in and about the *Republic*, in which I will ultimately focus on only a handful of prominent portions of the text. It is nonetheless intended to be rigorous and to be revelatory of the essential character and meaning of that work, while being only one of many possible studies. It is, effectively, an essay about the *Republic*: an essay in which I lay down what I have come to understand as the first coordinates, so to speak, for interpreting this work.

Plato's *Republic*, I believe, is about the distinctive nature of what it is to be a human being and, correspondingly, the distinctive nature of human society. More exactly, the *Republic*, I believe, addresses a kind of revolution in human history that emerged within the history of ancient Greece itself and that is decisive for all subsequent history. We are familiar with the world-transformative effects of the invention of the printing press or, in our own day, the internet; something similarly transformative happened in ancient Greece, and this, roughly, can be called the emergence of "politics," though the phenomenon is more varied than that simple word suggests. The emergence of politics in Greece is the emergence of the whole *world* of the *polis*—the "city-state"—a world that, along with introducing the world to the possibility of popular government—"democracy"—also brought about a revolution in virtually every aspect of social, artistic, economic, and personal life.

It has often been noticed that the classical Greek world underwent a major political change through the emergence of the "new men," the sophists and other intellectuals of the fifth century BC, and it is not new to construe Plato's writing in general, and the *Republic* in particular, as responding to this phenomenon.[1] This emergence is itself (rightly) tied to the more general issue of the emergence of literate society—a society of writing, rather than an oral society.[2] In fact, the history of ancient Greece in the few centuries before Plato was a time of vast change on many fronts, including the emergence of the world's first money-economy. Leslie Kurke describes this basic phenomenon well:

> The archaic period in Greece is one of great upheaval, for it sees, in addition to the rise of the polis, the development of tyrannies, the invention of coinage and the beginnings of a money economy, the crisis of the aristocracy, the slow spread of literacy, and the trend toward Panhellenism.[3]

In other writings contemporaneous with the world of Socrates and Plato, these changes are commonly construed as a loss of "the old ways," and it has been common to interpret the *Republic* and its discussion of a putatively ideal state as a gesture of resistance to these changes. My own interpretation of the *Republic* fits with this general recognition that the Athens of the century before Plato witnessed such a loss of traditional values and witnessed the birth of a new kind of *anomie* rooted in the liberation of the intellect from traditional religious ties, and that the perspective of the Platonic texts is defined by its critical engagement with this new order. In general, though, my interpretation of the *Republic* is at odds with traditional interpretations of it.

The presumption that Plato's writings are a conservative rejoinder to these new political and intellectual developments and that the *Republic* offers a blueprint for an (absurd) ideal state is long-standing.[4] In general, as I shall discuss in a moment, I think these conclusions are themselves rooted in a methodologically untenable approach to the interpretation of the amazingly rich and complex Platonic texts. On the specific theme of the political orientation of the *Republic*, moreover, I will argue that this standard interpretation could hardly be more wrong.[5] Instead of this interpretation, I will argue that the *Republic* analyzes the very roots of human political behavior, showing why the political transformations within ancient Greece were "probable or necessary," as Aristotle says in his description of tragic plots, and why they have laid bare the political reality with which it is precisely and always incumbent upon us to grapple.[6] Before addressing this theme, though, the nature of the Platonic texts in their own right needs to be considered.

I. The Nature of Platonic Writing

Plato's writings, which we generally classify as "philosophical" writings, are in fact a unique genre. Indeed, to classify them as "philosophical" is somewhat misleading, for there is good reason for identifying these works as effectively inventing what we call "philosophy."[7] Of course, one can recognize Parmenides's poem, Heraclitus's aphorisms, or the sage advice of Hesiod's narrator as works one might similarly class as "philosophical," but with all of these texts (in the case of Parmenides and Heraclitus) or traditions (in the case of Hesiod), it is only by comparison with "purer" examples of philosophy that we generally recognize these as colorful cases of philosophizing from which other, extraneous (for example, poetical) material has first to be removed.[8] Perhaps Thucydides offers us something closer to "pure" philosophy in the argumentative speeches that he presents in his *History* by the various statesmen or generals who propose strategies and give commentaries upon political and military events of the Peloponnesian War, but even here the work itself seems primarily dedicated to another purpose (namely, historical writing for the purpose of present political analysis and decision-making), and not to be philosophy as such for its own sake.[9] It is really with Plato's writings that we are first consistently and deliberately presented with the philosophical discourses of a philosopher (Socrates, typically, but also Parmenides, Protagoras, and others), discourses, that is, in which the practice we now typically call "philosophy" is taken up on its own terms and, indeed, called "philosophy." Further, in Plato's writings all the major themes of metaphysics, epistemology, ethics, political philosophy, aesthetics, and more are introduced, developed, and analyzed, such that, in this first introduction to philosophy as such, we are also offered something like a comprehensive presentation of philosophy as a whole: the discourse of philosophy is, as it were, both opened and closed, begun and completed, in the same gesture that is the Platonic *oeuvre*. If this is so, though, there is something fundamentally odd in classing the Platonic texts *within* the genre we call "philosophy," for, as the inaugural site of this very reality, this body of work cannot just be treated as an *instance of* it: later texts may well be "like" Plato's, but Plato's texts in their originality, that is, precisely, in their *inability in principle* to appeal to an already existent norm in order to define themselves, are not "like" the texts that follow them. Later texts may imitate and copy Plato's, but Plato's texts are not imitating and copying anything in those later works.[10]

And, in fact, these Platonic texts—these founding or "instituting" texts of the discourse of philosophy itself—turn out not to be so "pure" either, judged by the standard of "philosophy" to which they gave rise and by which we classify them. For these texts, too, like those of Parmenides or Hesiod, continue to be "contaminated," as it were, by what can appear to us as the uneliminated "residue" of other modes of discourse: these Platonic works, though obviously philosophical properly speaking, are also clearly "literary," employing a dialogic form notably similar to the form of tragic and comic dramatic poetry as their main medium for presentation of philosophical ideas, and, beyond this, they contain many clearly "poetic" elements, such as the so-called myths (i.e., colorful tales invented by Plato and put in the mouths of his characters, not myths properly speaking in the sense of the traditional, religious tales that a culture hands down to itself).[11] In this way, Plato's writings, from the perspective of the tradition of "philosophy" that they inaugurated, can appear to be "not yet" fully purified from their poetic past.[12] In fact, however, I believe the situation is quite the opposite of this. To explain why I reject this familiar opposition of philosophy and poetry—an opposition that is largely inaugurated by the Platonic texts themselves—I must first raise another familiar opposition (which will continue to occupy us throughout the book): the opposition between philosophy and sophistry—another opposition inaugurated in and by those texts.[13]

Though Plato's writings themselves are highly nuanced and, indeed, sympathetic in their treatment of the ancient Greek figures called "sophists," we, like the Greeks themselves, tend to treat this name as having a simply negative connotation.[14] Unlike a true philosopher, whose work is characterized by integrity and insight, a sophist, we imagine, is wrapped up in "making the weaker argument the stronger," that is, dishonestly relying upon the power of abstract argumentation or deceitful rhetoric, and obscuring rather than illuminating the real issues that define our human situation; proper philosophy, we imagine, should communicate with a pure conceptuality, devoid of rhetoric—an argumentation that has no "interest" beyond the abstract articulation of truth on its own terms.[15] The "purification" of philosophy with which we are rightly concerned—the demand that philosophy be rigorous and sincere, and that it answer to the demands of reality itself rather than pursuing some relative, self-interested agenda—and the distinguishing of this from dishonest imposters—from "sophistry" and "rhetoric"—is indeed a central concern of the Platonic dialogues.[16] But my contention, unlike our familiar sense that our academic institutions offer this purified practice in contrast to the still-contaminated works of Plato, is that it is Plato's text that offers us the antidote to the problematic practice of academic philosophy. In his early work *Against the Academics*, Augustine accused the professional philosophy of his day—the philosophy of "the Academy"—precisely of engaging in sophistry, and I similarly believe that the contemporary institution that we typically call "philosophy"—precisely the "purified" philosophy to which I have been referring—is guilty of this same charge. In contrast, I believe it is the Platonic texts that offer the "purest" philosophy, and, in so doing, they precisely show us the problem of the practice we more commonly call "philosophy."

The Platonic texts show us that the abstract "rationality" that "philosophy" construes to be primitive and autonomous is in fact derivative and dependent on a more basic kind of rationality: a *concrete* rationality that, like poetry, cannot be detached from its unique and specific conditions of expression and that, like sophistry, cannot be detached from the project of persuading particular individuals—cannot be divorced from rhetoric. As a consequence, it is also a rationality that we cannot simply analyze in an attitude of detached observation, but one instead that commands our *participation*.[17] This concrete rationality that does not easily allow the clear distinction of philosophy and sophistry or of philosophy and poetry is captured in the ancient Greek word *logos*, and this is the notion around which my study in this book revolves.

The ancient Greek word *logos* is properly translated, in different contexts, by a variety of different English words: "ratio," "speech," "reason," "expression," "rationality," and more. While each of these terms is appropriate in context, though, each captures only a facet of the meaning of the Greek term and does not by itself express the other dimensions of meaning that always hover in the background of any particular use of the Greek term.

While there is no single English term that exactly "translates" this Greek word, our English term "account" does come fairly close to mirroring its significance, both in the sense that it has a general richness of meaning analogous to that of *logos* and in the more specific senses in which "account" can also mean "speech," "reason," "rationality," and so on. Though *logos* can often mean the impersonal and objective reality of the inner "rationality" of some thing in the world, of a mathematical fraction, or of a written speech, *logos* also can also mean the subjective *ability of* speaking and reason: it can mean, in other words, the ability to "take account" of something or to "give an account" of something. It is this sense of *logos* that is specially central to my study.[18]

There are, of course, very many rich and vibrant themes explored throughout the Platonic dialogues. At the center of all these themes, though, is the relentless exploration of the distinctive ontological character of the human being, the being about which Aristotle, crystallizing the insights of Plato and the tradition of Greek thinking that provides the context for Plato's writing, famously says it is "the only animal having *logos*."[19] This notion that we are the animal having *logos* in the sense of the ability to "take account" and "give an account" of things is, I believe, the general interpretive framework for the study of the human being throughout the Platonic dialogues. It is also the specific theme of the speech given by the character Protagoras in Plato's dialogue *Protagoras* (*Protagoras* 320d–322d) in the form of a colorful story [*muthos*] (*Protagoras* 320c) rather than as a conceptual argument [*logos*] (*Protagoras* 324d).

According to Protagoras's story, which is his *mimēsis* or "interpretive retelling" of the myth of Prometheus, the natural world in general is characterized by the phenomenon of "fit"—that is, the different organisms we encounter have capacities suited to their needs and suited to their environments, and these different organisms in relationship to each other work out a kind of reciprocal balance (*Protagoras* 320d–321b). Human beings, however, though born into the natural world, are strikingly lacking in the resources with which other organisms are endowed: "While the other animals were well provided with everything, the human race was naked, unshod, unbedded, and unarmed" (*Protagoras* 321c). Humans, however, "have a share of the divine dispensation [*theias metesche moiras*]" (*Protagoras* 322a), which is the "wisdom in the practical arts together with fire [*tēn entechnon sophian sun puri*] (without which this kind of wisdom is effectively useless)" (*Protagoras* 321d). This wisdom is what allows this otherwise weak natural organism to survive (*Protagoras* 321d), and it is the source of our "articulating speech and words [*phōnēn kai onomata*] and [inventing] houses, clothes, shoes, and blankets, and [being] nourished by food from the earth" (*Protagoras* 322a–b). And beyond this practical wisdom, we have a further divine gift, "a sense of justice and shame [*dikēn kai aidō*]" (*Protagoras* 322c), which is responsible for our living together in society: it is the source of "order within cities and bonds of friendship to unite [humans]" (*Protagoras* 322c).[20] On this interpretation, what is distinctive of our nature as humans is the capacity we have (a) to make sense of our world and develop the arts by which we transform it into an environment in which we can live, and (b) to see this world in light of the good. These capacities, which put us apart from the rest of the natural world, are precisely what make it possible for us to engage effectively with that natural world. This "divine" power in which we participate is, broadly, the power of *logos*.

This *logos*—our ability to "give an account" of things—simultaneously puts us deeper into the world and holds us apart from it: the very power we have to comprehend the rich concreteness of our world also invites us to dwell in abstraction. It is this problematic temptation toward abstraction that has, I believe, characterized much of the tradition of "philosophy" that has developed from the Platonic inauguration, and this problem of abstraction is similarly at the heart of many other developments of our contemporary culture. It is the profound ambivalence of this *logos*-character, an ambivalence made powerfully manifest in the original historical developments of the Athenian city-state that provide the setting of the Platonic dialogues, that is the guiding theme of this book.

Like the other Platonic dialogues, the *Republic* portrays a unique conversational event, and it is a unique piece of writing. The dialogue begins with the word *katebēn*—"I went down"—thus beginning a narration by one character (whom we subsequently learn to be Socrates) and an unnamed conversational companion or companions.[21] The initial narration is very specific with respect to time and place: the narration, which is a recounting of a conversation Socrates had the day before, takes place the day after the celebration of a religious festival in the port associated with Athens (the Piraeus).[22] The details of the event and the details of the various interlocutors that are revealed through the subsequent narration should in principle allow one to date the conversation rather precisely, though our own lack of knowledge about various details of Athenian history leaves some of this uncertain. The main conversation is with the two brothers of Plato, Glaucon and Adeimantus, and it takes place in the home of the immigrant shield manufacturer Cephalus and his sons. Because of what we do know about the biographies of these various historical figures (and especially about the dates of their births and deaths), and because of what information we do have about the introduction into Athens of the goddess "Bendis" (who seems, according to I.354a, to be the subject of the festival), it seems most likely that the dramatic date of the *Republic* is around 421 BC.[23] Assuming that to be so (though in my analysis here nothing significant will depend upon this dating), we can note a few distinctive features of this unique conversational event: the central character (the narrator), "Socrates," would be roughly fifty years old; Glaucon and Adeimantus, the brothers of Plato with whom Socrates carries out most of the narrated conversation, would be in their early twenties (while Plato himself would be less than ten years old); and Athens itself would be enjoying the so-called Peace of Nikias, roughly ten years into an ongoing conflict with Sparta often designated "the Peloponnesian War." The opening of Socrates's narration is particularly rich with details of the setting: he and Glaucon were returning from the Piraeus, where they had witnessed the first celebration of a specific festival, when they were stopped on behalf of Polemarchus, who "saw them from a distance as they were setting off home," by a slave who "caught hold of [Socrates'] cloak from behind." Regardless of how one interprets these details, what they put on display is the intensely specific character that characterizes any of our experiences.[24]

The unique conversational event narrated in the *Republic* is a (complex) communication between Socrates and his (unknown) interlocutor(s). This communication in turn has as its primary material the portrayal of other conversations—the ones that took place between Socrates and Cephalus, between Socrates and Polemarchus, between Socrates and Thrasymachus, between Polemarchus and Cleitophon, between Socrates and Glaucon, and so on—that make up the "story" of the *Republic*. Those portrayed conversations are not abstract ideas, but are unique interpersonal events whose meaning cannot be understood apart from understanding what is happening between the interlocutors; in other words, the things said are gestures expressed from one person to another, and they must be understood as such.[25] To understand the conversational event that is the *Republic*, one must ask, for example, what Socrates is communicating to his unnamed interlocutor by telling him how Cephalus was dressed or how Polemarchus behaved.[26] To understand those portrayed conversations themselves, one must ask, for example, what the conversational impact is of Adeimantus's frequent interrupting of Socrates, or what the conversational impact is of Thrasymachus's apparent aggression and irritability: the things said by Socrates are not timeless expressions of timeless ideas, but are ways of responding to someone who is angry, in the latter case, or to someone preoccupied with his own concerns, in the former. Similarly, one must remember that it is "the *Republic*" that one is interpreting; that is, the question is, "What does *this* document mean?" This document, to be sure, *contains a discussion of* a particular form of state, but it is by no means a simple *advocacy* of that state (even if one or more of the *characters* might so advocate).[27] In Book III of the *Republic*, Socrates identifies tragedy and comedy—the new and distinct poetic forms that emerged in Athens in tandem with the emergence of democracy—as art forms that, in producing an "imitation" or "re-enactment" [*mimēsis*] of the speech of characters, are able to persuade us of the presence of realities that are not actually present while simultaneously effacing their own reality as artworks (III.394b–398b; cf. VIII.586a–d).[28] The "man who is able by wisdom" to thus "imitate" surely alludes as much to Plato himself as it does to the tragic poets who are explicitly identified (III.394d, 398a–b), and should thus remind us it is important that we resist our temptation simply to "believe in" the *mimēsis* offered by the *Republic*.[29] And, in any case, this state under discussion in the *Republic* is by no means a single, clear reality; on the contrary, over the course of the conversation this "state" is discussed in various different, even contradictory, forms, and it is precisely incumbent upon the reader to *think through* these various developments and complexities.[30] Again, while Socrates does at various points express his own view on matters under discussion, in large part the portrayal of this "state," and the discussion in general, takes its form from the contributions of the other interlocutors, and it is consequently a major task of interpretation to discern *through* this conversation what Socrates's views are. Far from being the dogmatic expression of a conservative reaction to the transformations in classical Athenian society, the *Republic* is the portrayal of a conversation about that topic (and many others) carried out by various members of that society, and its interpretation requires the subtle attention and insight that is needed to make sense of any extremely complex conversation. And, like the conversation of Socrates reported in the *Republic*, the *Republic* as a singular literary work is not an abstract idea, but is itself a unique communication inaugurated by Plato—it is Plato's written portrayal (presumably for unknown readers, though one can never know his intended audience) of Socrates's conversation about Socrates's conversation about *politeia*—and one must ask what is communicated by Plato's choosing to portray this conversation in this way.³¹

As was made clear in Protagoras's *muthos*, we are beings with *logos*: the "ability to take account" or "rationality." What the *Republic* puts on display from the start is that the characteristic form in which we experience that rationality is in *dialogue—dialegesthai*.³² Our rationality is our collaborative ability to make sense of our situations. We do make sense of our situations, such that the meaning of our exchanges can be lifted from our initial exchanges and subsequently shared with others—as Socrates is doing, for example, in reporting to someone else the conversations he had the night before. Nonetheless, however, those meanings have their roots in specific, concrete contexts, and it is their responsiveness to this concreteness that is the essential sense of that meaning.³³

The *Republic* is Plato's report on one part of a conversation that Socrates had with an unknown interlocutor. A thorough reading of the *Republic* as a whole would have to follow that conversation *as a conversation* in order to grasp what the *Republic* is saying. This conversational contribution by Socrates is itself the report on another complex conversation, and understanding that conversation (the one reported in the *Republic*) similarly would require following that conversation *as a conversation* in order thereby to grasp the meaning of the separate components of that conversation.³⁴ This book will not undertake to carry out that task; indeed, I will not even come close to addressing all these interpretive issues in their complexity. Partially, this is because that task is huge, but more importantly it is because this task has, in my judgment, already been carried out very well by others. In particular, Eva Brann and John Sallis have, I believe, compellingly interpreted the basic "drama" of this conversation that Socrates reports in the *Republic*. Brann, in "The Music of the *Republic*," argues that the conversation in the *Republic* is really Socrates's effort to bring about an existential transformation in his young interlocutor Glaucon, a drama that is portrayed through imagery that depicts Socrates as travelling through Hades;³⁵ Sallis in his study of the *Republic* in *Being and Logos*, develops further this analysis of the imagery of Socrates's journey through Hades, deploying it as a key to interpreting quite precisely the experiential weight of Socrates's metaphysical and epistemological discussion of the *eidē* ("forms," "species," or "looks") in Books V and VI. While one could no doubt improve on details of these interpretations or develop aspects of them further, these studies have, I believe, convincingly established what the basic form of the *Republic* is, and they should provide the starting point for any future study. My interpretation does not in fact depend on these interpretations, though it is, I think, highly compatible with them. Instead, my work will selectively focus on a prominent theme introduced within the conversation reported in the *Republic* and will work through the text only insofar as it contributes to working out the issues involved in that theme. In other words, though the comprehensive interpretation of the *Republic* must be oriented to making sense of it as a conversation, my reading does not have this intention and thus will not follow that method. Nonetheless, this selective reading, in order to be a rigorous engagement with the *Republic*, must still be contextualized by the methodological recognition that the text requires to be interpreted *as* a conversation; consequently, this recognition always provides the larger frame of my analysis, even though my focus will be on something a bit different.

II. The Method of This Work

Mine is a philosophical work, not a work of literary commentary, and its main method, therefore, is simply thinking (the meaning of which will itself be a significant theme of this work). Plato's text, in other words, will be read as an invitation to grasp intelligently the realities that we all confront in our everyday living. Plato's text offers profound—indeed, incomparable—resources for such grasping, but they cannot be accessed simply through passively following along with the unfolding conversation: these resources are accessed if and only if one takes what is said as a provocation to think for oneself and thus to engage critically with the conversation as it unfolds. Precisely because the text presents a conversation and not a treatise, there are no grounds for presuming that any of the interlocutors speaks in a philosophically satisfactory way; one cannot assume, that is, either that Socrates's interlocutors have done a good job of responding to his questions, for example, or, for that matter, that Socrates himself has a satisfactory perspective on the matter under discussion. Plato has portrayed a philosophical conversation, and one's task as a reader is to become, as it were, a further interlocutor to the conversation.[36] In other words, this work, as a work of philosophy, requires us to think through the issues raised and judge the quality of the conversation based on this analysis. In fact, as many readers have demonstrated, when one approaches this (or any) Platonic text in this way, the text rewards these efforts, and offers rich resources for further thinking that are themselves evident only to one who is actively engaged in thinking rigorously about the issues raised. Consequently, my method in this book will be to take seriously various claims made in the text and to do the work of *thinking them through*, which equally means to think *through* them; it amounts, that is, to turning to the realities of our everyday experience to assess the soundness of the interpretive claims that are advanced while simultaneously using those claims to illuminate the realities of our everyday experience. What I believe this analysis shows is that, if one follows this procedure rigorously, some of Socrates's most striking claims in the dialogue prove to be profoundly insightful assessments of our human reality: of the nature of the city, of the nature of knowledge, and of the nature of human psychology. Demonstrating this to be true is the central purpose of this book.

In the course of the attempt here to *think through* the *Republic*, there will also frequently be occasion to reflect on dialogues other than the *Republic*, as the conversation in the *Republic* addresses themes that are powerfully addressed in those other dialogues. Now, just as the *Republic* is a conversation and not a treatise, so, too, do the other dialogues portray unique conversational events. Consequently, there is no simple way to excerpt a portion of one of those other conversations as if "Plato says here" this or that. The interpretation of any portion of another dialogue requires just as much attention to the dynamics of the conversational event in which it is embedded as does the interpretation of the *Republic*. That said, however, it of course makes sense that things said in one conversation are pertinent to things said in another conversation, all the more so when both of the conversations in question involve (putatively) the same figure, Socrates, albeit at perhaps dramatically different stages in his life (in texts written, too, at dramatically different stages in the life of the author, Plato).[37] Consequently, it makes sense that, in the course of thinking through the conversation in the *Republic*, one might think, "This is like the time when Socrates said . . . ," just as one might think that about the history of one's own conversations while talking with someone about something on some occasion.[38] It is thus possible to cite, within a study of the *Republic*, the analyses—the thinkings-through—of different issues as those occur in other dialogues; but such citation is not a simple matter of reporting a simple statement of doctrine, but is a reminiscence of another conversation in which the things said bear within them the complex conversational baggage of that other event and must be interpreted accordingly. My writing, correspondingly, will draw upon my forty years of reading Plato roughly as if I were drawing on many years of living with Socrates as a conversational partner. I will at many points have reason to draw upon things said in dialogues other than the *Republic*—most notably in the *Protagoras*, the *Gorgias*, the *Apology*, the *Laws*, the *Phaedo*, the *Phaedrus*, the *Symposium*, and the *Charmides*—each of which will provide essential supplementary material for my study of the themes raised in the *Republic*. Such quotations will always have the problem that they carry within themselves a frame of reference that cannot be properly clarified without elaborate interpretation of those dialogues that is beyond the scope that is fitting to this work; consequently, such quotations will always be like promissory notes for fuller interpretations that must be presumed but cannot be adequately defended within this work. But even though an exhaustive justification of these texts cannot be offered within the scope of this work, my interpretation of these works, like my interpretation of the *Republic* as a whole, will, I hope, be made sufficiently compelling precisely by demonstrating the light that my use of these texts sheds on *ta pragmata*, on the matters of our familiar world.[39] And, indeed, I believe that the strength of this book in general will be revealed to the reader in the new light that it sheds on subsequent readings of the *Republic* itself.

What follows is an attempt to extract some of the most central insights of the *Republic*, accomplished by thinking along with the points made in conversation in a way that stays simultaneously focused on these thoughts and on the worldly affairs to which these philosophical thoughts pertain. In that sense, it is an attempt to think with, or think through, the *Republic*, as much as it is an attempt to think about it. My reading of the *Republic* therefore primarily takes the form of a philosophical engagement with *ta pragmata*: with the actual states of affairs that define our world. For that reason, my work (especially in chap. 2) draws as much upon historians, literary critics, and other great philosophers (especially Aristotle) as it does on other academic interpreters of Plato. Indeed, it is an unfortunate circumstance that, in the study of classical Greek texts, there has developed a significant division between those who study the Greek philosophers and those who study the rest of classical antiquity, whereas the interpretation of Plato's texts, to my mind, requires competence in both of these domains. A notable attempt to bridge this divide is Patricia Fagan's *Plato and Tradition*, a work that is exemplary for its attempt to bring the broader study of ancient Greek culture to bear on a reading of Plato's texts that is simultaneously alive to their philosophical richness and subtlety, and a work that, like Brann's "Music of the *Republic*" and Sallis's *Being and Logos*, should be, I believe, standard reading for anyone involved in the serious study of Plato. My own work cannot claim anything like Fagan's fluency with classical antiquity, but what I have endeavored to do is to rely on the results of the best contemporary work in the interpretation of ancient Greek literature and history to provide the essential context for understanding both the meaning of Socrates's conversation with Glaucon and Adeimantus and the nature of Plato's text.

My interpretation of the *Republic* is particularly indebted to the works of a variety of classical scholars, themselves influenced by the insights of nineteenth- and twentieth-century European philosophers that have been filtered through the writings of contemporary anthropologists and literary critics. These classical scholars have focused on the political significance of the different genres of ancient Greek literature, especially in their relation to the emergence of the *polis* in archaic Greece. More exactly still, it is their study of the emergence of a money-economy in archaic Greece and its relationship to the cultural conflict between an elite, aristocratic ideology and a collective ideology of the *polis* that has provided the central context for my interpretation of the basic "sense" of the *Republic*. My study of the *Republic* interprets this work as a subtle text that is powerfully attuned to precisely these political and cultural issues and then, within that context, uses what I believe are the best insights of contemporary philosophy as a guide to understanding the epistemological and psychological insights of Plato's text. In short, I believe that Plato's text is both a profound commentary on ancient Greek history and culture and a highly relevant contribution to the contemporary philosophical study of the nature of knowledge and action. I thus construe the present work not as an antiquarian study in the "history of ideas," but as a contribution to contemporary discussions of political economy, cognition, and psychology.

III. The Argument

The fundamental focus of my argument, and what I believe to be the organizing theme of the *Republic*, is the ambivalence of *logos*; more specifically, my thesis is that the central power that defines our *logos*-capacity—namely, what I generally call our ability to abstract, to "draw away" from something what, in that thing, exists only in immanent integration with the whole—is simultaneously what is most distinctly enabling and most distinctly disabling in our experience. Consequently, our "nature" as beings with *logos* is that we are fated, so to speak, to grapple with this ambivalence in all the concrete forms that it takes; it is this demand, constitutive of the human condition, that defines the distinctive nature of wisdom and hence the project of philosophy. After initially defining and demonstrating this problem, this book traces out the implications of this problem as they are worked out through the central analyses of the *Republic*, producing thereby an overall picture of the reality of politics and philosophy and their place in human life. More precisely, the two chapters of part A, "Politics, Money, and Persuasion," investigate the parameters of our distinctively human environment, demonstrating how and why our ability to take account—our *logos*—is of decisive importance in shaping that environment; the two chapters of part B, "The Vicissitudes of Opinion," which are the major studies in the book, then investigate in some detail, first, how we can bring our account-taking into a healthy state and, second, how we can, instead, corrupt that ability.

Chapter 1, "The Problem of Abstraction," draws on aspects of the conversation in Books I and II of the *Republic* to identify the distinctive environment of human life: this is the world of politics, science, writing, and money, themselves all distinctive phenomena of *logos*, of the ability to "take account." Each of these four realities is simultaneously natural and artificial, arising from an irremovable human need but requiring free human action to bring it into being. Each also is a reality that, precisely because it is not merely natural, requires human intelligence for its appropriate, healthy employment. Yet each in fact invites misappropriation such that, rather than fulfilling an essential human need, it becomes an essential structure for crippling human flourishing. We find ourselves in a world structured by these realities and we take them for granted without understanding them, and it is the failure to understand this, our own distinctively human environment, that precisely encourages the corruptive functioning of those realities. Understanding these realities is what makes possible their healthy employment, and it is that task to which, I maintain, the *Republic* is devoted; my remaining three chapters work out how this is so.

Chapter 2, "The Currencies of Power," uses Socrates's central argument of Book VIII of the *Republic* to investigate how the *polis* with its money-economy comes into being. I argue here that Socrates's analysis of the "decline of states" accurately and insightfully grasps the changing character of Greek—and specifically Athenian—history from the Homeric world through post-Periclean democracy in Athens. The analysis focuses on the changing ways in which these different forms of society recognize the founding role of *logos* within political life. Specifically, the analysis argues that political life has an intrinsic trajectory toward the development of democracy, because this is the form of political life that explicitly recognizes the ineffaceable role of *logos* in politics, and it investigates how and why the development of a money-economy is intrinsic to this development. That democracy and money are integral to the human political environment, though, makes tyranny an ever-present threat in human life. Thus, this is not a simple advocacy that democracy is the best regime (nor a simple renunciation of democracy); on the contrary, it is an argument that it is our "destiny," so to speak, to inhabit this inherently ambiguous political environment. Democracy is the ultimate form of human politics because it recognizes that our social self-interpretation is essential to our lives; democratic politics, therefore, is the form of our social self-organization that is most vulnerable to the weaknesses in our self-interpretations.

Our fate is determined by the quality of our ability to interpret and understand—to take account of—our situation, and chapter 3 investigates in detail what "taking account" properly involves. Turning primarily to the image of the "divided line" in Book VI of the *Republic*, chapter 3, "True Opinion," argues that our knowing happens at a variety of levels that become progressively more rigorous as they become progressively more absolute: more superficial forms of knowledge are relative to epistemological and metaphysical contexts that are precisely the objects of more substantial forms of knowing. The "divided line" demonstrates both how knowledge is possible for us and why the accomplishment of knowing ultimately cannot be divorced from moral development—from turning to the good. It is only in the wholesale commitment of our lives to the pursuit of the good that our nature as beings with *logos* is fulfilled: this fulfillment is philosophy, and it is this philosophical perspective that provides the norm—the wisdom—that answers to the demands of our political situation. Because knowing takes this manifold form, however, it is possible for us to mistake relative forms of knowing for absolute knowing. To mistake the relative for the absolute is a permanent temptation in our experience, and doing so is the foundation of sophistry, which is thus an ever-present threat in our interpretive experience.

Because it is only in philosophy—in the thoroughgoing pursuit of the good in all aspects of our lives—that we are ultimately fulfilled, it is much easier for us to miss the mark than to hit it and, correspondingly, it is always easier for sophistry and tyranny to come on the scene than it is for our politics to be guided by wisdom. Chapter 4, "Persuasion," investigates the nature of the human soul to determine how and why we typically fail at becoming philosophers, drawing primarily on the account of the "division of the soul" in Book IV of the *Republic*. Specifically, our nature as beings with *logos* entails that we are *always* taking account, at every level of our experience. Much of our taking account, in other words, is not at the reflective level we explicitly avow, but at pre- or nonreflective levels; specifically, we become habituated to ways of assessing situations that operate "before" and "beneath" our reflective assessment, crippling our powers of critical reflection by determining in advance the *terms* of reflection. Because this habituation is largely socially enforced, our social and political systems, we will see, can actually become powers that work against our becoming the kinds of people who can govern ourselves effectively.

Overall, my work emphasizes the tight connection between the life of the city and the life of the soul, demonstrating both the crucial role that human cognitive excellence and psychological health (or the lack thereof) play in political life and the crucial role that our social and political culture plays in facilitating (or inhibiting) our healthy cognitive and psychological development. In other words, the healthy development of city and soul each depend on the other. In short, as Socrates says in Book V of the *Republic*, until "philosophy and political power come together in the same," there will be no end of evils for cities (V.473d); our analysis shows both why this is the case and why it is so difficult to bring about this reconciliation of philosophy and politics. *Chalēpa ta kala*: noble things are difficult.[40]

Notes

1. For this broad theme, see Guthrie, *A History of Greek Philosophy*, vol. III, *The Fifth Century Enlightenment*.
2. Havelock, *Preface to Plato*, is the classic statement of this position.
3. Kurke, *The Traffic in Praise*, p. 2.
4. This interpretation has been prominent since antiquity, and in modern scholarship it is most famously advanced in vol. I of Popper's *The Open Society and Its Enemies*; it is generally the assumed starting point—rather than a reasoned conclusion—of most contemporary study of the *Republic*. Nonetheless, as I will note below, the challenge to this traditional interpretation has become quite well developed; see especially Sallis, *Being and Logos*, and Recco, *Athens Victorious*, both works that, though quite different in style and

focus, parallel my work in overall interpretive orientation and to which I will make repeated reference in endnotes.

5. Compare Roochnik, *Beautiful City*, p. 2: "Despite appearances to the contrary, . . . the *Republic* actually offers a qualified and cautious defense, rather than a resounding condemnation, of democracy. This defense, however, . . . is not stated as an isolated political thesis expounded explicitly and then substantiated at a particular juncture of the work. Instead, it emerges from the dialogue as a whole, from the very fabric of the work understood as a dialectical activity." Though I think Roochnik ultimately does not make a compelling argument for his interpretation of the *Republic* as a whole, many of his specific observations helpfully complement the arguments I make in this book.

6. Aristotle, *Poetics* 9.1451a35–36.

7. Compare Klein, *A Commentary on Plato's Meno*, p. 9: "But there is this one difference: between them [Plato's contemporaries] and us there is the immense philosophic—and philological—tradition of the ages which stems, for the most part, from Socrates' and Plato's teaching. It is not in our power to remain untouched by it. And as much as this tradition may help our understanding, it may also obstruct and distort it."

8. An analogous attitude also pertains to Asian works such as the *Upanishads*, Buddhist discourses, the *I Ching*, and so on.

9. The specific purpose of Thucydides's *History* is studied in Munn, *The School of History*.

10. Though one might, of course, say they are copying an ideal, better copied by those later works, such that, in a sense, the earlier is copying the later.

11. On the distinction between myth properly so-called and the "myths" in Plato, see Fagan, *Plato and Tradition*, p. 81.

12. This attitude towards the Platonic texts is evident, for example, in Annas's reaction to the story of Er in Book X of the *Republic* as a "painful shock" (*An Introduction to Plato's Republic*, p. 349). More fully, Annas writes of Books VIII and IX that although "they have been admired for their creative power," these books "leave a reader who is intent on the main argument unsatisfied and irritated. Plato's procedure is both confusing and confused" (p. 294). Compare the "initial shock and disgust" she first experienced when reading the work (p. v).

13. See *Republic* X.607b for the "old quarrel between philosophy and poetry," a quarrel unheard of before the *Republic*, except perhaps in the case of Pythagoras; see Brann, "Music of the *Republic*," p. 60.

14. The cultural perception of the distasteful and threatening character of the "sophists" is displayed at *Protagoras* 312a, when Hippocrates blushes and admits that he would be ashamed to admit his desire to become a sophist; see also Anytus's angry expression of distaste for "sophists" at *Meno* 91c. A similar cultural prejudice against the dangers of "free thinking" is the central theme of Aristophanes *Clouds*, a stinging condemnation of the dangerous anti-intellectualism of Athenian popular culture. See McCoy, *Plato on the Rhetoric of Philosophers and Sophists*, pp. 7–8, on the range of meanings of the term *sophistes* in the fifth and fourth centuries BC.

15. Compare Hyland, *Finitude and Transcendence*, p. 20: "When we read a book of more orthodox philosophical format, such as the *Critique of Pure Reason*, the almost complete absence of reference to context invites us to suppose that Kant is speaking as a "pure mind," that he is speaking universally, that he would say much the same thing to anyone, at any time." See also p. 25.

16. See in particular *Gorgias* 464b–466a.

17. On this relationship between philosophy and sophistry, see Hyland, *Finitude and Transcendence*, p. 23: "They [Socrates's arguments in the *Crito*] are not comprehensive, context-neutral arguments against anyone escaping from jail, and they certainly do not present 'Plato's position on civil disobedience.' But they do succeed in their existential intention: they convince Crito"; see also McCoy, *Plato on the Rhetoric of Philosophers and Sophists*, pp. 3–5, for the idea that Plato resists the normal distinction between philosophers and sophists, and pp. 16–17 on the essential poetic and rhetorical dimensions of philosophy in Plato; see pp. 193–196 for the summary of her interpretation of the distinctively philosophical use of rhetoric. For an extremely insightful account of the relationship between poetry and philosophy in Plato generally and in the *Republic* in particular, see Freydberg, "Retracing Homer and Aristophanes in the Platonic Text"; see also Freydberg's "'Oracles and Dreams' Commanding Socrates"; and compare McCoy, *Image and Argument in Plato's Republic*, p. 7: "In the *Republic*, there is no image-free way of speaking about philosophical objects. That is, there is no philosophical language that can wholly free us from the limits of images."

18. For a discussion of the whole range of meanings of *logos*, see Aygün, *The Middle Included*, pp. 3–6, and Sparshott, *Taking Life Seriously*, pp. 46–48. On *logos* as "the ability to give an account," see Brann, "Music of the *Republic*," p. 54.

19. *Politics* I.2.1253a9–10.

20. For the careful interpretation of the speech of the character Protagoras in the *Protagoras*, see Corey, *The Sophists in Plato's Dialogues*, and Gonzalez, "Caring and Conversing about Virtue." Gonzalez, like most other interpreters, treats Socrates as the hero and Protagoras as the villain in the *Protagoras*, while my interpretation is roughly the opposite: in the *Protagoras*, I believe, it is (the young) Socrates who displays classically "sophistical" behavior in the presence of Protagoras, who generally says quite wise things. Corey interprets both the speech of Protagoras and the character of Protagoras in a way very close to my own; see, among other things, his remark that "Protagoras and Socrates appear not as antagonists but as allies in the grand and meaningful attempt to describe the foundations of politics in a way that can promote civic health and well-being" (p. 66); see also McCoy, *Plato on the Rhetoric of Philosophers and Sophists*, chap. 3, for a rich discussion of the *Protagoras* that also emphasizes that there is not a clear winner or loser in the exchange between Socrates and Protagoras. See Zuckert, *Plato's Philosophers*, pp. 217–228, for an analysis of the *Protagoras* that is focused on how it portrays the stage of Socrates's philosophical development; Zuckert, too, treats Protagoras as the villain.

21. Many interpreters have addressed the importance of this first word, *katebēn*. Brann, in "Music of the *Republic*," pp. 8–12, draws on the implications of this word as the basis for her interpretation of the defining metaphorical trope of the *Republic*, namely, that Socrates is portraying himself as in Hades; Sallis, *Being and Logos*, pp. 314–316, richly builds on Brann's analysis. On the significance of the word *katabēn* in the larger ancient Greek cultural context, see, for example, Bernabé, "What Is a Katábasis?"

22. See Fagan, *Plato and Tradition*, pp, xiv–xv, on the specificity of the settings of Platonic dialogues. In his unpublished manuscript, *Verbs of Seeing in Plato's Republic*, George Gregory does a masterful job of showing how much is communicated through this narration of the physical setting of the opening scene.

23. Brann, "The Music of the *Republic*," p. 9, takes the dramatic date as between 411 BC and 405 BC; this is a date by which Cephalus would be dead, but that fact is consistent with her interpretation of Socrates as being in the "land of shades." For a helpful overview of

the controversies surrounding the dramatic date of the dialogue, see Nails, "The Dramatic Date of Plato's Republic" and *The People of Plato*, pp. 154-155 and 324-326; the difficulties include the possibility that the dramatic date of Book I is inconsistent with the dramatic date of Books II-V (primarily because of Glaucon's age). Gifford, "Dramatic Dialectic in *Republic* Book I," states the problem of dating Book I concisely in n. 18 (p. 53): "Since in the very first sentence of *Republic* I Plato indexes the time of the conversation to a specific and highly public event . . . there is some reason to suspect that the date might be significant here. Unfortunately, the event Plato refers to cannot be placed with any certainty." On Bendis, see Planeaux, "The Date of Bendis' Entry into Attica."

24. Hyland emphasizes this theme of the specificity of conversational situations for his interpretation of Plato; see *Finitude and Transcendence*, pp. 5-9, 14.

25. As Roochnik writes (*Beautiful City*, p. 108): "There are not general claims in the Platonic dialogues. There are only characters, often drawn in stunning detail, who occasionally make abstract claims."

26. I refer to the unknown interlocutor as "him," since almost all interlocutors in the dialogues are male, though Socrates could be talking with his wife, Xanthippe, who appears in the *Phaedo*, or with someone like Diotima, who appears in the *Symposium*, or Aspasia, whose speech is invoked in the *Menexenus*.

27. Contrast Annas, *Introduction to Plato's Republic*, who describes the *Republic* as Plato's "manifesto" (p. 1), explaining that "the rest of the book [after Book I] is a continuous exposition of what we can only take to be Plato's own views on people and society" (p. 5).

28. Aristotle discusses this distinctive social and political power of tragedy in the *Poetics*; on this theme of the conception of the public force of poetry in Aristotle's *Poetics*, see Schmidt, *On Germans and Other Greeks*, chap. 2, "Aristotle." On the intimate connection of tragedy and democracy, see Seaford, *Reciprocity and Ritual*, chaps. 7-10. See also Goldhill, "The Great Dionysia and Civic Ideology." As a translation of *mimēsis*, I generally favor "re-enactment" (which is the meaning of the term in ritual contexts) over the familiar but misleading "imitation"; on the translation of *mimēsis*, see also Benardete, *Socrates' Second Sailing*, p. 69.

29. See Brann, "The Music of the *Republic*," pp. 33-34, on the relationship of the *Republic* to mimetic art. In *Beautiful City*, Roochnik identifies a similar self-referentiality running throughout the *Republic*, such that the state imagined in the dialogue rules out the very conditions by which this dialogue in which it is imagined is possible; see especially pp. 69, 71-72, 81-82. and 91. In *Image and Argument in Plato's Republic*, pp. 30-31, McCoy argues that Plato's writing uses *mimēsis* in a way that encourages critical reflection on it. Hyland, *Finitude and Transcendence*, p. 88, also notes the parallel of Platonic authorship with the tragic and comic poets outlawed from the city.

30. Indeed, even ignoring the contradictions and inconsistencies that emerge in the discussion, at least four different versions of the *polis* are discussed. This issue is precisely analyzed in Brann, "The Music of the *Republic*," pp. 12-17, 22, and 24-25, and in Sallis, *Being and Logos*, especially pp. 357-358. We will have reason to address this specific issue of the different "versions" of the city in chap. 1.

31. In other words, whether or not Socrates is advocating some form of ideal state, the fact that Plato gives us a portrayal of that conversation does not in and of itself give us any basis for determining whether he himself endorses that conversation or whether he wants, for example, to offer an exemplary portrayal of ridiculous behavior (just as Shakespeare's portrayal of Macbeth, for example, does not in and of itself allow us to conclude that

Shakespeare advocates murderous ambition). For a provocative and insightful interpretation of the narrative form of the *Republic*, see Benardete, *Socrates' Second Sailing*, pp. 9–10, 124. Baracchi offers a very rich interpretation of the "literary" elements—the Platonic "myths" and images—in the *Republic* in *Of Myth, Life, and War in Plato's Republic*. The "seventh letter" is often invoked to justify interpretations of Plato's views, but there is no convincing evidence of the authenticity of the letter; as Annas writes ("Classical Greek Philosophy," p. 285), it is "such an unconvincing production that its acceptance by many scholars is best seen as indicating the strength of their desire to find, behind the detachment of the dialogues, something, no matter what, to which Plato is straightforwardly committed."

32. Compare Roochnik, *Beautiful City*, p. 7. The distinctive meaning of Socratic *dialegesthai* is studied through Metcalf, *Philosophy as Agōn*; see especially pp. 54–56, 74.

33. Compare Hyland, *Finitude and Transcendence*, p. 32: "It is always possible to transcend the specific situation out of which philosophic discourse arises, to, as we say, generalize from this or that instance; but that transcendence is always *finite*. Part of one's understanding of a given 'theory' must always be a consideration of the kind of situations out of which and in terms of which it might arise."

34. The most concise and compelling carrying-out of that analysis with which I am familiar is by Sallis in chap. V of *Being and Logos*, though Sallis's analysis does not include the discussions of the decline of states and tyranny in Books VIII and IX. Benardete's *Socrates' Second Sailing* is also a very insightful and textually sensitive interpretation that offers a commentary on the whole presented as a sequence of individual conversations about distinct themes. For an attempt to provide a commentary on the whole book by reconstructing the *Republic* strictly as a sequence of arguments, see Dorter, *The Transformation of Plato's Republic*. Rothleder, *Fraught Decisions in Plato and Shakespeare*, offers a particularly insightful interpretation of the *Republic* that focuses on it more as a literary text than as an argument; Rothleder takes her orientation from the "Myth of Er" in Book X, and interprets the *Republic* as a rich reflection on what is involved in interpreting the "success" of one's own life (i.e., judging it as a tragedy or as a comedy), a theme that powerfully illuminates the stakes—personal, familial, and political—of "justice."

35. Roochnik, *Beautiful City*, pp. 55–56, gives a helpful summary of the significant conversational contributions by Glaucon that mark him as the central interlocutor. Xenophon, in *Memorabilia* III.vi, describes a conversation in which Socrates convinces Glaucon (who was not yet twenty years old, according to Xenophon) not to try to become an orator and pursue the leadership of Athens; one could imagine that the conversation portrayed in the *Republic* is Plato's version of that event. Corey, *The Sophists in Plato's Dialogues*, pp. 74–77, provocatively refers to the *Republic* as Plato's "Choice of Glaucon," modeled on Prodicus's "Choice of Herakles," as that is portrayed in Xenophon, *Memorabilia* II.i.

36. This same point is made by Klein, *A Commentary on Plato's Meno*, pp. 6–9, and Sallis, *Being and Logos*, p. 28. Compare McCoy, *Image and Argument in Plato's Republic*, who shows (especially in the introduction and chap. 1, but also throughout the book) that Plato's use of images is a means of requiring the reader to exercise independent philosophical effort—imagination and thought—to engage with the text.

37. I do not find efforts to assess the changing character of Plato's thought and hence to date the different dialogues (as "early," "middle," or "late") convincing. Though such a chronological interpretation is in principle possible, all existing interpretations with which I am familiar have relied upon unconvincing assumptions by scholars about what Plato thought—the very sorts of presumptions that are given the lie both empirically and

in principle by a reading that attends to the literary form of the Platonic works. For a nice summary of these issues, see Lane, "Socrates and Plato: An Introduction," pp. 157–160. For a detailed history and critique of all methods, including stylometric, of dating the dialogues, see Howland, "Re-Reading Plato."

38. Compare McCoy, *Plato on the Rhetoric of Philosophers and Sophists*, p. 18: "Socrates' arguments are not always persuasive to all individuals, even when logically valid. Sometimes they are even fallacious. But Socrates' character and his love of the good make him the hero of Plato's dialogues; they ground his philosophy. In an important sense, Plato's defense of philosophy goes hand in hand with his defense of his teacher, Socrates."

39. Though it is not documented in detail within the text, my reading of this material is nonetheless the distilled result of a long history of close reading. I have demonstrated what I take to be readings that answer to the demands of such precision in a very early essay of mine, "Hermeneutics and Plato's *Ion*," and more recently (and I hope more maturely) in "Education in Plato's *Laws*." In the twelve YouTube lectures that make up "Plato's Republic" (https://www.youtube.com/playlist?list=PLZyk__e49-Cv86nHOUeQWzoKI8U9VkWni), I offer a somewhat fuller reading of many of these texts from the *Republic* (especially Books II, III, and IV).

40. This idiom is cited, first by Glaucon and then by Socrates, in the *Republic* at IV.435c and VI.497d; the expression is also used in the *Hippias (Major)* (304e) and the *Cratylus* (384a–b). On the dialogical significance of Socrates's use of this idiom, see Mintz, "*Chalepa Ta Kala*."

A.
POLITICS, MONEY, AND PERSUASION

1

THE PROBLEM OF ABSTRACTION

For children growing up in the modern world, handheld computers, cars, and fences are a part of the immediate given environment to which the children must accommodate themselves, just as much as dogs, trees, and rain are. But though experientially these realities are all roughly equal to the children, ontologically they are in fact quite different; the former are artifacts of human culture and learning, while the latter are naturally occurring. For growing children, this crucial distinction is obscured by the circumstance that they take the fact of these realities for granted and precisely must learn to live on the basis of them: it is this already-human world into which they are born and in which they must learn to live, so, from their functional, living perspective, it is just as "natural" to ride in a car as it is natural to get wet in the rain. It will be an important part of their education, though, eventually to recognize and appreciate this distinction between the artificial and the natural, and to understand, at least broadly, the workings of computer, car, and fence in a way that, on the contrary, the "workings" of dogs, trees, and rain will always remain significantly mysterious.

For all of us, our human environment is one we have inherited. But, whereas we generally come to understand the basic workings of computer, car, and fence, there are other, more fundamental aspects of our distinctively human environment that we typically do not understand. In our ongoing lives, we generally take for granted the existence of government, learning, writing, and money. We treat these as, so to speak, "natural" dimensions of our world—generally without even recognizing that there is something here to be understood. This lack of insight into our own condition, furthermore, is not just a matter of individual understanding, but is true at a collective level as well: though there have been, to be sure, powerful philosophical forays into the comprehension of these realities—in such figures as Aristotle, Adam Smith, John Dewey, and Jacques Derrida, for example—these insights, unlike the insights into the working of car and computer, have generally not been diffused into our broader cultural self-understanding. Consequently, we live, both individually and culturally, on the basis of realities for which we, collectively, are responsible, but which we have not, so to speak, "owned." It is the philosophical comprehension of just these realities that provides the central framework of the *Republic*, realities that Socrates introduces in his conversations in Books I and II.

In Book II of the *Republic*, Socrates explores the way in which the *polis*—the city, state, or city-state[1]—emerges from human need, and is in that sense "natural," but depends on our *logos*, our "making sense of things," in order to be realized. The discussion of these matters—the discussion that sets the frame for the remainder of the *Republic*—brings into focus the distinctive problem that this, our human environment, intrinsically poses for us: when it is not guided by wisdom, the power of government becomes a threat to our development rather than a support for our development; we need government, but the successful working of government is contingent on the quality of our own agency and insight, of our *logos*.

In fact, our *logos* as such has a character that is logically (and ontologically) analogous to that of the *polis*: enacting *logos* or "taking account" is natural to us, but doing it well is a matter of cultivation. *Technē* or "expertise"—excellence in taking account of something—is itself a central theme of Socrates's conversation in Book I of the *Republic*. The analysis of *technē*, however, reveals a problem intrinsic to it that is analogous to the problem intrinsic to government: we can fail to understand our own understanding, and mishandle its power. Furthermore, this "rogue" science—*technē* unleashed from insight—is itself intimately connected with the emergence of the very money-economy toward which, as is suggested in the conversation in Book II, the *polis* characteristically develops. In the phenomenon of money, therefore, the problems of *polis* and *technē* dovetail, and the proper handling of the world made possible by a money-economy becomes the distinctive challenge of our human condition.

Through these analyses in Books I and II of the *Republic*, Socrates introduces us to our central theme: the ambivalent power of our *logos*, which makes it possible—and, indeed, necessary—for us to live on the basis of realities we do not understand, but which are not "naturally" good, realities that precisely call on us to handle them wisely. These opening discussions introduce us to these problems—these realities—that it will be the project of the remainder of the *Republic* to analyze and comprehend in detail, and that define the context for the distinctive problems of opinion and persuasion that will be our ultimate focus.

I. The *Polis* and the Problem of the Guardians

It is in Book II of the *Republic* that the particular question is asked that it is the task of the bulk of the ensuing conversation to answer: the question of how just rule is possible. This question emerges in the context of a discussion, by Glaucon, Adeimantus, and Socrates, of what the nature and origin of the *polis*—the city—is. In order to appreciate the specific question as it is asked there in the form of the "problem of the guardians," we must first grasp the context in which the question emerges.

It is a clear feature of our life today that we live in developed societies. Each of us was born into such a society, and we were not there to witness or take part in its emergence. That is likewise the situation of Athenian citizens in 421 BC (the likely dramatic date of the conversation in the *Republic*), though it is interesting to recognize that those individuals were in fact much closer historically than we are to some of the most powerful, formative moments in the development of human society. The Greek city-states themselves emerged in the so-called Dark Ages of Greece, between roughly 1200 BC and 700 BC, and the democracy in Athens developed between, roughly, 580 BC and 450 BC, so these revolutionary transformations within shared human life occurred within the immediate cultural memory of the society within which Socrates, Glaucon, and Adeimantus lived, rather as the American Revolution remains immediately culturally alive to contemporary American culture (and, no doubt, with a comparable degree of ignorance and misrepresentation in how it was remembered). Nonetheless, Socrates, Glaucon, and Adeimantus, like each of us, did not themselves take part in those cultural processes, and so they, like us, face the challenging task of working backward from an existent reality to the understanding of where this reality came from—a question that is both historical (empirical) and ontological. In Book II of the *Republic*, Socrates, Glaucon, and Adeimantus decide to consider how and why there are *poleis*.

In fact, this initial, rich conversation by Socrates, Glaucon, and Adeimantus that provides the context for the remainder of the conversation in the *Republic* involves a good number of unnoted and rather important conceptual confusions.[2] First, Socrates in fact offers three different types of analysis, without ever acknowledging that the very "logic" of his account is changing. Initially, Socrates offers a sort of derivation of the city through an anthropological account of its origins in the division of labor (II.369b–372d). Glaucon claims that this does not speak to the realities of life nowadays, and Socrates then specifies the meaningful relationship of elements within this different form of society (II.372d–375d). In doing so, however, he does not continue the form of his initial analysis, that is, he does not show *how* this second "luxurious" or "soft" city [*truphōsan polin*] (II.372e) emerges from the first city;[3] instead, his analysis shifts from *derivation* to *description*. Finally, in response to the "problem of the guardians" that is diagnosed within the city nowadays, Socrates abruptly switches the logic of the analysis again, this time to a *prescriptive* study that responds to Adeimantus's earlier critical assessment of contemporary culture that launched the conversation about the city (II.376d–IV.427c).[4] Furthermore, as I will go on to indicate, though Socrates calls the first city a "*polis*," this is actually a rather loose usage given the very specific meaning that reality—the *polis*—came to have in ancient Greece, and the social form he is deriving would perhaps better be called a *kōmē*, or "village." That is, though it is not itself simply a household—*oikos*—it is nothing more than a connected network of households, and thus it is a form of society that still operates with a social "logic" of the household.[5] I will argue in chapter 2 that it is the unexplained transition from this form of society to the society "nowadays"—the society of the contemporary *polis*—that is effectively analyzed in Book VIII of the *Republic*. As we read this text, we must be careful ourselves to be clear about these various differences, even if Socrates's interlocutors are not thus careful. In any case, it is in relation to this second city "nowadays" that the distinctive problem of the guardians arises, and this is the issue with which we will be concerned. First, though, let us consider Socrates's original derivation of the *polis* (loosely so-called).

Socrates begins the discussion of the coming into being of the *polis* by identifying its founding principle: "I think a *polis* comes to be because none of us is self-sufficient, but we all need many things" (II.369b).[6] Socrates then expands on the import of this basic principle:

> And because people need many things, and because one person calls on a second out of need and on a third out of a different need, many people gather in a single place to live together as partners and helpers. And such a settlement is called a *polis*. (II.369b–c)

"And if they share things with one another, giving and taking," he asks, "they do so because each believes that this is better for himself?" "It is,"

Adeimantus replies (II.369c). At its root, the *polis*—here meaning something like "society"—is a collaborative effort of living together, in which we each contribute to the accomplishment of a whole that exceeds any of us singly and that provides for each of us an essential, supportive context for our individual lives.

In the ensuing exchange, Socrates works out more fully how this idea explains our social reality. His argument is that we flourish in a context of division of labor in which we each develop specialized activities, relying on our ability to exchange the products of our specialized labor with the products of the specialized labor of others who have themselves specialized in the tasks that we neglect for the sake of pursuing our own specializations. "The result, then," Socrates notes, "is that more plentiful and better-quality goods are more easily produced if each person does one thing for which he is naturally suited, does it at the right time, and is released from having to do any of the others" (II.370c). Socrates, Glaucon, and Adeimantus then go on to articulate the basic needs that must be met by such a city.

Socrates identifies three main sorts of needs. First, there must be the basic services—food production, the building of shelters—that are the minimal conditions for our living (II.369d–370e). Second, though, because in any physical setting it is difficult to establish a city that can supply all of its own needs, there is a need for trade with other centers and this in turn points to the need for markets and currency (II.370e–373d). It is in the context of discussing this point that Glaucon intervenes in Socrates's account, requiring Socrates to address the city "nowadays" [*nun*], in which people are accustomed to living a more culturally "refined" life than Socrates has described so far (II.372c–d). In discussing the resources required to fulfill the desires for this more "luxurious" [*truphōsan*] life (II.372e), Socrates identifies the third need: their competing desires for resources lead cities into conflict with each other, and there is thus a need for the city to attend to its own self-protection (II.373d–375d).[7] This third need—the need for self-protection—has a dual form.

Though this need for self-protection is initially discussed in the specific context of noting the acquisitive character of "the luxurious city," the point being made has a more universal significance (which is itself gradually but implicitly recognized throughout the ensuing conversation).[8] In general, society has an internal integrity of its own: it is a self-defined, basically self-sustaining community. Like a natural organism, it is an organized system of constitutive member-parts, but, again like an organism, it also participates in a larger world with others, and though its internal form is normative for itself, that form is not automatically normative for others: the society needs to protect its own organization, since those outside with whom it is in contact need not care about the preservation of its organization. The protection of its integrity is thus one of the needs that must be met in the city. This role of "guardian" is itself an inherently differentiated task that is both internally directed and externally directed. Externally, there is the need to protect the city militarily from foreign assault, whether in the context of its own initiation of aggression or in the context of its being the object of the aggression of another; internally, there is the need to maintain the organization that defines the city. The role of "guardian," the third essential need that Socrates identifies, though it initially is addressed only in terms of military defense in the context of intercity conflict, thus essentially comprises the various functions with which we are familiar under the names of "army," "government," "police," and so on, a point that is ultimately made clear at the end of Book III, when within those called "guardians" a distinction is made between the rulers (the government) who are most properly the "craftsmen of the city's freedom" (III.395b) and their helpers (the military) (III.412c–414b).[9]

Precisely because the city is not a natural organism, though, all of its "parts" are not naturally occurring but are matters of nonnecessitated human action: individual persons must deliberately direct their action to the tasks that allow the city to exist and function, whereas, in the natural organism, the functioning of the parts is not different from the functioning of the organism itself. For each of the city's functioning parts, persons must conform their lives to enacting that function—there must be farmers who devote themselves to food production and tradespeople who devote themselves to buying and selling—and this is no less true for the function of self-protection: individual persons must take on the responsibility for acting as guardians for the city. We will see that this fact has important implications.

Now, historically, different societies have, of course, fulfilled this essential function of self-protection in different ways. Notably, for example, the Greek *poleis* famously relied on "hoplite" armies for defense during much of their early history. The hoplites were citizen-soldiers: it was a fundamental structure of these cities that the individuals who had a stake in the maintenance of the community also had the responsibility of defending it, and those citizens who were wealthy enough to supply their own armor were the city's "guardians" in external combat.[10] Rome, similarly, presumably relied on some such structure in its early history, and this image is romantically projected back by Livy in his *Ab Urbe Condita*, especially in the figure of the farmer-soldier Cincinnatus.[11] Internally, too, the democratic Greek *poleis*—most prominently Athens, Syracuse, and Argos, for example, but also many smaller communities—strove to unite the role of "guardian" with the other essential roles, making community decision-making—"government"—a matter of popular, collective action; this non-separation of the role of government into a separate group of individuals is the essential structure of Greek democracy and, indeed, the core of the ideal of the "citizen," who rules and is ruled in turn.[12] And, though the Athenians, for example, had no real "police" force, the executing of law still remained largely in the hands of the citizens through their participation in the juries of the law-courts. In these ways, Greek democracies, and Athens in particular, did not give the role of "guardian" over to a separate group of individuals. It is also common, however, for these roles of military, legislature, police, and so on to be handed over to specialized groups of individuals. This is, in fact, the approach taken up in the conversation in Book II of the *Republic*.

Socrates emphasizes the importance of specialization, recognizing that, in general, our chosen fields of endeavor require each of us to commit our whole life to "what we do" if we are to do it well:

> But we prevented a cobbler from trying to be a farmer, weaver, or builder at the same time and said that he must remain a cobbler in order to produce fine work. And each of the others, too, was to work all his life at a single trade for which he had a natural aptitude and keep away from all the others, so as not to miss the right moment to practice his own work well. (II.374b–c)

As a reflection on the realities of the development of individual life, this is a very sensible account: with good reason, we do generally define ourselves by a single activity by which we "make a living."[13] Socrates goes on, though, to relate this insight to the work of the warfare:

> Now, isn't it of the greatest importance that warfare be practiced well? And is fighting a war so easy that a farmer or a cobbler or any other craftsmen can be a soldier at the same time? . . . To the degree that the work of the guardians is most important, it requires most freedom from other things and the greatest skill and devotion. (II.374c–e)

Contrary to the actual practice of Athens, Socrates here identifies the reason it makes sense for communities to rely on a discrete group of individuals as soldiers (and, though the argument here does not take up this broader theme explicitly, as guardians more broadly in their role of governors).[14]

While it is noted by Glaucon only in passing, when he asks, "Aren't they adequate by themselves?" (II.374a), it certainly should be noted more pointedly by us as readers that the very *premise* of the distinctively "democratic" Athenian *polis*—the *politeia* that Socrates, in both the *Apology* and the *Crito*, endorses with his words and with his very life—speaks against this argument for the separation of the guardians. As competent readers, we must here ask of the text, "But what about democracy?" And, indeed, we must maintain this concern as we evaluate the implications that Socrates draws from this analysis. For the moment, though, it is more important to appreciate the consequence that emerges from this reasoning.

"Our job, it seems," Socrates remarks, "is to select, if we can, the kind of nature suited to guard the city" (II.374e). Comparing the guardian-soldier to a young dog, Socrates notes that

> both of them need sharp senses, speed to catch what they perceive, and finally strength if they have to fight it out with what they have caught.... To say nothing of courage, if they are to fight well.... As for the body's characteristics, it's plain how the guardian must be.... And, as for the soul's—that he must be spirited [*thumoeidē*]. (II.375a–b)

It is from this essential nature of the guardian that the central problem of the *Republic* emerges:

> With such natures, how will they not be savage to one another and the rest of the citizens? ... Yet, they must be gentle to their own and cruel to enemies. If not, they'll not wait for others to destroy them, but they'll do it themselves beforehand.... Where will we find a disposition at the same time gentle and great-spirited? Surely a gentle nature is opposed to a spirited one.... If a man lacks either of them, he can't become a good guardian. But these conditions resemble impossibilities, and so it follows that a good guardian is impossible. (II.375b–d)

What Socrates notes in the guardians is the ambivalence present in any weapon: its function is simply to kill, without regard to any particular target. In the case of the city, investing an independent body with the agenda of using violent force to achieve its ends produces a group that is as much a threat to those whom it is to protect as it is to those whom it is supposed to oppose.[15] This is the form of the problem as it presents itself in the context of the guardians construed militarily, but it also applies to the role of guardian more broadly, for there is a second, more universal, problem implicit in this first: Investing an independent body with the objective of "self-defense" introduces a problematic ambiguity with respect to this notion of "self"—by defining that independent group as essential to the city, *its* needs can easily appear to it to *be* the city's needs, and this applies as much to the rulers as it does to the military "helpers"; indeed, at the beginning of Book IV, Adeimantus will himself propose that the guardians are "they to whom the city in truth belongs" (IV.419a). There is thus a problem built into the very notion of "guardians." The need for guardians is a need that arises from the rest of the city, and thus the very meaning of the guardians is that they are "for" the city; as we noted, they must "very precisely be craftsmen of the city's freedom" (III.395b). And yet, when the role of guardian is enacted as an independent group of persons who are identified with the power—military or governing—that defines the city, there is a constitutive tension in the very nature of that group that threatens to make them, not the salvation of the city, but the very thing they were needed to protect against.

The city is not a natural organism, so, whereas in the organism all functions are functions of the whole and, as such, are constitutively directed toward their own "proper" functioning without ulterior motive, in the city each of the functional parts has the potential to separate itself from its coordinated role in the maintenance of the city as a whole and to pursue its own agenda as a separate agent.[16] In other words, the successful, "proper" functioning of the city depends on the free commitment of its member-parts to that collective goal. In the context of any of the parts—farmers, merchants, and so on—the stance of alienated, self-interested action can be a problem, but it is most profoundly a problem when it is the guardians—the member-parts precisely responsible for the maintenance of the city's integrity—that abrogate their constitutive responsibility and "go rogue," so to speak.[17] What is striking and powerful in Socrates's assessment is the recognition that this "going rogue" is not an alien contamination of the guardians' role: it is, rather, the predictable—almost natural—action of the guardians, given how they have been defined.

With respect to military guardians, the insight of Socrates's observation is amply and forcefully demonstrated by human political history. In the contemporary United States, for example, it is widely documented that the police, who are typically advertised as protectors of the people—"to serve and protect," as the slogan of many police departments runs—are often involved in the forceful and illegal oppression of Black Americans and are often highly partisan agents who use their powers in the support of causes (typically very conservative) that are in fact against the interests of the citizens and, indeed, against the laws.[18] This phenomenon is nothing new, however. Perhaps the most decisive case of all in human history is the Roman army. Whereas, as noted above, there is a Roman tradition of celebrating the farmer-soldier, what is actually historically striking about Rome is its development of a professional army, and these "legions" famously became tools of their generals, who used them to seize power within Rome, rather than as the protective servants of "the senate and people of Rome."[19] Even in Livy's romanticized history of early Rome, the army is consistently portrayed as forcefully repressing popular unrest against the unjust and oppressive conditions imposed by the ruling "aristocracy";[20] by the time of Sulla and Caesar, the army became the tool for installing a new king, resulting in the end of the Roman Republic, and subsequently (initially in the "year of the four emperors," AD 68, and after that as a matter of course), the army itself became in effect the ruler of Rome.[21] Whether in the case of the police in the United States or the army in Rome, it is clear that an armed force that has been put in power by the state commonly functions not primarily as a protector of public interest, but as a power that operates in its own interests and advances causes that in fact oppose the public interest. As Socrates claims, this is not an aberration, but is rather the predictable, "normal" functioning of such bodies.[22]

Analogous concerns surely apply to rulers, and this is, indeed, the explicit theme of Socrates's rather heated exchange with Thrasymachus in Book I of the *Republic*. There, Thrasymachus maintains that rule properly speaking is rule in the interest of the rulers, and it is the prima facie compelling character of his portrait of human psychology that launches the subsequent conversation between Glaucon, Adeimantus, and Socrates about justice.[23] This, then, is the profound question raised in the discussion of Book II of the *Republic*: How can the "guardians" be a body that actually guards rather than exploits? It is in Book V of the *Republic* that Socrates ultimately answers this question. It is not, he says, until "political power and philosophy come together in the same" that there will be "rest from ills for cities ... or for human kind" (V.473d). In other words, until it is the case that the appointed "guardians" do in fact recognize and care for the good, cities are destined to be sites of oppression and exploitation. For the moment, my point is not to pursue the political analysis, but only to note the structure of the problem here, for it reveals something essential both about the ontology of society and, more basically, about the human condition as such.

The human being needs social life, and society itself needs functional differentiation and organization, in both inwardly and outwardly directed ways. But, unlike the organic structures of natural organisms, which are naturally responsive to their needs, the social structure necessary to the fulfillment of human needs does not itself occur by nature. Aristotle describes this exact situation in the *Politics*:

> When several villages [*kōmōn*] are united in a single complete community, large enough to be nearly or quite self-sufficing, the state [*polis*] comes into existence, originating in the bare needs of life, and continuing in existence for the sake of a good life. And therefore, if the earlier forms of society [*hai prōtai koinōniai*] are natural, so is the state, for it is the end [*telos*] of them, and the nature of a thing is its end. . . . The impulse to form a partnership of this kind [*hē hormē epi tēn toiautēn koinōnian*] is implanted in all men by nature, and yet he who first founded the state was the greatest of benefactors. (*Politics* I.2.1252b27–32, 1253a29–31 [translation, modified])

Though the state provides, for us, our "natural environment," that is, the environment in which it is possible for us to fulfill our native potential, that natural environment does not itself occur naturally, but requires historical, human agency to come into being, which is why "he who first founded the state was the greatest of benefactors." In this sense, we are naturally beings of "culture," beings whose fulfillment depends on creative human effort.

Aristotle describes further how our distinctive natural orientation toward the *polis* is evident in the characteristic form of life that defines our organism:

> That man is more of a political animal than . . . any other gregarious animal is evident. . . . Man is the only animal whom [nature] has endowed with the gift of speech [*logon de monon anthrōpos echei tōn zōiōn*]. And whereas mere voice is but an indication of pleasure and pain, and is therefore found in other animals, . . . the power of speech [*logos*] is intended to set forth the expedient and the inexpedient, and therefore likewise the just and the unjust. And it is a characteristic of man that he alone has any sense of good and evil, of just and unjust, and the like, and the association of living beings who have this sense makes a family and a state. (*Politics* I.2.1253a7–18)

We are not naturally situated within the environment that supports us, and it is incumbent on us to generate this environment for ourselves. The distinctive natural capacity that makes this possible (and, indeed, necessary) for us is *logos*: the ability to take account, which means the ability to grasp things in terms of the norms by which they are defined and to express this to each other. It is our status as "animals having *logos*" that makes us in principle subject to the problem of the guardians diagnosed above.

What is definitive of the problem of the guardians is that there is a constitutive contradiction in the very being of the guardians: (i) There is *a reason for* the existence of the guardians—a natural need—that explains why it is that there should ever be such things in the first place: as we saw above, it is the human need for a self-sufficient community that introduces into reality the demand that the role of "guardian" be something defined for us in our experience and, hence, addressed in our behavior. (ii) The very form in which the guardians exist, however—the way in which this constitutive need must be realized—allows this body to adopt an independent existence that is determined by its own limited values rather than being determined in its action by the constitutive reason that justifies its existence in the first place—a situation clearly described and, indeed, advocated by Thrasymachus in Book I of the *Republic*. It is the very definition of the guardians—their very "being"—that they are to protect the needs of the community *of which* they are the guardians: otherwise, they *are not* "guardians." Once inaugurated into being, though, this body exists in separation from this, its founding meaning, and can use the powers it has only because of this founding meaning without regard for this meaning. In the guardians, we see the problem of the separation of surface, so to speak, from substance, the emergence of a reality that is capable of forgetting the origin to which it is in debt for its very being. This ability to separate surface from substance, fruit from origin, is, I shall maintain, the distinctive character of *logos*.

The formation of the city, a process rooted in natural need but enacted through human decision and practice, has no ontological guarantee of its success. The city imitates nature, in that it approximates a self-organized whole, but it is not, in fact, a natural whole but instead is a reality enacted only in and through the practice of actual individuals.[24] The bond in this fabric is not organic but is, as Aristotle says, only the sense of justice of the agents from which the city is composed. Because the city *in its very being* relies on the sense-making—the *logos*—of its constituent members, there is never a guarantee that it will function as the whole that it is called on to be. The functioning of the city depends on the way in which the participants in the city make sense of their situations, which most fundamentally is a matter of how they interpret themselves and their goals; but the fact that we are sense-making beings—beings with *logos*—precisely means that the truth of things is not immediately manifest to us, that understanding is for us a challenge, and that we can therefore be fundamentally mistaken about our own reality. The power of governance is assigned to individuals *as if* they were natural organs immediately committed to using those powers for the good of the "organism" from whom the assignment comes, but this dream of good governance would be realized only if the individuals thus empowered properly understood their reality in the ontological terms in which it is actually defined. In fact, however, individuals typically do not recognize their own debts: they receive the power without simultaneously acknowledging the debt they thus assume for the reality that gives rise to those powers. The individuals, because of the limitations of their *logos*, separate the surface of the power from its source, and thus, in the context of the city in which these individuals are assuming the powers of governance, the city itself has its government separate from its human substance and thereby become an independent, exploitative force.

II. Expertise and Writing

We are beings with *logos*, beings who "make sense of" our situations. We are beings, in other words, whose nature it is to know: just as we are destined to political life, so are we destined to understanding. As we will see in detail in chapter 3, our knowing takes a variety of forms, many of them studied within the *Republic*, but the core of knowing is our developing of *technē*—"expertise"—with respect to some particular *pragma*—"state of affairs."

In the *Gorgias*, Socrates has a discussion—an argument, really—with Polus, a student of the Sicilian sophist Gorgias, about whether oratory [*hē rhētorikē*] is a matter of expertise, and this exchange is helpful for bringing the nature of expertise into focus. About oratory, Socrates maintains that it is not a *technē*, not a matter of expertise; instead, he says to Polus, "It's the thing that you say has produced *technē*, in a treatise I read recently . . . I mean *empeiria*" (*Gorgias* 462b–c). This relationship between *technē* and its source in *empeiria* is helpfully clarified by Aristotle.

Aristotle begins *Metaphysics* A(I) with the remark that "all human beings by nature strive to know" (A[I].1.980a21). In his subsequent description of the process of learning, Aristotle discusses the notion of *empeiria*:

> From memory experience [*empeiria*] is produced in men; for the several memories of the same thing produce finally the capacity for a single experience. And experience seems pretty much like science [*epistēmēi*] and art [*technēi*], but really science and art come to men through experience; for "experience made art," as Polus says, "but inexperience luck." Now art arises when from

> many notions gained by experience one universal judgment about a class of objects is produced.... With a view to action experience seems in no respect inferior to art, and men of experience succeed even better than those who have theory [*logon*] without experience. (*Metaphysics* A[I].1.980b27–981a13)

Empeiria here is properly translated by the English word "experience" in the sense in which we use that word when we say, for example, "She's an experienced sailor." "Experience" in this idiom names a developed state of familiarity, the situation in which one has come to grasp some particular *pragma* or state of affairs ("a class of objects") in such a way that one has a basic "know-how," a basic competence for interacting with that *pragma* effectively. In this sense, "with a view to action experience seems in no respect inferior to art."

Technē, however, takes us a step beyond this know-how. *Technē* comes about when, through reflection on our developed state of experience, we explicitly grasp the principles animating this know-how: "when from many notions gained by experience one universal judgment about a class of objects is produced." One truly has *technē*, "expertise," when one explicitly grasps the cause or principle [*hē archē*] of what one is doing: it is here that we would typically say that one "understands." This is the point Socrates makes when he explains why he does not believe oratory to be a *technē*:

> I say that it isn't a *technē*, but an *empeiria*, because it has no account [*logon*] of the nature [*phusin*] of whatever things it applies by which it applies them, so that it's unable to state [*eipein*] the cause [*aitian*] of each thing. And I refuse to call anything that lacks such an account a *technē*. (*Gorgias* 465a)

One of the most distinctive things about us—about human beings—is the twofold fact that (i) we can develop an educated familiarity with the things we encounter and (ii) we can then give an explicit account [*logos*] of the sense—the rationality—of this developed situation.[25]

Throughout Book I of the *Republic*, Socrates identifies many distinctive features of *technē*. In the course of his discussion—or, rather, again, his argument—with Thrasymachus, about whether rulers are always self-interested, Socrates points to what is ultimately most defining of a *technē*.[26] In his argument about the nature of rule, Socrates first makes a point complementary to that which we made above, distinguishing between rule properly speaking and exploitation (I.340e, 342e). We saw above that the very notion of rule emerges out of a need within the nature of human experience, but that, once defined, the role thus marked out within society can be enacted in a way that betrays this founding significance that gives the notion of rule meaning in the first place. In the course of his argument, Socrates also addresses the notion of *technē*, relying on this distinction between the definitive nature of something and its derivative misappropriation.

Taking as an example the *technē*—the expertise—of medicine [*hē iatrikē*], Socrates asks Thrasymachus, "Is the doctor in the precise sense ... a money-maker or one who cares for the sick?" (I.341c). The issue here is understanding what in principle the very notion of "doctor" (or "ruler" or "pilot" and so on) is that is presumed in all our casual uses of that designation. We may well say that "the doctor builds a house," but in that case we are using "the doctor" as the designation for identifying a particular individual who *in addition to being a doctor* also is engaged in the activity of building a house: it is not *insofar as the individual is a doctor* that the person is building a house. In the context of his argument with Thrasymachus, Socrates uses this notion to pry apart analogously the proper practice of medicine as such from the fact that the doctor makes money: a doctor is a human individual who may well make money through a medical practice, but it is not money-making *by virtue of which* the doctor is a doctor; on the contrary, it is *in virtue of caring for the sick* that the doctor is a doctor.[27] If we reflect on what it means in principle to *be* a doctor, we can recognize that the doctor must have the *aptitude* for caring for the sick, for this is the qualification that makes the person an expert and, indeed, she or he must *actually care* for the sick or else will have only the potential to be a doctor. Thrasymachus is thus rightly forced to concede that the doctor is "one who cares for the sick" (I.341c). Observing thus that "the art [of medicine] was devised for the purpose of providing what is advantageous for a body," Socrates further wins from Thrasymachus the recognition that "it isn't fitting for an art to seek the advantage of anything else than that of which it is the art" (I.342b). The argument with Thrasymachus aside, the point about *technē* is crucial: as is implied in the account of *technē* in Aristotle's *Metaphysics* with which we began, it is the very sense of *technē* that it is the capstone, so to speak, of the process one engages in so that one can learn *to be responsive to the nature of the object*.

This point about the proper object of *technē* is expressed especially powerfully by Socrates earlier in Book I, in his discussion with Polemarchus about the nature of justice. Polemarchus introduces a line from the lyric poet Simonides that it is just to give to each what is owed [*to ta opheilomena hekastōi apodidonai dikaion esti*] (I.331e), which Socrates explicates as follows: "It looks as if he thought that it is just to give to everyone what is fitting [*to prosēkon hekastoi apodidonai*], and this he gave the name 'what is owed'"[28] (I.332c) This explication of "what is owed [*ta opheilomena*]" as "what is fitting [*to prosēkon*]" is a helpful one, for it makes it clear that the proper treatment of something must be assessed in terms of the object being treated; that is, it is the nature of the object that determines what is proper to it. Socrates then asks Polemarchus,

> If someone were to ask him, "Simonides, the art called medicine gives what that is owed and fitting to which things?" what do you suppose he would answer us? (I.332c)

Polemarchus replies, "'It's plain,' he said, 'drugs, food and drinks to bodies.'" What this analysis in the discussion with Polemarchus adds to the analysis of *technē* in the argument with Thrasymachus, then, is the notion that *technē* is precisely a matter of doing justice to its object: *technē* in its founding, defining nature, is a matter of "taking care"—*technē* as such seeks *the good of* its object (I.343b, 345b–347a; cf. I.352d–353e, 335b).[29]

It is possible for medicine to care for the body precisely because the body has its own immanent norm—health. The living body has a [dynamic] state of functioning that it naturally tends toward. This goal of the body—this "good"—is not defined by something other than the body, and it cannot be discerned by any means other than observation of the body. This orientation toward the primacy of "the good of the thing" is precisely the principle identified by Socrates in the *Phaedo*, when he describes what he had initially imagined to be the meaning of Anaxagoras's identification of "mind" [*nous*] as the cause of all things:

> If then one wished to know the cause of each thing, why it comes to be or perishes or exists, one had to find what was the best way for it to be or to be acted upon, or to act. On these premises then it befitted a man to investigate only, about this and other things, what is best.... As I reflected on this subject I was glad to think that I had found in Anaxagoras a teacher about the cause of things after my own heart. (*Phaedo* 97dc–d)

Inasmuch as it is itself a naturally occurring reality, the body has its own inherent good—its own defining trajectory—and medicine is possible only inasmuch as we can first recognize this native trajectory of the body; medicine develops through further observation and experimentation by which we learn how to support and supplement this state of the body, but it is already rooted first in answering to the terms—the nontranslatable terms—set by the body itself. Medicine does not "create" health, but rather learns how to support the body's natural tendency to rest in its proper state; indeed, as Socrates observes in the *Lysis*, "Suppose we consider a healthy body. It has no need of a doctor's help. It's fine just as it is" (*Lysis* 217a).[30] This same orientation to the good of its object is analogously true for the other *technai*.

Not all *technai* are matters of directly caring for natural bodies: house-building and piloting, for example, are each fundamentally defined by reference to something artificial, namely, houses and ships, respectively. Even in these cases, however, the notion of answerability to an immanent norm still obtains. In the case of house-building, it is the notion of "house" itself that sets the terms for the art, and it is by first grasping the meaning of that term that we can determine what counts as expertise in this domain. At root, housing is a reality emergent from our need for shelter, our need to make for ourselves a home within the challenging (natural) world. Piloting, similarly, is rooted in our need to navigate within the surrounding, challenging world (and thus is surely rooted ultimately in this same need as housing). *What it means* to be housed and *what it means* to sail cannot be separated at root from a grasp of the nature and the needs of the human being. Then, within that context, there is such a thing as competence at house-building and such a thing as competence at sailing. In each case, competence is a matter of being able to pursue the founding need that defines the art through the materials that constitute its domain of operations: the competent—and ultimately, the expert—house-builder *knows how* to work *within* the norms intrinsic to wood, plaster, and so on to satisfy the norm of human shelter, and the competent—and ultimately, the expert—sailor *knows how* to work *within* the norms intrinsic to ocean, wind, sail, and rudder to satisfy the needs of human travel. While these *technai*, unlike medicine, are intrinsically "open-ended" in their specific objectives, in that human shelter and human travel are both realities intrinsically shaped by our desires and thus intrinsically open to varied forms of realization, they are nonetheless matters of possible expertise precisely insofar as they are at root answerable to the given norms, themselves rooted in the demands of human nature, of sheltering and travel, and, within that context, answerable to the norms that the materials of their realization project for their effective employment: the expert house-builder and the expert pilot must first develop *empeiria* within these domains, these *pragmata*.

And, as we noted in our initial discussion of *technē*, the experienced house-builder or sailor will become a *technitēs*—an expert, properly speaking—when, going beyond know-how, that person explicitly grasps the principles that have been operative in the successful practice of building or sailing. *Technē* is experience we have in which we actually formulate explicitly—put into words—the rationality that has already been guiding our practice, and so *technē* naturally results in a product: it is the natural flowering of expertise to produce and thence share articulations of principles—"to state [*eipein*] the cause [*aitian*]," as Socrates said in the *Gorgias* (*Gorgias* 465a)—whether in the form of written treatises or through oral teaching. As Aristotle writes,

> In general it is a sign of the man who knows, that he can teach, and therefore we think *technē* more truly knowledge than *empeiria* is, for artists can teach and men of mere experience cannot. (*Metaphysics* A[I].1.981b7–9)

Technē, then, precisely produces a kind of model of itself—an encapsulation of its meaning, housed now in words rather than in action: the expert house-builder is simultaneously a builder of houses and a portrayer of what it is to build houses. It is the production of this separate product—the teaching—that allows the art to be passed on to others.

This separable teaching can be passed on only because the principle of the relevant *technē* can be formulated in language, thus allowing the fruitful culmination—the *anthos* or "blossom," so to speak—of one's own experience to be passed on to another.[31] Our language—*logos*—allows us to separate the lesson—the *leçon*, or "reading"—from the experience, and this particular power of language can itself undergo development. When our language is oral only, transmission is always local, in both time and space. With the development of writing, however, the lesson of the language can itself be further separated from the immediate activity of linguistic communication, and can become, as Thucydides says of his *History*, a *ktēma es aei*, a "possession for all time." With writing, we more powerfully secure our learning against the frailties and vicissitudes of finite human life.

And this passing on of our learning is itself, like sheltering and travel, another activity rooted in the needs of human nature: we are beings inherently constituted by the need to learn, and so *education* is a defining feature of human reality. As human beings, we begin with a relatively meager natural endowment for navigating the world—we are weak and vulnerable animals, as Protagoras noted (*Protagoras* 321c)—but our cultural inheritance is huge: we are born into worlds that carry on the accumulated product of centuries of human learning, and, by assimilating ourselves to this body of cultural riches, we are able to act with powers that massively exceed what any of us could ever achieve individually.[32] It is that crucial dimension of *technē* that is the formulation of the distilled essence of our know-how into a *logos*, an articulated account—and most especially a written record—that allows for this handing down of cultural learning.

As we noted earlier, we, like the characters in Plato's *Republic*, have grown up in a world shaped by government, but the roots and meaning of that reality are largely opaque to us. This is true more broadly of the entirety of our cultural inheritance: we have the handed-down wisdom of generations offered to us as ready-to-use powers, but we (necessarily) do not have the rich, developed *empeiria* that was defining of those generations and that is the real substance of that accumulated learning.

The very source of the power involved in learning—the source of education—is equally the site of its weakness. Our learning is essentially a "second sailing," as Socrates says in the *Phaedo*, in that rather than "looking at *ta pragmata* with our eyes and attempting to grasp them by each of the senses, ... we take refuge in *logoi* and look in them for the truth of beings" (*Phaedo* 99d–e). It is because the essential core of our learning can be formulated as a detached lesson that it can be passed on; equally, though, this means that what we pass on is inherently distanced from that which gives it its core meaning. Socrates raises this issue in relation to writing specifically in the context of his narration of a somewhat complicated "myth" in the *Phaedrus*. There, the king (called a god by the Greeks) Thamus discusses the "pros and cons" of the many arts introduced by the god Theuth; about letters (writing), he says,

> This will produce a forgetting in the souls of those who learn these letters as they fail to exercise their memory, because those who put trust in writing recollect from the outside with foreign signs, rather than themselves from within by themselves. . . . Your students will appear rich in knowledge when for the most part there's an absence of knowledge, and they will be difficult to be with since they appear wise rather than being really wise. (*Phaedrus* 275a–b)

The essence of understanding is that it is the grasp of the principle that is *already animating our engagement with a state of affairs*. Properly speaking, understanding is understanding *of* something familiar: the *anthos* or "blossom" of a rich process of connecting with our situation. When we formulate the principles of our engagement abstractly and turn them into a lesson that can be passed on to others, we massively empower others to elevate the level of their engagement with the world; equally, though, we allow others to live with the illusion that they have mastered some domain because they have the "theory" [*logos*] of it, even though they have no practical knowledge of that domain. As Aristotle noted in the quotation from *Metaphysics* A(I) that we studied above, "men of experience succeed even better than those who have theory [*logon*] without experience" (*Metaphysics* A[I].1.981a14–15), and this truth is surely familiar to all of us: by cultivating the detached, "cognitive" relationship to the world, our involvement in education can lead us to believe ourselves to be learned and wise when in fact we live an insulated life without real, meaningful engagement with those dimensions of reality with respect to which we consider ourselves learned.[33]

III. Money

Our *logos*-capacity allows us to "give an account" of things, and this is what allows us to develop *technai*. Developing an account [*logos*] of some state of affairs [*pragma*] entails that we are not utterly absorbed in that state of affairs: giving an account of things requires that we have some distance from those things, and that we thus have some capacity to deploy our powers freely. Thus, even though the development of a *technē* is a matter of putting us more deeply into contact with the thing studied, it is simultaneously the establishing of our independence from it, the instituting of the reality of our power over it. Our general theme in this study is the ambivalent character of our *logos*, and through this analysis of *technē* we can now identify (at least) three ways in which this *logos* can separate itself problematically from the very substance that gives it meaning: we will see this in the reduction of *technē* to exploitation, to money-making, and to the possession of an abstract rule.

We can see a bit more of the complexity integral to *technē* if we contrast two descriptions of *technai*, one in the *Republic* and one in the *Apology*. In the *Apology*, Socrates recounts his conversation with Callias regarding the education of Callias's sons:

> So I asked him—he has two sons—"Callias," I said, "if your sons were colts or calves, we could find and engage a supervisor for them who would make them excel in their proper qualities, some horse breeder or farmer. Now since they are men, whom do you have in mind to supervise them? Who is a supervisor in this kind of excellence, the human and social kind?" (*Apology* 20a–b)

Here in the *Apology*, Socrates points to horse-breeding and farming as *technai* that precisely and obviously are oriented toward the good of their object: it is the commitment of these arts to raise colts and calves to their proper development as horses and cows. In his argument with Socrates in the *Republic*, Thrasymachus challenges Socrates's analysis of *technē* as something answerable to the good of its object, using just such an art as his example:

> You do not even recognize sheep or shepherd ... because you suppose shepherds or cowherds consider the good of the sheep or the cows and fatten them and take care of them looking to something other than their masters' good and their own; and so you also believe that the rulers in the cities, those who truly rule, think about the ruled differently from the way a man would regard sheep, and that night and day they consider anything else than how they will benefit themselves. (I.343a–b)

Thrasymachus here rightly points to the fact that shepherds, like the horse-breeders and farmers above, are not solely involved in caring for the animals they supervise, but are also involved in the practice of using those animals for their own ends.[34] It is precisely this complexity—the conjoining of the care for the end of the object and the care for the interests of humans with respect to those objects—that we must understand in order to grasp the problematic abstractions to which *logos* is prone.

In fact, there is no contradiction between the truths noted by Socrates and Thrasymachus in the two passages just cited: it is true that *technai* are answerable to the good of their objects and also true that *technai* are answerable to human interests. We noted earlier that, in the case of house-building, the commitment to human dwelling must also work expertly with the natural materials that must be drawn on in order to provide human shelter. Here, caring for human dwelling competently cannot be separated from the demands of *learning* how to interact competently with wood and weather. Analogously, we should recognize that shepherding is itself a subspecies of dwelling (as we also noted with piloting); that is, establishing an adequate human home cannot be separated from using the natural environment as much for food and clothing as for shelter and travel. (Indeed, food, shelter, and clothing are the initial examples Socrates identifies of the type of human need that the *polis* must address [II.369d].) Herding cattle or sheep for food, leather, and wool, however, is not at odds with caring for the needs of the animals, but in fact presupposes precisely that care: the very ability to "harvest" resources from these animals, like the ability to harvest crops from the earth, requires *learning* how to interact competently with those animal and plant realities. In other words, as we noted in our initial reflections on *technē*, it is only *from those realities themselves* that we can learn what it is that they make possible, and, hence, any *technē* with respect to these realities is necessarily rooted in *empeiria*: one must become experienced with those realities in order to be powerful with respect to them. Shepherding, thus, is indeed committed to the good of the object—the sheep—though this good is itself held answerable to the good of humans, who must themselves rely on the resources made available by the sheep. There is no living thing—human, animal, or plant—that does not use environmental resources, and thus one cannot be committed to the care of any form of life except by caring for its use of the other natural forms in its environment that it relies on for food, shelter, and so on.[35] Use and care are thus coordinate orientations rather than contradictory orientations. It is this nexus of use and care, however, that allows us to define a relationship of use that is not a matter of care but a matter of exploitation.

Thrasymachus portrays the (unjust) ruler as being like a shepherd for whom his subjects are like sheep to be sheared. In fact, historically, the shearing of sheep for wool went hand in hand with the careful maintenance of flocks, and the relationship of shepherd to sheep was more symbiotic than exploitative. Thrasymachus's image (which is indeed one we often employ idiomatically in the same way) is thus in fact poor, given the point he wants to make: while it does no doubt capture the passivity of the "victims" of shearing, it does not in fact portray the exploitative relationship of self-interested rule for which he is using it as an analogy. We can, nonetheless, recognize that there are such exploitative pseudo-*technai*, as in the case, for example, of contemporary "factory farms." In our contemporary economic world, sheep are not cared for by shepherds but are managed as "inputs" in massive, technological businesses for which these sheep exist only as raw material—only as resources from which a product is extracted. As animal rights activists regularly complain, these farms are not at all concerned about caring for their animals but instead do the minimum necessary to maintain the existence of those animals as product-producing resources. Something analogous is also notably true in the contemporary lumber industry, which replaces healthy forests with massive fields of uniform tree species that are repeatedly planted, cut, and replanted, in contrast to whatever *technai* of lumbering or forestry have functioned in earlier societies, and, indeed, in a wide range of other contemporary technological enterprises. In contrast to the symbiosis that is definitive of *technē*, these industries are truly exploitative.

What defines these industries as exploitative, and what specifically distinguishes them from *technai*, properly speaking, is that they *take advantage* of their objects.[36] More than just taking advantage of their objects, though, these industries also take advantage of *technē* itself. The key to understanding this is to recognize that this industrial exploitation is *possible* only because it relies on the learning about the objects that comes from *technē*, which, as we have seen, itself comes from *empeiria* with respect to that object. Industrial exploitation relies on the knowledge of *how* to interact with sheep, trees, rock, or whatever else in order to extract wool, lumber, ore, and so on, but *it does not itself produce this knowledge*: this knowledge owes its existence to the historical development of various *technai* that themselves owe their existence to a long history of *empeiria*. This *empeiria*, further, is not just a personal matter—though it is, of course, always persons who have to develop this experience—but is also a cultural matter in that it is a matter of generations of cooperative experience (of the sort identified by Socrates, Adeimantus, and Glaucon when they introduce the notion of the *polis* [loosely so called]) to learn to make bronze, herd sheep, or cultivate wheat.[37] Modern technological industry has inherited this massive body of cultural learning—learning that is inherently dependent on, and indeed defined by, generations of careful engagement with the natural world—without the need to go through the practice of developing *empeiria* with respect to the natural world, precisely because of *logos*: precisely because of the separability of the lesson—the explicit account—from the process of learning. It is because *technē* is precisely realized in the production of a result separable from the practice that gives rise to it that its learning can be passed on in a way that absolves future generations of the need to learn the meaningful relationship to the world of nature *of which* that lesson is the distilled essence.

These modern industries are exploitative in that they have inherited a learning that they did not earn, and they thus "take advantage," simultaneously, of their objects and also of the *technai* that have offered them the powerful rules for interacting with the world on which they depend. In principle, the powers operative within exploitative, modern technology have a debt to learning, but it is a debt they do not acknowledge. Here, then, we see the first aspect of the ambivalent character of *logos* in the context of *technē*, in contemporary "technological," economic exploitation. There is a second, important economic aspect to this ambivalent character as well.

In the context of such "technological" industry, it is not just the intimate connection to object and *technē* that is lost. The product is similarly alienated from the industry. In the contemporary factory farm, the wool or the eggs are produced, not because of a desire for wool or eggs, but because those goods are "commodities," that is, they can be sold. No doubt there is someone who wants wool or an egg, and the factory farm functions on the premise that that person will pay money for such a product. For the factory farm, the concrete character of its product is irrelevant to it: all that matters is the capacity of that product to be sold. In other words, value, from the point of view of technological industry, is money, not goods.

One does not, of course, have to enter the world of contemporary technological industry to encounter money. Indeed, we already encountered it in the argument with which we began our study of *technē*, in which we considered the *technē* as such. Socrates there asked Thrasymachus, "Is the doctor in the precise sense . . . a money-maker [*chrēmatistēs*] or one who cares for the sick [*tōn kamnontōn therapeutēs*]?" (I.341c).[38] "To make money" is a goal, and one that can be pursued by operating on the sick, but it is not the same goal as "to care for the sick"; indeed, if one's goal is to make money, then the sick have become a means to that end, whereas, on the contrary, in order to care for the sick, they must precisely be taken as the end. And within the *Republic* itself, we have the example of Cephalus, the father of Polemarchus and the host of the conversation that is the *Republic*, who grew quite rich through his shield manufactory. In situations like Cephalus's shield manufactory, we can see that, though massive, modern, technological industry did not exist in ancient Greece, the pursuit of money-making did.[39] Indeed, as we shall see in more detail in chapter 2, Plato's ancient Greek culture was itself historically a prominent site for the emergence of money-culture.

Like government, money is a reality with which we are already engaged without in fact grasping what it is. Also like government, money is a distinctive phenomenon of the world of beings with *logos*. Most basically, money is the medium in and by which different goods share in a single measure of value.[40] To establish money is to establish a system of valuation by which the worth of anything and everything can be assigned a specific quantity of a uniform value—a "price." Historically, grain, for example, has been a common "currency," with different goods being defined by agreement to be equal in value to specific quantities of grain. As Aristotle writes,

> So the builder has to get the shoemaker's product from the shoemaker, and he has to give him some of his own.... But nothing prevents one person's product from being worth more than the other's; so they have to be equalized.... So all things that are exchanged have to be somehow comparable. For that purpose, coinage came about, and it becomes a sort of medium, for it measures all things, so that it also measures the excess and the deficit, how many sandals are equal to a horse or to food. (*Nicomachean Ethics* V.5.1133a8–22)

In fact, in ancient Greece, the more developed system of using precious metals and the coinage they make possible as the money-standard had some of its earliest beginnings and, as David M. Schaps writes in *The Invention of Coinage and the Monetization of Ancient Greece*, "the invention of coinage and its adoption by the Greeks involved an intellectual change of great importance—to put it clearly, if too simply, ... the notion of money as we think about it, although it surely had antecedents, was something that had not been thought of before the Greeks adopted coinage."[41] Whatever its material form, money, at its root, is a way of "taking account of" one's worth, in the sense of translating and recording the meaning of one's goods into the terms of a shared standard.[42]

Like the explicit formulation in *technē* of the principle of some form of *empeiria*, money, as the interpretive expression of the value of some good, is a reality separable from its roots. One can study the principle of a *technē* without establishing any contact with *to pragma*, the state of affairs, of which it is the principle, and one can engage with money without establishing any contact with the goods, of which it is the value. One can imagine, for example, that Cephalus (or his father or grandfather) might well have gone through a disciplined process of learning about shields in order to develop his shield-making business, but one can also imagine that Cephalus's son, Polemarchus, might well inherit and thus carry on this already-established business without himself ever learning the trade. Unlike traditional societies, in which the father's way of life is typically passed on to the sons by initiating them into that *practice* from an early age (which sociologists call "narrow socialization"[43]), in Cephalus's situation it is the case both that his children have been raised with greater independence than in traditional societies and that it is a *business* (which apparently relied on the labor of about one hundred slaves[44]) that is handed down. Indeed, this issue of one's relationship to what one inherits is precisely the theme that initially emerges in the conversation that Cephalus begins with Socrates (and which begins the central conversation of the *Republic*):

> "Cephalus," I said, "did you inherit [*parelabes*] or did you earn [*epektēsō*] most of what you possess [*hōn kektēsai ta pleiō*]?"
>
> "What do you mean, earned, Socrates!" he said. "As a money-maker, I was a sort of mean between my grandfather and my father. For my grandfather, whose namesake I am, inherited pretty nearly as much substance [*ousian*] as I now possess, and he increased it many times over. Lysanias, my father, used it to a point where it was still less than it is now. I am satisfied if I leave it not less, but rather a bit more than I inherited, to my sons here." (I.330a–b)

Socrates goes on to make a further point about inherited wealth:

> "The reason I asked, you see," I said, "is that to me you didn't seem overly fond of money. For the most part, those who do not make money themselves are that way. Those who do make it are twice as attached to it as others. For just as poets are fond of their poems and fathers of their children, so money-makers too are serious about money—as their own product [*hōs ergon heautōn*]." (I.330b–c)

The interesting theme here is that it is one's actual product—that in which one has invested oneself—that one cares about. Socrates here makes that point about money, and one can indeed imagine that one could demonstrate real skill—even expertise, *technē*—in the practice of making money and hence be proud of one's accomplishment; people who simply inherit that money, though, receive its power without themselves having to develop the discipline—the *empeiria*—that "earned" that wealth and hence can "harvest" the result without acknowledging the source of that harvest to which it is indebted. But similarly, this argument applies to money as such, for, as we have just been arguing, the making of money is an "abstract" process that can proceed without any meaningful engagement in the worldly practice that actually generates the source of that wealth. Thus, Greek "gentlemen farmers," for example, might well have grown wealthy from farms on which they effectively operated as estate-managers, without learning anything of the work of farming as such—work, that is, that was carried on by employed laborers and, to some extent, slaves.[45] In this sense, then, money itself, like the principle of a *technē*, is a reality that can exist in abstraction for the very source that gives it its meaning, and, as with the principle of a *technē*, it is thus a reality with which we can engage as if it were independently meaningful and valuable without acknowledging its, and hence our, indebtedness to the reality—the goods and the *empeiria*—on which it is intrinsically dependent.

IV. *Technē*, Money, and the Commercial *Polis*

Government, *technē*, writing, and money each offer the possibility of involving oneself with what is really the flowering, the "bloom" [*anthos*], of an inherently worthwhile engagement with the world as if that engagement were a detached, independently valuable reality. When the governors govern for their own sake rather than for the sake of the governed, when students desire to learn the theory while disdaining meaningful engagement with *to pragma*, when writing is imagined to convey context-free meaning, or when money-making is pursued at the expense of the very trades that make it possible, a kind of exploitation is being carried out. In the very case of reading the *Republic*, for example, students—and their teachers—can be engaged merely in the sort of "thought experiment" undertaken in Book II by Socrates, Glaucon, and Adeimantus in their making "a city in speech [*logos*]," and take themselves to be studying political philosophy simply because they read the presentation of various ideas about politics within these pages and then exercise their own ungrounded imaginations to determine whether or not they "agree" with the ideas rather than, say, studying Thucydides and Livy to learn first *ta phainomena*: to learn what the basic reality of political life is that these written presentations of ideas gather and unify. Such processes of imagining are, to be sure, valuable—indeed, they are educationally essential—but they should not be confused with knowledge. When such ungrounded imagining is confused with studying, a veneer of learning has been substituted for learning, and both the reality of politics and the reality of philosophical study are sacrificed to the trivial accomplishment of self-satisfaction in the student. And, similarly, even the more rigorous engagement with the written work—and this is even more true with textbooks that relay the theoretical accomplishments of the natural, social, or historical sciences than it is with a singular text like the *Republic*—can encourage one to imagine that the ideas one is encountering are simply timeless realities, rather than recognizing the historical, human interaction with the world of which the work is the condensed expression. In the case of money-making, the businessman who prides himself on his accomplishment of vastly increasing his wealth through trading goods between cities while in fact knowing nothing about olive oil production or pottery manufacture is in fact able to enrich himself only because the quantity of his accumulated wealth allows him to control the market and hence to compel the manufacturers of oil and pots to sell their goods to him for less that they are worth and then to sell them himself to others for more than are worth, his profit coming solely from the bulk of his trade.[46] Similarly, the estate-manager can grow very wealthy, imagining himself to be a great farmer and a great contributor to his society, when in fact his wealth comes from the intelligent labor of his workers, a wealth that he, rather than they, enjoys only because of the historically and institutionally structured situation that has put him and others of his social class in the position to force peasants and slaves to subordinate their work to his desire. In the case of governing, one can take one's position of authority as an invitation to impose one's own views and advance one's own interests rather than embracing the responsibility to think and act on behalf of the community that affords one such power. In all of these cases—the "study" of political philosophy, the reading of scholarly texts, the trade in oil and pots, estate-management, or self-interested governance—an enjoyment is had that rests on the workings of a reality that is invisible to the one enjoying. In each case, it is a kind of (innocent) misapprehension or (intentional) misrepresentation of the true nature of that reality, and it is thus a kind of dishonesty.

Government, money, writing, and *technē*, as phenomena of *logos*, manifest a fundamental ambiguity. Because of their ability, dishonestly, to be taken up as realities independent of their founding conditions, each of these is a manifestly dangerous reality, a reality that has the capacity to undermine the meaningful relationship with the world on which we ultimately depend. At the same time, however, each of these realities also has something extremely powerful to offer to the enhancement of our engagement with the world.

(i) The establishment of government—an independent system for the generation and maintenance of a network of human laws—offers persons quite a profound liberation. Human social life takes various forms, and, as we will note again in chapter 2, the law-governed *polis* is fundamentally a response to the limitations of a society built around the intimate, familial household—the *oikos*.[47] The Athenian Stranger describes this emergence of this structure in Book III of the *Laws*. In the oldest societies ("within the past one or two thousand years" [*Laws* III.677d]) of "those scattered in single households [*kata mian oikēsin*] or clans [*kata genos*]" (*Laws* III.680b)—societies that are matters of "dynasty" [*dunasteia*], (*Laws* III.680b)—he says,

> Isn't it the case, though, that they didn't need lawgivers, and that such a thing wasn't likely to occur in those times? For writing doesn't yet exist among those born in that part of the cycle, and their lives are governed by habits [*ethesi*] and what are called ancestral laws [*patriois nomois*]. . . . The eldest rules with an authority handed down from father and mother, whom the others follow, like birds forming a flock. (*Laws* III.680a, e)[48]

These communities grow, however, and "as these dwellings are growing bigger out of the smaller original ones, each of the small family groups arrives clan by clan, possessing both its own eldest who rules, and its own particular customs [*ethē*] because it has lived apart" (*Laws* III.681a–b). It is this situation, the Athenian Stranger remarks (*Laws* III.681c), that gives rise to legislation:

> Surely, after this, those who come together are compelled to choose certain men common to them who look over the customs of all the clans and, having picked out the ones they find especially agreeable for the community, display them clearly and present them for the approval of the leaders and chiefs, the monarchs as it were, of the populace. The men who do this we called lawgivers. (*Laws* III.681c–d)

The law-governed *polis* emerges, that is, because of the need to negotiate the differences of habitual modes of life that different, cohabiting groups are committed to, and to establish a shared way of life that is not partisan in its embrace of any particular group's traditional expectations. The impartial, deliberative council and the rule of the law that the *polis* offers make possible a norm of equality, a degree of complexity, and an openness to innovation that are not available in the isolated family or in a traditional society based on the "clan" structure. Though our families give birth to us and raise us, it is nonetheless of great value to us that we can be *liberated* from the parameters of family life and can participate in a culture and a system of decision-making that is detached from that—a world of human autonomy and self-definition.

(ii) The distillation of experience in the principles of *technē* is what makes possible the progressive advance in learning between generations. It took many generations for earlier humans to learn the forms of edible food, for example, and we are now very fortunate to be able to rely on those results without having to repeat the earlier generations' experiments; similarly, the ability to smelt and alloy metals is one of the greatest revolutions in human history, a scale of accomplishment captured by the divine characterization of this in the myths of Hephaistos and Prometheus, and we are again fortunate that we can benefit from the results of the long, difficult labors that produced these abilities without ourselves having to repeat the processes of learning that led to their discovery. The *liberating* character of *technē* allows us to bypass its experiential foundations and engage directly with its results, and we are all reliant on the fact that such results have been recorded.

(iii) Writing is itself particularly powerful in serving this end of the passing down of learning. Writing precisely separates the lesson—the *leçon*—from the human situation, allowing the focused appropriation of the "bloom" of experience without the need to engage with the complex human, material circumstances of its emergence. Writing, in other words, precisely makes possible the *impersonal* relationship to ideas, *liberating* us from the need to navigate the idiosyncrasies and the power structures of personal relationships in our desire to ascertain the truth, while simultaneously making possible a spatial and temporal dissemination of learning that would be unimaginable within the context of oral transmission.

(iv) Money, similarly, and the world of trade that it makes possible, has a transformative effect on the possibilities of our civilization that is analogous to the effects of government, *technē*, and writing. Socrates introduces this theme in Book II:

> "And further," I said, "just to found the city itself in the sort of place where there will be no need of imports is pretty nearly impossible.... Then, there will also be need for still other men who bring to it what's needed from another city.... And similarly, surely, agents as well, who will import and export the various products.... Out of this we'll get a market and an established currency as a token for exchange." (II.370e–371b)

From the beginning, we have recognized that the city exists to allow us to fulfill the needs of our life and development, and these needs in fact take us beyond any single city to the relationship between cities. Our interests bring us into relationship with others with whom it is in our mutual interest to trade; it is precisely in a world where we must engage with people who are not our intimates, however, that a recognized standard and medium of exchange becomes essential. *Technē* allows the fruits of our learning to be extracted and recorded in writing such that they can be saved, transported, and shared; money, similarly, allows the worth of our enterprises to be extracted and recorded such that it can be saved, transported, and shared. Money, in thus *liberating* us from the limitations of immediate exchange, vastly expands the spatial and temporal parameters of our shared existence, thereby increasing the scale and scope of possible human enterprise.

In the narrower scope of the initial society imagined by Socrates, Glaucon, and Adeimantus, when "many men gather in one settlement as partners and helpers" (II.369c) it is possible for "each one of them [to] put his work at the disposition of all in common" (II.369e). In such an intimate setting, it is possible to live in a situation of reciprocity, each of us offering to each other our work and benefiting from the work of the others without any explicitly formulated terms for our sharing of effort and accomplishment. In such an environment, the "medium" of our exchange is trust: we depend on each other, and we live in the comfortable confidence that the vulnerability entailed by that dependence will be appropriately cared for. In an intimate social world—the world of *oikos*—we live with the assurance that our dependency will be protected in our immediate dealings or that, if a problem arises in those dealings, our community as a whole will have a way of responding to and correcting that problem. In a society where we must interact with strangers, though, this trust is what is lacking. What it means for others to be "strangers" is precisely that, in some crucial way, we and they do not share the same life: we do not share expectations with them and hence do not know what to expect from them. With strangers, the terms of interaction cannot be presumed and must be established. In economic terms, this means establishing a way of exchanging our goods that does not require such trust: with money we establish a way to guarantee the successful completion of our exchange in the moment, without depending on a personal relationship of trust with the stranger with whom we exchange. Once the price has been paid—in wheat, cattle, olive oil, precious metal of certified weight and purity, or state-sanctioned coin—the exchange is done, with no expectation of future care from the other. In an intimate community—the *oikos*—the members of this community live with the trust that the appropriate reciprocity of their shared situation will be protected in their relationships with each other, and indeed "somewhere in some need these men have of one another" is precisely where Adeimantus locates justice (II.371e-372a); in the world of trade with strangers, this bond of "justice" becomes instead the establishing and policing of a system of exchange in which money—tokens and the attendant laws and guardians that control their use—has been exchanged for trust. Money, thus, does not simply translate the worth of goods into a single, universally shared value; it also translates relationships of trust into relationships of law. Money is definitive of a society that welcomes relations with aliens but, for that very reason, has an alienated relation to law.

The world of trade with strangers and the money that is its medium bring about a radical change in the form of human social life compared with the isolated life of the self-contained and minimally self-sufficient *oikos*. It is a world that operates with a different scale of operations than is possible in the simple *oikos*-community: the coordination of wealth and the organization of enterprises allow for undertakings that are larger, both temporally and spatially, such as massive architectural building projects or extensive naval trade to foreign markets. It is a more culturally diverse world, initially through its establishing of contact between cultures and subsequently through the uniting of diverse peoples in the same locations through embassies and immigration.[49] It is a world of class difference that, as Socrates notes in Book II, generates both a class of wage-laborers and a trade in luxuries for those able to afford them (II.371d–e, 372e–373a). And, as we just noted, it is also a world with a different orientation to law and justice, specifically, with justice conceived as law, as the regulation of transactions between anonymous individuals. This is the world—the reality—of the fully developed *polis*.

Conclusion

The *polis*, *technē* with its development in writing, and a money-economy are all phenomena of the being with *logos*, the being who can take account. They are all ambivalent realities that open up vast new possibilities for human life: the *polis* by allowing us to share a world with others who are not our intimates and about whom we need not care, *technē* and money by making it possible for us to engage with the results of other people's experience without ourselves having to be involved in that work and thus again in separation from the care that is integral to that work. This ability to "forget," so to speak, the preconditions of what we receive also opens up vast new possibilities for exploitation. Because we are beings of *logos*, we cannot fail to inherit much of our reality; the question, then, like the question Socrates posed to Cephalus, is how we handle this inheritance. We can never, strictly speaking, "earn" our own reality; the question, though, is whether we honor our debt or whether we live like dissolute, spendthrift children of wealthy parents, "the youth who become licentious . . . spending and wasting what belongs to them" (VIII.555c). What it takes to properly honor this debt is the subject of our remaining chapters, beginning, in our next chapter, with the fuller investigation of where the city we now live in—the commercial *polis*—came from.[50]

Notes

1. Indeed, Raaflaub argues for "citizen-state" as the more exact meaning in "Foreward," p. 3. See also "Homer to Solon," p. 44.

2. In my experience, the most thorough analysis of these complexities may be found in Benardete, *Socrates' Second Sailing*, pp. 44–54. Among other themes, Benardete especially points to the conflation of three different senses of the "city in speech" that Socrates, Glaucon, and Adeimantus are bringing into being: the community of discussion that they themselves constitute, a community they invent imaginatively, and a naturally occurring community whose emergence they are describing.

3. In order to continue the form of his initial derivation, Socrates would have to show how the second city emerges from need; in fact, in Book VIII, Socrates distinguishes between necessary desires and unnecessary desires (VIII.558d–559c), and, according to this distinction as it is interpreted there, the second city does not emerge out of need, but precisely out of unnecessary desires. This conception of "necessity," however, presumes merely an organic model of need, which, like the "geometrical necessities" that Glaucon refers to in Book V, is an insufficient model for understanding human need, because humans must also answer to "erotic necessities" (V.458d). The distinction between the first and second cities, according to which the second is the "luxurious" or "soft" city [*truphōsan polin*] (II.372e), resonates strongly with Aristotle's later analysis in Book I of the *Politics* according to which the village [*kōmē*] comes into being for the sake of living, while the *polis* comes into being for the sake of living well.

4. This third discourse is a prescriptive account, not of any existing society, but of a society that Socrates and Adeimantus are imagining. Socrates portrays the view they are developing as Adeimantus's view (III.389a, cf. IV.427c), and, indeed, the view they articulate does seem to be fairly straightforwardly a working-out of the perspective Adeimantus expressed at II.365a–367a.

5. Socrates's usage is not incorrect, for "*polis*" is a somewhat flexible term that, as Robinson notes (*The First Democracies*, p. 28, n. 51), can mean "society" and need not carry the specialized "political" sense it came to develop; on the history of the term and the reality of the *polis*, see especially Raaflaub, "Homer to Solon." Regarding the theme of *oikos*, as Brann ("The Music of the *Republic*," p. 16) and Sallis (*Being and Logos*, pp. 376–378) both note, Socrates in fact actually fails to mention households at all and identifies only individual men as members of this city, a point that is crucial for interpreting the unfolding of the conversation of the *Republic* as a whole; for my purposes, though, this need not detain us, for if one imagines this as a simple, sensible anthropology, this description would be a kind of synecdoche, and households would be implicit in these references to men.

6. Benardete, *Socrates' Second Sailing*, pp. 47–53, analyzes the unacknowledged complexity in this language of need.

7. According to Raaflaub, war for control of land began in Greece in the second half of the eighth century BC, a situation integral to the emerging reality of the *polis*; see "Homer to Solon," p. 51.

8. This changing sense of self-protection and the related change in the defining character of the "guardians" is the central focus of Brann, "The Music of the *Republic*." From the point of view of analyzing the dramatic development of the conversation—and especially its role as an educational experience for Glaucon—it is crucial to attend carefully to when and how these changes are noticed; I here "telescope" these developments, however, since my concern is not with the conversation as such but with the overall insight that the conversation offers into the nature of the very institution of "guardian." I offer a fuller discussion of the textual and conversational details in my YouTube lecture series, "Plato's Republic" (https://www.youtube.com/playlist?list=PLZyk__e49-Cv86nHOUeQWzoKI8U9VkWni).

9. On the distinctive significance of the conversational and conceptual issues raised by the notion of "craftsmen" of freedom, see Benardete, *Socrates' Second Sailing*, pp. 57, 71.

10. See Aristotle, *Constitution of Athens*, chap. 4, discussing the constitution of Draco: "The franchise was given to all who could furnish themselves with a military equipment." On the issue of whether there was a "hoplite revolution," see Raaflaub, "Homer to Solon," p. 80. For rich discussions of the controversy surrounding the nature and significance of hoplite warfare, see the essays collected in Kagan and Viggiano, *Men of Bronze*.

11. Livy, *The Early History of Rome*, Book III, chap. 26.

12. Aristotle, *Politics* III.4, IV.11.

13. Compare Plato's *Laws* VIII.846d–e: "There's almost no human nature that is capable of laboring with precision at two pursuits or two arts, or even of practicing one adequately himself while overseeing someone else who is practicing another."

14. On the idea that the "one man, one art" model fits uncomfortably with the notion of the guardians, see Benardete, *Socrates' Second Sailing*, p. 71.

15. This passage from Book II of the *Republic* and the issue of "savagery" that it raises is analyzed by Recco in *Athens Victorious*, pp. 58–60. Dorter analyzes the argument here in *The Transformation of Plato's Republic*, pp. 67–68. In my experience, the most thorough analysis of this discussion of the nature of the guardians—and especially of the correlation of the nature of the guardian with that of the "philosophical" dog—is found in Benardete, *Socrates' Second Sailing*, pp. 54–58; Benardete demonstrates, in particular, the complex and problematic employment of the notion of *thumos* and its entanglement here with the complex and problematic introduction of the notion of philosophy. This passage will be relevant when we investigate the nature of *thumos* directly in chap. 4.

16. This notion that the city is not an organism, and that in its place we must rely on *logos*, is the central theme of Protagoras's speech in *Protagoras*.

17. I use this expression in order to allude to Derrida's work *Rogues*, which discusses many of the themes of this chapter and the next and includes a substantial interpretation of the discussion of "democracy" in Book VIII of the *Republic*.

18. For documentation, see, for example, Davis, *City of Quartz*; Macaré, Schenwar, and Price, *Who Do You Serve, Who Do You Protect?*; and Woodiwiss, *Organized Crime and American Power*. See also Ivković, "To Serve and Collect." According to Transparency International's *Global Corruption Barometer* (2017), police in 119 countries were judged the most corrupt public institution, tying with elected representatives and followed closely by government officials, business executives, and local government.

19. Adam Smith has an insightful discussion of the impact of the professionalization of the Roman army in *The Wealth of Nations*, Book V, chap. 1, pt. I.

20. Livy, *The Early History of Rome*, Book II, especially chaps. 22–35.
21. On the "year of the four emperors," see Fagan, "Philosophical History and the Roman Empire."
22. Compare Althusser, "Idéologie et appareils idéologiques d'État," on the "repressive state apparatus."
23. In *Politics*, III.7, Aristotle similarly identifies three basic types of regime—monarchy, aristocracy, and democracy—and there are powerful reasons why each of these can be a good governing structure. But these positive features are all secondary to the more basic question of whether the government governs in the interest of the people or whether it governs exploitatively, in its own interest.
24. For the comparison of the city to a natural whole, see Aristotle, *Politics*, I.2.
25. For a provocative discussion of what is involved in Socrates's conception of *technē*, see Kirkland, *The Ontology of Socratic Questioning*, pp. 74–80.
26. On Socrates's argument with Thrasymachus about *technē*, see Sallis, *Being and Logos*, pp. 339–340. Sallis also notes that Thrasymachus is the only character in the *Republic* who claims to have an art; see *Being and Logos*, p. 338.
27. Dorter, in *The Transformation of Plato's Republic*, pp. 37–42, gives a detailed analysis of the argument separating *technē* from money-making.
28. According to Adam (*The Republic of Plato*, commentary ad loc. vol. I, p. 13), this is likely not a quotation but a popular paraphrase of a passage in Simonides of which there are no extant remains in the fragments we possess.
29. Thrasymachus here uses just these terms in his attempt to distance himself from the conclusions he has been forced to acknowledge.
30. This passage is the beginning of a longer argument that identifies anything in its natural state and inherently defined by the possibility of deterioration as "a friend of the good" (*Lysis* 218b–c). If, however, we construe this to mean that the good is defined only derivatively from the bad, we will face an infinitie regress, and we thus must recognize more fundamentally the originality of the good: "We have to arrive at some first principle which will no longer bring us back to another friend, something that goes back to the first friend, something for the sake of which we say that all the rest are friends too" (219d–e).
31. This separability of the principle of *technē* is the subject of the conversation between Socrates and Polemarchus at I.332c–334b, there emphasizing that this knowledge can in fact be turned against the object toward whose good it should be directed, a theme we will consider in our discussion of exploitation.
32. The discussion of history in Book III of *Laws* makes this point quite powerfully.
33. Grappling with this issue is one of the central themes of John Dewey, *Democracy and Education*—probably the single most important book in philosophy of education written since Plato's *Republic*; see especially chap. 14.
34. See Sallis, *Being and Logos*, pp. 339–340, on the intertwining of *technē* with money-making. Benardete's subtle analysis of this conversation in *Socrates' Second Sailing* (pp. 23–24) is worth careful attention; note in particular his conclusion that it is only in the art of money-making that self-interest and care for the good of the object coincide.
35. Many of the specific forms of such environmental relationships are documented in Aristotle's *History of Animals*.
36. See I.332c–334b, where Polemarchus and Socrates discuss the exploitative use of *technē*.
37. On this exact history, see in particular Anthony, *The Horse, the Wheel and Language*.
38. The Greeks have no unambiguous word for *money*, but use a number of designations, many of which are found throughout the *Republic*, including "*chrēmata* [wealth, or, more

exactly, "things used"], *argurion* [silver], and *nomisma* [currency, or, more exactly, "thing produced by customary division"]. Metaphors drawn from the realm of money are also pronounced in the discourse of the *Republic*; though it would be an extremely worthwhile endeavor, I will not here study the monetary "metaphorics" of the text. On the emergence of the money-culture in ancient Greece, see Seaford, *Money and the Early Greek Mind*, and Schaps, *The Invention of Coinage*; on the politics of coinage, see Kurke, *Coins, Bodies, Games, and Gold*.

39. Compare Demosthenes 27, *Against Aphobus 1*, secs. 9–11.

40. In fact, money functions are somewhat more complicated, though those complications are not relevant to the level of our analysis. For a particularly good account of the precise nature of money (and its emergence in Greek history), see Seaford, *Money and the Early Greek Mind*, especially pp. 16–20. In general, Seaford's account of money is excellent, but whereas his own interpretation of Greek culture and literature is based on the best methods of contemporary anthropology, themselves indebted to the insights of European philosophers of the nineteenth and twentieth centuries, he relies, for the interpretation of the pre-Socratic philosophers, on the work of scholars who are explicitly committed to the renunciation of those very insights.

41. Schaps, *The Invention of Coinage*, p. vi.

42. On the nature of money in general, see Adam Smith, *The Wealth of Nations*, Book I, and Ingham, *The Nature of Money*. Typically, money is defined with four parameters, as a standard of value, a medium of exchange, a way of storing value, and a final means of payment. Compare Hippias's claim, in *Hippias (Major)* 289d–e, that that which makes the fine [*to kalon*] fine is gold (*chrusos*).

43. For discussion of this concept, see Arnett, "Broad and Narrow Socialization."

44. According to Lysias's autobiographical remark in *Against Eratosthenes* 19. For a helpful account of the nature of Cephalus's family, see Gifford, "Dramatic Dialectic in *Republic* Book I," pp. 52–58.

45. The Romans developed huge slave-based farms that resulted in the generation of incredible wealth for a small financial aristocracy; Greek farms operated on a smaller scale and, according to Meiksins Wood, *Peasant-Citizen and Slave*, chap. 2, were not primarily based on slave-labor; on this point, see the parallel analysis of Osborne, "The Economics and Politics of Slavery at Athens." Xenophon's *Oeconomicus*, in *The Shorter Socratic Writings*, is a discussion between Socrates and Critoboulus about "estate-management"; it communicates, among other things, how detached such a "gentleman farmer" could be from the realities of his agricultural enterprise.

46. See *Statesman* 260c–d. The character of money and trade is also richly discussed in Book XI of the *Laws*.

47. The opposition of *polis* and *oikos* is hyperbolically illuminated throughout the "comedic" Book V of the *Republic*, in which it is made clear that the monolithic, paternalistic authority of "the state" is fundamentally challenged by the proper "element" of the *oikos*, namely, the natural reality of childbirth and its attendant familial structures of upbringing. It is noteworthy, too, that the discussion of the emergence of the *polis* in Book II makes no mention of childbirth or family life, but instead imagines the city emerging from already-formed individuals. Brann, "The Music of the *Republic*," pp. 22–23, notes the comic resonance of Book V. Sallis, in *Being and Logos*, pp. 371–396, demonstrates in considerable detail the "comedy" of Book V, a theme that runs throughout his analysis. Freydberg also discusses the comedy of Book V in *The Play of the Platonic Dialogues*, pp. 118–122. See Brann, "The Music

of the *Republic*," p. 16, for the idea that the "first city" includes no birth; Sallis builds on this point in *Being and Logos*, pp. 376–378, 452.

48. For the analysis of these situations of *dunasteia*, see Fagan, "He Saw the Cities and He Knew the Minds of Many Men"; Fagan especially exploits the Homeric references of this discussion in the *Laws* to reveal the inherent xenophobia of such *oikos*-communities.

49. Compare *Laws* III.681d: "A third pattern of regime emerges, in which all forms and experiences of political regimes and of cities come together."

50. Rothleder, *Fraught Decisions in Plato and Shakespeare*, gives a particularly rich interpretation of the theme of "debt" in the *Republic*. How this relates to the intersection of matters of polity and matters of economy in the *Republic* is a central theme of the prologue to part II; its relevance to the character of Cephalus in particular and to the figures of Book I in general is provocatively analyzed in the prologue to part I.

2

THE CURRENCIES OF POWER

Our investigation into the nature of money led us to consider the *oikos*-community and the intimate relations of trust in an economics of reciprocity and distinguish that community from the more varied and "multicultural" community of the society involved in a money-economy. In distinguishing these principles of how a society is organized and, hence, how its members behave toward themselves and others, we are distinguishing how each of these societies "takes account" of itself. Social organization—social self-interpretation, in other words—is itself a matter of *logos*. This particular distinction, between the *oikos*-community and the money-economy, is itself a distinction within the range of possibilities for such social self-interpretation.

In our investigation of economics, we saw that money is the embrace of a way of taking account of things such that the qualitatively different worth of different goods is taken up as a matter of simple quantitative difference within a uniform domain of value. Something analogous happens in the "taking account" of ourselves that defines community life: we, as persons, are each unique and thus qualitatively distinct from each other, but in our social relationships we take ourselves to be all variants of the "same"; in other words, in our social relations we similarly embrace a practice of translating qualitative difference into measurable, quantitative uniformity. As Socrates says of social life, "What happens to be honored is practiced, and what [is] without honor is neglected" (VIII.551a). Different forms of society are built around different forms of measuring this, our social "value"—different forms of honoring—and thus establishing the hierarchy that organizes our social life.

Like all the conversations in the *Republic*, the discussion that Socrates, Glaucon, and Adeimantus have in Book VIII about the forms of political life is textually and conversationally complex, largely because of Socrates's interweaving of the political analysis of different regimes with the psychological analysis of putatively exemplary individuals within those regimes, and in part because of the usual dialogic complexities of interruption, idiosyncrasy, ambiguity, and so on;[1] at the root of Socrates's political narrative, though, is the identification of three "currencies" of social life, three different ways a social group can interpret what is important and defining about itself. These three currencies of social self-definition are honor [*timē*], money [*chrēmata*], and freedom [*eleutheria*]. Socrates's provocative comments about these currencies are powerful, not just because of his recognition of the independent importance of each of these principles of social organization, but because of his demonstration of the dynamic relationship between them.

In fact, we will see that, though what Socrates offers is not a properly historical account, the dynamic relationship that Socrates identifies between different political regimes does correspond closely to the conflicts and developments that define the actual history of Greece from the late Bronze Age society idealized in the Homeric epics to the emergence and flourishing of democracy in Athens. And, as we gradually move in our analysis from Homer to Athens, we will in fact be witnessing the transformation of an *oikos*-community into a democracy involved in international trade. We will eventually see that the virtue and tyranny are the two extremes that define the possibilities for this last regime, the regime of *logos* itself.

I. Timocracy

The Homeric epics portray a world of "heroes" who accomplish great deeds [*erga*] in war and who thereby win undying glory [*kleos aphthiton*] among mortal men. The Homeric portrayal (like analogous portrayals in the oral poetry of other Indo-European traditions in India, Iran, and so on) is a kind of poetic fiction, reflecting the historical imagination of the culture and time of the performance of these epics, but it nonetheless contains a memory of a real social world.[2] As Richard Seaford writes,

> Although Homeric epic does not give us a photograph of an actual society, neither is it *merely* an ideological construction.... Aspects of the internal consistency of the society described in the poems, taken together with its complex resemblance to known comparable societies, ensure it a degree of historicity. An example of this consistency and this resemblance is provided by the combination in Homeric society of a weak state, a relatively autonomous family, the importance of honour (*timē*), and a more central role for reciprocity and

ritual in the creation and maintenance of social relations than for abstract and generalized "co-operative" virtues.³

Roughly, filtered through the lens of the emerging *polis*-culture of the Greek Dark Ages, the epics portray a Bronze Age world in which an especially powerful "great man" has preeminence among a number of other powerful chieftains, all of whom are recognized as quasi-divine by the many other members of the society who do the primary economic work of that society. That actual Bronze Age world appears to have had its beginning in cattle-herding societies in the Eurasian steppes from roughly 3500 BC, which continued into the Mycenean culture that ended abruptly around 1200 BC.⁴ Archaeological investigations suggest that this was a world characterized by a "redistributive" economy, wherein the many producers deliver their goods to the central power of the dominant lord, who enriches himself vastly from these goods while also using them to supply the needs of the population and simultaneously carrying out various lavish celebrations, whether for internal religious occasions or for external expressions of gift-giving and hospitality.⁵ In this world, the "great men" with their households [*oikoi*] look to other great men with their households as their equals, with whom they compete for glory in public exploits, whether of warlike deeds [*erga*] or of hospitality [*xenia*], while the ordinary population is construed by them as inferior and subordinate.⁶ As portrayed in the Homeric epics (and other, comparable Indo-European works), these "great men" consider themselves to be good, where this goodness means both their adherence to a divinely sanctioned code of valor and their recognition by their elite peers. In this sense, the "good" that is the definitive currency for determining the social hierarchy in this society is "honor" [*timē*] in the ambivalent sense both of "doing what is inherently good" and of "being praised by others."

In Book VIII of the *Republic*, Socrates begins his account of the dynamic unfolding of (imperfect) political forms by describing what he calls a "timocracy" or "timarchy": a city in which honor [*timē*] rules. Socrates himself associates this notion with the regimes in Crete and Sparta (which we will consider below); nonetheless, it is these Homeric communities that are truly "timocracies," for the Homeric society is truly organized around honor.⁷ In this society, the dedication to the "heroic code" is equated with virtue (when construed as a matter of individual worth) or justice (when construed as a measure of the worth of deeds). It is this dedication to a code that defines nobility within the society, and it is why the society defines itself as noble [*kalon*]. Now, as an interpretation of "the good," this sort of social order is ultimately restrictive and myopic, favoring extreme inequality between the elite and the ordinary members of society and favoring blood vengeance in response to violations of hospitality. Indeed, virtue, in this context, is basically equated with martial courage [*andreia*—"manliness"].[8] As a model for virtue and justice, this form of society is no doubt ultimately unsatisfactory, but it nevertheless entails commitment to an objective standard by which individuals are measured.

Even this dedication to the code, however, is by no means "selfless." The honorableness of the warlike deeds and lavish hospitality commands the praise of other honorable individuals, and the earning of praise generates status and power. Initially, the elite warrior-class in these societies justifies to itself its commandeering of wealth on the grounds that its members are the "better" people, masking thereby this ambivalence of living for duty and living for gain. It is this ambivalence—an ambivalence that directly resonates with the ambivalence of the guardian class diagnosed in Book II of the *Republic*—that becomes more pronounced in the history of subsequent Greek culture.

There is a significant historical gap between this "heroic" age and the classical world of Socrates's Athens and other city-states [*poleis*]—a gap typically referred to as the Greek Dark Ages. In that time, the social world underwent a radical change: whereas the earlier, Bronze Age communities were built around the *oikos*—the household of the chieftain and his extended family, itself construed ultimately as absorbing the other households of his domain—the emerging communities were *poleis*; that is, exactly as interpreted by the Athenian Stranger in the *Laws* and as Aristotle claimed in the passage from the *Politics* that we considered in chapter 1, they were self-governing communities that, through their collective establishment of law, precisely resisted being defined by the *oikos*.[9] During the transitional period of the Greek Dark Ages, however, it appears likely that members of this former elite class continued to occupy powerful positions in the self-sufficient peasant communities that emerged in these intervening centuries—the communities that eventually became the city-states of the classical age—though not in the same way as before, and they were thus an ambivalent presence; indeed, within these collective communities, there gradually emerged a tension between the logic of collective autonomy and the endorsement of a hereditary aristocracy.[10] As Victor Ehrenberg writes, describing the emerging *polis*,

> The internal structure of such a community . . . differed strongly from its Mycenaean predecessor. . . . Increasingly, the settlement acquired an urban character. . . . The tribal order of the people was maintained . . . ; so was the *oikos*—the family unit, though tribe and family were subordinated to the urban community. This was to be the polis, not quite appropriately translated as the city-state, since it always included the agrarian countryside outside the town. It was, in fact, both more and less than a state, rather a human community, often very small indeed, always held together by narrow space, by religion, by pride, by life. . . . Monarchy . . . gradually lost its position and had to give way to the growing power of an aristocracy of rich and independent families ("clans") of landowners and warriors. . . . In possession of most of the land, relying on dependent peasants or even serfs, the nobles . . . exercised political power. Though owners of comparatively large estates, they began to concentrate in towns whose political and economic importance slowly increased. The market-place (*agora*) became the centre for meetings and jurisdiction as well as a place of worship and trading. The non-nobles, too, mostly farmers and tenants, tended as far as possible to live in town where most of the artisans and other professions, up to then migrant, also settled. It was in the town [that] . . . the polis started its long life as a completely new form of human community, a community of citizens—or those who were to become citizens—living either in the city or the countryside, ruled over by a class of noble land-owners.[11]

Though they were a fundamentally new form of society, these later *poleis* identified themselves as continuous with the earlier, Bronze Age culture through their (poetic) memory of that culture, and in significant ways they interpreted themselves in light of the values they imputed to that culture.

Within the later city-state culture of Greece, Sparta and Crete—the societies that Socrates calls "timocracies"—were generally esteemed as the most honorable cities for their warlike, "virtuous" character.[12] Crete had the oldest system of law known to the Greeks, and Sparta in particular was popularly held to be the epitome of a society that held to the "ancient ways" laid down for it by its mythical legislator, Lycurgus.[13] The "*Politeia* of the Spartans," a short document generally believed to have been written by Xenophon, helpfully captures this perception of the Spartan constitution. Sparta, he writes, is "the most powerful and famous of all Greek states," largely thanks to "Lycurgus, the man who established the laws under which they flourished" ("*Politeia* of the Spartans" I.1–2.). What is celebrated as great about the Spartan society (and, likewise, the Cretan, though our literary evidence for that is slimmer) is that its citizen-males, who deem themselves equals ["the same," *hoi homoioi*], dedicate themselves without reserve to the good of the city, a dedication primarily understood as military. In this sense of adherence to a standard we can indeed see that such a society, like the Homeric society, is like a virtuous society in the way that a society of self-interested individuals is not, and this, presumably, is why, in Book VIII of the *Republic*, timocracy is portrayed as only one step removed from "*Kallipolis*," the society of virtue (VIII.545c). Indeed, according to Xenophon, "In Sparta Lycurgus forbade free citizens from having anything to do with making money, and ordered them to devote themselves solely to activities which ensure liberty for citizens" ("*Politeia* of the Spartans" VII.2). He writes, further,

> Everyone knows the outstanding obedience of the Spartans to their rulers and laws.... Another aspect of Lycurgus' institutions which may properly be a source of wonder is his establishment of the principle that a noble death is preferable to living in dishonour.... It would be difficult to find anything meriting attention in military matters which the Spartans have overlooked. ("*Politeia* of the Spartans" VIII.1, IX.1, XII.7)

"The same" are thus construed precisely as "guardians" in the sense introduced in Book II of the *Republic*.[14] Beyond this work of Xenophon, these values are clearly expressed in the "*Politeia* of the Athenians," a work preserved with the works of Xenophon by an unknown author often referred to as "the Old Oligarch," and in the archaic poetry of Tyrtaeus, and they are generally recognized as being the values held by the educated and wealthy population generally. These are also the values typically espoused by Socrates's (aristocratic) interlocutors throughout the Platonic dialogues.[15] Like the world of the Homeric heroes, these idealized societies of post–Dark Ages Sparta and Crete were thus construed as timocracies. The ambivalence of the currency of "honor" that we identified above, however, is the key to Socrates's analysis of these contemporaneous "timocratic" societies, an ambivalence thematized in Plato's *Protagoras*.

In the *Protagoras*, Socrates criticizes the "epinician" poetry of Simonides (c. 556–468 BC), who is the oldest known professional poet in this tradition of archaic praise poetry that celebrates the deeds of the victors in the great, aristocratic athletic contests. Socrates's argument in the *Protagoras* is a kind of cultural criticism that sees in the emergence of this tradition the development of a "trade" in praise, whereby the praise of the poets became the currency—the propaganda, really—that could establish the greatness of the subject of that praise, despite the actual lack of virtue of that person.[16] Whereas in the heroic world it appeared to be the honorableness of the deeds that resulted in their celebration in *epos*—the epic poetry of Homer—in the world of the epinician poets it has become the poetic praise that generates the value of the deed.

In general, epinician poetry, especially in the hands of its most famous exponent, Pindar (c. 518–438 BC), celebrates the *areta*—"virtue"—of athletes, where this virtue amounts to sporting prowess or excellence in bodily competition.[17] In these Panhellenic athletic competitions—most prominently the Olympian, Nemean, Pythian, and Isthmian games—the only competitors were aristocrats. These athletic competitions, together with the celebratory poetry—*epinikia*—of professional poets such as Simonides, Pindar, and Bacchylides, function as a popular public institution that legitimizes aristocratic existence and authority within the otherwise anti-aristocratic environment of the *polis*, a form of public honoring that resonates with the tradition of gift-giving between powerful households that structured the elite world of the Homeric timocracy.[18] These athletic contests and *epinikia* go hand in hand with other structures by which the aristocratic presence affirmed its power within the city-state, such as the massive displays of wealth through public works, which Aristotle identifies with the virtue of *megaloprepeia*.[19] Through these public celebrations, elite families secured their power in the city through winning honor—the prestige reflected in public praise—in a way that has no intrinsic connection to any virtue other than athletic prowess or public expenditure; but beauty and wealth have a powerful rhetorical force.

This "debasing" of the code of honor in which the powerful aristocrats in the *polis* are revealed to be involved in a propaganda war to maintain their social position in the context of a self-interested pursuit of wealth and power in fact makes clear the ambivalence that was always at the heart of timocracy: whether the code is construed as the heroic code of Homeric society or as the martial dedication to the city in Sparta and Crete, celebration by others was in fact the quantitative "currency" that was all along being substituted for the quality of virtue. Truly being virtuous entails finding virtue "its own reward," that is, according to the distinction Glaucon makes at the beginning of Book II of the *Republic*, it is an *inherent* good, a good done for its own sake, not an instrumental good that is good only because of some further good that it brings;[20] in seeking the good in honor, however, one has already substituted something else for the good, made something else one's "absolute." From the start, in other words, the society of *timē* equates—confuses—being virtuous with being deemed good by powerful others. The later debasement of the world of honor into the world of praise makes clear that a kind of hoarding of wealth—a kind of nascent "money-loving"—was always operative in the society of honor. Indeed, it is in just these terms that Xenophon interprets contemporaneous Spartan society as a timocracy in decline; he writes, for example, that

> I know that in the past the Spartans preferred to stay in Sparta in moderate prosperity rather than expose themselves to the flattery and corruption involved in governing other cities. In the past they were afraid of being proved to have gold, but there are those now who even pride themselves on possessing some. . . . There was a time when they worked to be worthy to lead, but now they are far more interested in ruling than in being worthy of their position. ("*Politeia* of the Spartans" XIV.2–3, 5)

It is in this sense, then, that the timocracy can be seen, as Socrates proposes, as "a certain middle between [virtuous] aristocracy and [money-loving] oligarchy" (VIII.547c): because of the inherent ambivalence of its ideal [*timē*], it vacillates between commitment to an objective standard and pursuit of self-interested gain.[21]

The social and economic realities of Greek society changed dramatically from the Bronze Age communities through the settlements of the Greek Dark Ages to the city-states of the classical period. The "traffic in praise" brought to critical reflection by Socrates in the *Protagoras* is the mark of a society no longer governed by the "heroic code" for which *timē* is an almost natural reality to which one is answerable; *timē* here has become a commodity to be deployed in the pursuit of prestige and power that now operates along lines other than those regulating the interactions of Bronze Age chieftains. Thus, what "markets itself" as a dedication to honor can in fact be simply greedy self-interest. There remains a superficial resemblance to an older code, which Socrates notes:

> In honoring the rulers, and in the abstention of its war-making part from farming and the manual arts and the rest of money-making; in its provision for common meals and caring for gymnastic and the exercise of war—in all such ways won't it imitate the preceding regime? (VIII.547d)

The "timocratic" society of Socrates's era, that is, has retained from traditional society the commitment to the primacy of war and the separation of the elite warriors from the disdained and subordinated *technai* that actually generate the economic wealth of the society (precisely the separation of the guardian class envisioned in Socrates's discussion with Glaucon and Adeimantus in Book II of the *Republic*). But the driving force of this society is no longer the commitment to honor that was the living soul of that traditional society; on the contrary,

> such men ... will desire money just as those in oligarchies do, and under cover of darkness pay fierce honor to gold and silver, because they possess storehouses and domestic treasuries where they can deposit and hide them; and they will have walls around their houses, exactly like private nests, where they can make lavish expenditures on women and whomever else they might wish. ... They seek out expenditures for themselves and pervert the laws in that direction; they themselves and their wives disobey them. (VIII.548a–b, 550d)[22]

The "debased" timocracy of Socrates's day maintains a veneer of motivation by socially grounded honor when in fact its real motor is self-interested desire that seeks wealth and power for private enjoyment. Even if, then, honor is explicitly endorsed and money explicitly disdained as a social good in this society, money is implicitly what is governing this social hierarchy, both in the sense that money itself is secretly what is driving the actions of the powerful and in the sense that honor has itself become a "bankable" currency, so to speak, in this pursuit of wealth and power.

Implicitly, then, timocracy has given rise to another sort of regime: a regime in which social relations are interpreted and a hierarchy organized around money [*chrēmata*] rather than honor [*timē*]. Thus, Socrates remarks,

> "And, I suppose, oligarchy would come after such a regime."
>
> "What kind of arrangement do you mean by oligarchy?" he [Adeimantus] said.
>
> "The regime founded on assessment [*Tēn apo timēmatōn politeian*]," I said, "in which the rich rule and the poor man has no part in ruling office." (VIII.550c–d)

Exploiting the implicit pun in the word *timēma*, which in Athenian legal contexts meant "property assessment" but which grammatically simply refers to the bestowing of *timē* [honor], Socrates notes that the truth of the society of honor is that it honors money, and thus ultimately gives rise to a society governed by the rich.[23] In fact, Athens itself underwent a revolutionary transformation that resulted in the social organization being dictated by just such a property assessment.

II. Oligarchy

The emergence of the classical *polis* as such—that is, as a community self-governed through a suprafamilial body, a legislative "state"—was a revolutionary transformation in Greek culture, and indeed, in world culture, and it did not immediately appear in the highly developed form it took in the city-states of Socrates's age. On the contrary, the development of the *polis* was a gradual process that required overpowering the governing authority of elite, "aristocratic" families.[24] In Athens, this revolution—the revolution that eventually produced the classical Athenian democracy—is especially associated with the actions of the lawgiver [*nomothetes*] Solon [c. 640 BC–c. 560 BC].[25]

By Solon's time, money had indeed, as Socrates's analysis indicates, become a dominating force in the shaping of social life, and Solon, himself an aristocrat, was asked to play the role of mediator [*diallaktēs*] in the context of a virtual civil war between the rich and the poor in Athens. Solon's legal reforms were especially important for limiting the aristocratic control of that society by designing a system in which the ability to participate in government offices and to participate in the council that formulated proposals for decision by the public assembly was determined by wealth, not birth.[26] This reliance on the criterion of wealth to determine eligibility to rule makes a society what Socrates calls an "oligarchy" (literally, "governance by the few"), and, as Socrates says about such a regime, "Where it's more of an oligarchy, the sum [required for participation] is greater, where less of an oligarchy, less" (VIII.551b).[27] Solon's reforms, in which property assessment is formally recognized as the principle of government, were an attempt to deal with a problem that had already emerged in a world in which money, rather than honor, had become the actual defining force of social organization; it was an attempt, in the terms of Socrates's description, to make the regime in Athens "less" of an oligarchy.

In fact, one can recognize a fundamental way in which this notion of a property assessment makes sense as a qualification for participation in governing. Those who possess wealth can be presumed to have a stake in the protection of their society, and, indeed, one can imagine, too, that the experience of generating or managing such wealth affords those with such wealth insight into what is required to care for it. Indeed, one is reminded again of Socrates's remark to Cephalus in Book I:

> Those who do make [money] are twice as attached to it as others. For just as poets are fond of their poems and fathers of their children, so money-makers too are serious about money—as their own product. (I.330c)

In fact, Solon's constitution, by recognizing various degrees of wealth and allowing varied degrees of participation in government according to wealth rather than allowing power only to the hereditary nobility, created a broader-based decision-making body that better reflected the range of interests in the city; he also created a system that allowed one to increase one's level of participation in governance through increasing one's wealth, and, indeed, paved the way over the next century for a series of progressively more radical developments of popular governance that ultimately produced the classical Athenian democracy.[28] In this sense, then, a city in which the level of one's wealth determines the level of one's participation in government appears more rational and fair than timocratic rule by elite families. Socrates's discussion of oligarchy, however, takes no time to address these potentially progressive aspects of a government based on property qualification; instead, he immediately draws attention to the problems in this approach to social self-interpretation.

Socrates first identifies the logical problem intrinsic to this approach to governance:

> "Reflect: if a man were to choose pilots of ships in that way—on the basis of property assessments—and wouldn't entrust one to a poor man, even if he were a more skilled pilot—"
> "They would make a poor sailing," he [Adeimantus] said.
> "Isn't this also so for any other kind of rule whatsoever?"
> "So I suppose, at least."
> "Except for a city," I said, "Or does it also apply to a city?"
> "Certainly," he said, "most of all, insofar as it is the hardest and greatest kind of rule." (VIII.551c)

Rule requires care, skill, and insight—the same *empeiria* and *technē* we earlier considered in other contexts of human engagement with the world—and whether or not one has developed these is a factual matter independent of the factual matter of whether one has money. And beyond this problem in principle (to which we will return), there is a second, empirical problem. Before identifying that problem, though, we must first reflect on the notion of a "money-economy."

Though a version of money is surely operative in the Homeric world—various things are often described as being worth a certain number of cattle, for example—that world does not operate according to a money-economy: the fundamental mode by which wealth changes hands is through gift (between elite households in relations of hospitality) or through redistribution (within elite households and their attendant population), and goods are construed as of relatively autonomous value.[29] When honor is the "currency" of social relationships, the very "economy"—how the very value of "goods" is construed and how these goods are distributed—is a matter of honor.[30] The move from the city of honor (timocracy) to the city of money (oligarchy) is also the shift from a "gift"-economy of reciprocity and redistribution to an economy of money.[31]

It is a radical shift in the very conception of social life when "money" is what is honored in society: when money, that is, becomes the "absolute" in terms of which the value of all things is defined. For a money-economy to be adopted, it must become the functioning perspective within a social world that goods operate in a system of exchange and that the values of exchange are what one must answer to for one's social standing. It is such a money-economy that was embraced by the Greek city-states of Solon's day and, indeed, some of Solon's reforms may have been associated with the recent introduction of coined money within ancient Greece.[32] In fact, the emerging money-economy had a fundamentally contested character in this society, for, though the introduction of coinage (initially in Lydia) was in fact a practice associated with tyrants, the monetary interpretation of worth was pointedly identified with the popular, "civic" (i.e., democratic) perspective, in contrast to the aristocratic gift-economy.[33] Specifically, the use of precious metals—traditionally interpreted precisely as the exclusive marks of aristocracy—to make coins bearing the seal of a civic authority announced a universal and nonhierarchical basis for calculating worth, and inasmuch as currency does not function without a system of public trust in which the participants rely on the future recognition of the worth of their monetary tokens (coins), the functioning of such currency itself depended on and reinforced a communal commitment to this system of valuing.[34] Thus, just as government based on property assessment challenged institutionally the authority of traditional elites, so, more fundamentally, did the very introduction of coined money represent the opposition of the self-defining *polis* to traditional elite rule.

The introduction of a money-economy, however, brought with it problems of its own, and just as Solon's policies for the distribution of public offices were an attempt to deal with the already existent reality of the dominating force of money, so was another of his reforms a matter of addressing another unique social reality introduced by the money-economy: the phenomenon of financial debt.

"Debt," in the sense of "what is owed," is a universal phenomenon in human life because to be a being with *logos* is to be a being that takes account, and hence a being that is accountable, answerable: a being that owes. This "owing," though, is open to different interpretations. Indeed, it is this question of the meaning of "what is owed" that emerges in Socrates's initial discussion with Cephalus (I.331b–c), a question brought out most clearly in the immediately ensuing exchange between Socrates and Polemarchus:

> "What was it Simonides said about justice that you assert he said correctly?"
>
> "That it is just to give to each what is owed," he [Polemarchus] said....
>
> "He is a wise and divine man. However, you, Polemarchus, perhaps know what on earth he means, but I don't understand." (I.331e)

Like the value of goods, the meaning of what one owes is also construed differently in a money-economy than it is in other forms of social self-interpretation. Debts exist in the world of honor, but they are, accordingly, debts of honor. Honor societies have ways of handling the debts incurred between people, typically involving the giving of gifts and the performance of various rituals, but the canceling of debt never involves a quantitative calculation of exchangeable value.[35] Indeed, particularly striking are the "incalculable" debts that are definitive of the narratives of the *Iliad* and the *Odyssey*: Hector's killing of Patroclus and the suitors' "besieging" of Penelope, for which Achilles and Odysseus, respectively, will accept no compensation.[36] The society of honor has ways of dealing with the ways in which one person is answerable to another—generally, through hospitality and vengeance—but there is no appeal in this system of interpretation to a universal standard of exchange. In the money-economy, though, everything "has a price."[37] One of the most striking ways this reality showed itself in the context of the Greek city-states was the phenomenon of debt-servitude: nonelite Greeks generally existed on the basis of subsistence agriculture; especially in the context of difficult seasons, economically weaker peasants grew dependent on the loans of larger landholders, and when they were unable to repay these debts, they lost their lands and themselves became the slaves of those larger landholders.[38] Such debt-servitude is possible only because of the presumption that there is a specific price to be repaid, and the very substance of a person's life has its value calculated as a resource for repaying that debt. Solon, in addition to introducing the property assessment and possibly standardizing weights for coinage, is reputed to have canceled debts and to have outlawed debt-servitude in Athens. This problem of debt-servitude is closely related to what Socrates himself identifies as "the greatest" of the "evils" of the oligarchical society.

After identifying the problem in principle with a system that equates wealth with the capacity to rule well, Socrates identifies the empirical problem with the society of money, namely, that it produces a society at war with itself, rich against poor: "Such a city [is] not one but of necessity two, the city of the poor and the city of the rich, dwelling together in the same place, ever plotting against each other" (VIII.551d). It is in this context that Socrates points to "the greatest of these evils":

> "Now see whether this regime is the first to admit the greatest of all these evils."
>
> "What?"
>
> "Allowing one man to sell everything that belongs to him and another to get hold of it; and when he has sold it, allowing him to live in the city while belonging to none of its parts, called neither a money-maker, nor a craftsman, nor a knight, nor a hoplite, but a poor [*penēta*] man without means." (VIII.552a)

In the money-economy, everything is a *commodity*, everything is defined by its value-for-exchange, and thus nothing is of intrinsic worth and, equally, nothing is "inalienable." In such a society, one can buy anything and, equally, one can sell anything. This means it is possible, while living properly according to the principles of this society, for a buyer and a seller to unite to destroy the functional participation of the seller in the society. Let us consider how this is so.

A society is not simply a "heap," as Aristotle describes quantities of water or earth.[39] Rather, a society is a group of people who are "with" each other: like an organism, a society has "members" whose presence in the society is itself functionally relevant to that society—each has a role to play. In this sense, society is characterized by "belonging": the members of a society are not—and do not experience themselves as—isolated individuals, but are each a "part" of something. To a large degree, *who* we are is defined for us by *how* we participate. This point was already voiced in the discussion we considered above of the "division of labor" that Socrates has with Glaucon and Adeimantus in Book II:

> "Different men are apt for the accomplishment of different jobs. Isn't that your opinion?"
>
> "It is."

> "And, what about this? Who would do a finer job, one man practicing many arts, or one man one art?"
>
> "One man, one art," he [Adeimantus] said....
>
> "I don't suppose the thing done is willing to await the leisure of the man who does it; but it's necessary for the man who does it to follow close upon the thing done, and not as a spare-time occupation."
>
> "It is necessary."
>
> "So, on this basis each thing becomes more plentiful, finer, and easier, when one man, exempt from other tasks, does one thing according to nature and at the crucial moment." (II.370a–c)

Generally, we will, each of us, devote ourselves to—and hence define ourselves by—a particular social (economic) task, such that we will regularly find it appropriate to ask another, "What do you do?" and to say in response, "I *am* a lawyer" or "I *am* a construction worker" or "I *am* a chef," and so on. *By* what we "do," we become part of the fabric of our society. For this reason, we can see from another angle the insufficiency of the equation of economics and money.

Our economic activity is not simply a matter of accumulating wealth but is equally integral to our social belonging and to our sense of self-definition. For this reason, it is essential to society—both from the perspective of the society as a whole and from the perspective of its parts—that its members be preserved in their functioning. This, though, is what is destroyed in the money-society, in which one's functional membership is converted into a cash price such that one can sell off one's meaningful social existence, thereby becoming "a poor man [*penēta*] without means [*aporon*]" who "belong[s] to none of [the society's] parts" (VIII.552a). In this way, the principle (money) of the society has become a power that overpowers the needs of the society as such, as the organized economic functioning that is the very fabric and substance of the society is "sold off."[40] The "proper" functioning of this society is thus, in a sense, "cannibalistic": by translating its very fabric into exchangeable wealth, the commitment to the primacy of exchange entails the destruction of some of the society's membership. Socrates develops this point further, precisely in relationship to the theme of debt:

> I suppose that because the rulers rule in it thanks to possessing much, they are unwilling to control those among the youth who become licentious by a law forbidding them to spend and waste what belongs to them—in order that

by buying and making loans on the property of such men they can become richer and more honored.... These money-makers ... wound with injections of silver any man among the remainder who yields; and carrying off from the father a multiple offspring in interest, they make the drone and the beggar great in the city. (VIII.555b–c, 555d–556a)

Within the society that honors money, one portion of the society grows rich at the expense of another portion that, so to speak, mortgages to it its very substance (hence Socrates's designation of this city as an "oligarchy"—rule by the [rich] few). This is the problem Socrates identified of "such a city's not being one but of necessity two, the city of the poor and the city of the rich, dwelling together in the same place [*en tōi autōi*], ever plotting against each other" (VIII.551d). Exemplifying in an extreme form the problem of the guardians that was diagnosed in Book II, this city has become only a location, a site for this exploitation, rather than a shared reality.

Whereas the characteristic behavior within a society that honors honor—the timocracy—is dedicated to the preservation of the society, the characteristic behavior within the society that honors money—the oligarchy—undermines and erodes the very substance of that society. Describing the psychology intrinsic to money-making, Socrates says,

> Don't you suppose that such a man now puts the desiring and money-making part on the throne [of his soul], and makes it the great king within himself? ... And, I suppose, he makes the calculating and spirited parts sit by it on the ground on either side and be slaves, letting the one neither calculate about anything but where more money will come from less; and letting the other admire and honor nothing but wealth and the wealthy, while loving the enjoyment of no other honor than that resulting from the possession of money and anything that happens to contribute to getting it. (VIII.553c–d)

In a money-economy, money-making replaces dedication to the heroic code as one's fundamental "duty," so to speak. This means that, in place of a socially oriented world, the society of the money-economy generates a world of self-interest and private desire: in place of a society whose members think in terms of "we" and "ours," this is a society whose members think in terms of "I" and "mine." This exact issue is thematized by Socrates in his earlier discussion with Glaucon.

In Book V of the *Republic*, Socrates and Glaucon are discussing the distinctive demands relevant to healthy formation of those who would be "guardians" of the city.[41] In that context, Socrates and Glaucon discuss the theme of what is "one's own" within the context of the cohesion of a society:

> "Have we any greater evil for a city than what splits it and makes it many instead of one? Or a greater good than what binds it together and makes it one?"
>
> "No, we don't."
>
> "Doesn't the community of pleasure and pain bind it together, when to the greatest extent possible all the citizens alike rejoice and are pained at the same comings into being and perishings?"
>
> "Of course."
>
> "Doesn't that sort of thing happen when they don't utter such phrases as 'my own' and 'not my own' at the same time in the city, and similarly with respect to 'somebody else's'?"
>
> "Entirely so."
>
> "Is, then, the city in which most say 'my own' and 'not my own' about the same thing, and in the same way, the best governed city?"
>
> "By far." ...
>
> "I suppose, then, that when one of its citizens suffers anything at all, either good or bad, such a city will most of all say that the affected part is its own, and all will share in the joy or the pain." (V.462a–e)[42]

As we have noted since our initial discussion of our inherent need for society—the theme that is central to the discussion of Book II of the *Republic*—we are always dependent on our relations to others, and thus our reality is a shared one: we live our individual lives only in a way that is inherently indebted to others; that is, what is "my own" is necessarily always a matter of what is "ours."[43] This sense of "owning" as a public matter is reflected in the timocratic society of the Homeric epics, for example, in the recognition that wealth intrinsically brings responsibility: the wealthy chieftain's position depends on his using his wealth in a redistributive relationship with those dependent on his household and in the reciprocity of hospitality to other elite chieftains who similarly maintain redistributive economic relationships within their own communities. A society is built on a fundamental sharedness of endeavor, and in a fundamental way, therefore, a society is deceived about itself if in its social self-interpretation it imagines its individual members to be ontologically self-sufficient, and thus it is fundamentally deceived when it allows individual members to construe "property" as exclusively and intrinsically their "own," individually. Yet this misrepresentative individualism is precisely the social self-interpretation that operates within the society of the money-economy.

Economic relationships are not separable from relationships of social self-interpretation and hence are not separable from relationships of individual self-interpretation. The money-economy is, however, premised on the falsehood that economics is thus separable, that is, that the only value is exchange value—a version of the problem of abstraction that I thematized in my discussion in chapter 1 of the distinctive phenomena of *logos*. This economic model goes hand in hand with a form of social life that is inherently self-destructive, producing a polarization between a small, ruling-elite of the rich and a large, exploited, poor populace. These social and economic relationships are themselves premised on an individualistic interpretation of human life. This individualism is itself the vehicle for further political developments.

III. Democracy

The oligarchic society of the money-economy does not spring onto the scene with a "blank slate," so to speak, but is itself a development within an inherited social world that is already defined by historical structures of myth, trade, settlement, social institutions, and so on. In the case of Greece, the money-society emerged within the developing city-states that themselves carried on various cultural and institutional remnants of earlier, Bronze Age society and that themselves were uniquely shaped by the geographical and demographic specificities of their individual formation in, for example, Attica, Euboia, and so on.[44] The money-economy is a transformative development within these historically specific structures, and this means that these inherited structures do not remain unchanged through this development. The society of money itself goes through various changes as its innovative and transformative principle gradually takes hold of the social world and recasts it from the form that was the product of earlier forms of social self-interpretation to the form that corresponds to the intrinsic demands of the money-economy itself.[45]

Following its establishment, the initial tendency of the money-society, as Socrates indicated, is to become not a single society but an antagonistic relationship between two different "cities": "the city of the poor and the city of the rich, dwelling together in the same place, ever plotting against each other" (VIII.551d). Once this divided form of the money-society has developed, there are two broad possibilities: this antagonistic relationship can tend more toward the successful maintenance of power by the relatively small population of the rich, or it can tend more toward the seizing of power by the relatively large population of the poor, "the one called oligarchy, a regime filled with throngs of evils, and this regime's adversary, arising next in order, democracy" (VIII.544c; compare VIII.560a). This ongoing struggle between these two possible forms is the dominant reality of the Greek city-states of the classical period and, as Aristotle writes, it was the very context for Solon's reforms at Athens.[46]

> Not only was the constitution at this time oligarchical in every respect, but the poorer classes, men, women, and children, were the serfs of the rich. . . . Since this, then, was the organization of the constitution, and the many were in slavery to the few, the people rose against the upper class. (*Constitution of Athens*, chaps. 2, 5)

Solon was appointed as archon and mediator in this "civil war."[47]

As I noted above, Solon's establishment of the varied property qualification as the primary basis for participation in government, though manifestly an equating of wealth with power, was a progressive measure that challenged the hereditary authority of the aristocracy and substantially broadened participation in government, and it proved itself in fact to be paving the way to the first real emergence of democracy—popular government—in history. Solon did not invent the property classification, and he did not invent the rule of money; rather, he brought about a significant development within that already-functioning system that, in the context of a popular revolution, paved the way for the eventual emergence of democracy. Solon himself, so far as one can tell from his poetry and the handful of quasi-historical legends of his law-giving, sought to establish a balance between the opposed desires of the rich and the poor, limiting some powers of the rich but not championing the needs of the poor *tout court*.[48] But a series of further reformers in Athens—Cleisthenes, Themistocles, Ephialtes, and Pericles—built on this foundation, progressively broadening the popular base of city government. Cleisthenes, who is generally credited with the creation of actual democracy, in about 508 BC redefined the system of "tribes" [*phulai*] to which citizens belonged, creating a geographically based model that cut across traditional clan membership; these new geographic groups became the basis for participation in the council [*boulē*], which proposed legislation to the popular assembly [*ekklēsia*]. This, the original democracy, was further developed by Themistocles's successful effort in 483 BC to turn civic wealth to the project of building a navy to be manned by unpropertied citizens, and then by Ephialtes, who succeeded in limiting the power of the aristocratic Areopagus court in 462 BC, and Pericles, who made it possible for all citizens to participate in legal decisions by establishing pay for jurors in 451 BC.[49] This original emergence of democracy in Athens was consistent with parallel developments of popular governments in various other cities, generally taking the form of the overthrow of an otherwise oligarchic regime.[50] The antagonism between proponents of oligarchy and proponents of democracy remained an ongoing tension within these cities throughout their subsequent history.

Politically, democracy was unprecedented in its institutional recognition of the worth of an otherwise exploited social class. As Socrates says,

> Then democracy, I suppose, comes into being when the poor win, killing some of the others and casting out some, and share the regime and ruling offices with those who are left on an equal basis [*ex isou*]; and, for the most part, the offices in it are given by lot. (VIII.557a)

In liberating the poor and identifying them as equal in status politically to the rich and the traditional elites, democracy involves a sense of justice—a sense of the good—that is fundamentally different from that recognized in either timocracy or oligarchy.[51]

This different sense of the good that is operative in democratic regimes is made explicit in Socrates's response to Adeimantus's question:

> "What do you say [democracy] defines that good to be?"
> "Freedom [*tēn eleutherian*]," I said. (VIII.562b)

Socrates describes this defining character of democracy more fully:

> "And what is the character of such a regime? . . . In the first place, then, aren't [the citizens] free [*eleutheroi*]? And isn't the city full of freedom [*eleutherias*] and free speech [*parrēsias*]? And isn't there license [*exousia*] in it to do whatever one wants [*ho ti tis bouletai*]?"
> "That is what is said, certainly," he [Adeimantus] said.
> "And where there's license [*exousia*], it's plain that each man would organize his life in it privately [*idian*] just as it pleases [*areskoi*] him." (VIII.557a–b)

In this society, unlike the societies that equate the good with honor or money, the good is interpreted as freedom:[52] democracy allows all citizens to participate in government rather than making some subject to the rule of others. There is a fundamental way in which the democratic regime is thus true to our nature in a way that the other regimes we have considered are not; Socrates says as much:

> For surely in a city under a democracy you would hear that [freedom] is the finest thing it has, and that for this reason it is the only regime worth living in for anyone who is by nature free [*phusei eleutheros*]. (VIII.562c)

Democracy recognizes us as by nature [*phusei*] free, and requires that this be reflected in society as our equal ability to participate in social decision-making.[53] In doing so, it thereby equalizes, from the point of view of political legitimacy, the *logos*—the account-taking—of every citizen, a political empowering of individual *logos* that equally means that individuals are free to determine the shape of their own lives.[54]

Democracy manifestly rejects the need for a separate guardian class that was discussed in Book II of the *Republic* and puts social decision-making directly in the hands, largely, of peasant-citizens rather than reserving this privilege for the rich and the traditional elites.[55] Decision-making rests on interpretation: it rests on how one construes the fact of a situation and on what values one holds relevant to those facts. This "democratizing" of decision-making is thus a democratizing of social self-interpretation; that is, the perspectives that are in the position to determine what "we" think and do are no longer simply those of the few rich and powerful but are also those of the many poor. In other words, the determination of the shape of "our" reality precisely depends on the *logos* of the individual participants, on how individuals "take account" of their situations.

As a form of social organization, democracy is a way of taking account of our nature, a social self-interpretation that is fundamentally different from that of the other regimes we have considered, and in a crucial way this principle of the democratic society is precisely the interpretation of human nature that philosophical investigation itself defends, namely, that we are beings with *logos*.[56] It does not follow from this, however, that the democratic regime is automatically philosophical, automatically wise. Socrates in fact pointedly asks, "Does the greediness of what democracy defines as good also dissolve it?" (VIII.562b). Indeed, in being the regime that honors *logos*, democracy as a regime precisely reflects the ambivalence that, we argued in chapter 1, is definitive of human nature as such.

We have seen that what defines a society is what it honors, what it takes to be the good.⁵⁷ Honoring—taking to be good—is thus what is really the moving force in human affairs.⁵⁸ In honoring *logos*, democracy is thus honoring honoring. Every other society has produced some currency—honor or money—as a substitute for the good; that is, it has made an interpretation and then failed to acknowledge its nature as an interpretation, instead treating it as a simple equation, as something natural. In honoring honoring as such, in recognizing the primacy of our account-taking, democracy has thus in a way found the root of social life, the suppression of which is precisely definitive of these other regimes. In so doing, it embraces the perspective in which the recognition of the good *as such*, and not *as* something else, is actually possible.

In this fundamental way, then, democracy marks a fundamental—indeed, virtually an ontological—advance in human life. The earlier regimes are *definitively* plagued by a conceptual problem in that they equate the good with something it is not—namely, something specific—thus making recognition of the good as such, and hence true virtue and justice, actually impossible.⁵⁹ Democracy, in acknowledging the primacy of *logos*, is, on the contrary, the regime in which true virtue and justice are actually possible. The price of thus making virtue possible, though, is that it is *only* possible—it cannot be guaranteed.

The institutional recognition of the ultimacy of *logos* recognizes that it is incumbent on us as free beings precisely to *recognize* what matters: to hold ourselves accountable to something we take to be the good. Installing this recognition of freedom in the position of authority does not, however, entail the rule of the good: it empowers only that which makes the recognition of the good possible.⁶⁰ In other words, the authority for determining the good has shifted from the authority of the regime as such to the authority of the citizens. But precisely insofar as it is *up to us* (up to each of us, individually) to recognize the good, it might or might not happen that we (each or any of us individually) make that recognition. By empowering the individual *logos*—the individual "voice"/vote—the democracy empowers opinion, whether or not that opinion is sound.

Democracy liberates the otherwise unrecognized voices of the community, offering the possibility of self-government at both the individual level and the collective level (which is to say, at the level of virtue and at the level of justice). It also, however, makes the form of government highly volatile, for its character is constantly being renegotiated in and as the ongoing collective discourse of the citizens. Socrates identifies this character of the democratic regime in his discussion with Protagoras in the *Protagoras*:

> I maintain, along with the rest of the Greek world, that the Athenians are wise. And I observe that when we convene in the Assembly and the city has to take some action on a building project, we send for builders to advise us; if it has to do with the construction of ships, we send for shipwrights; and so forth for everything that is considered learnable and teachable. But if anyone else, a person not regarded as a craftsman, tries to advise them, no matter how handsome and rich and well-born he might be, they just don't accept him.... But when it is a matter of deliberating on city management, anyone can stand up and advise them, carpenter, blacksmith, shoemaker, merchant, ship-captain, rich man, poor man, well-born, low-born—it doesn't matter—and nobody blasts him for presuming to give counsel without any prior training under a teacher. (*Protagoras* 319b–d)

In a democracy, the maintenance and development of the regime depends on the skill and insight of the citizens in recognizing what is the good for the city, both at the level of ends and at the level of means: both what the city should do and how it should do it. As we have already seen in our discussion of *technē*, though, this skill and insight is not a natural ability of persons but is something that is acquired only through learning. Consequently, the opinions of the citizens involved in the collective decision-making that *is* the *polis* are by no means automatically correct. In his discussion of democracy in the *Republic*, Socrates makes the problem in principle with the democratic city clear in a way that is strongly resonant with the reality of the democracy that was put on display in Greek history.

Most simply, individuals can be fooled. Opinion runs democracy, and opinion can itself be manipulated.[61] The democracy is particularly vulnerable to being controlled by self-interested individuals who manage, deceptively, to convince the citizens that they are allies of the democracy when they are in fact its exploiters. Such individuals pursue their own advancement while pretending to act on the good of the city. When successful in controlling popular opinion, these individuals succeed in establishing themselves as tyrants, replacing democracy with autocracy—a pattern repeatedly documented in history, from the time of Caesar's overthrow of the Roman Republic to the time of Hitler's overthrow of the Weimar Republic.[62]

The concern that powerful men, appearing to be allies of the city, would actually establish themselves as tyrants was a live concern in the Greek cities themselves, and, in fact, it was a reality in those cities.[63] It was precisely the three alternatives of oligarchy, democracy, and tyranny that defined the parameters of the ongoing dynamism of the Greek cities. In Athens, for example, Peisistratus became tyrant after Solon's reforms, and, indeed, the very reforms introduced by Cleisthenes that brought the democracy in Athens into being were themselves part of the effort of Cleisthenes to establish his own power in the city against his political rival Isagoras by, as Aristotle says, the typical tyrannical tactic of "taking the people into his party."[64] In a democracy, "the people" are empowered to rule themselves, but, precisely because this rule depends on the individual opinions that the citizens form, the decision-making of the citizen-body can be manipulated and the city can become vulnerable to its overthrow by tyrannical individuals who use deceitful populist policies to appeal to the ignorance and prejudices of the individuals, encouraging them to make decisions that actually have the effect of empowering the self-interested rule of a tyrant.[65]

Democracy, then, is on the one hand the accomplishment of the "natural" environment for beings with *logos*, that is, it is the regime that is uniquely premised on the recognition of our distinctive nature as human beings.[66] Precisely because democracy puts the community's self-interpretation in the position of rule, however, the structure of rule changes within the community as that community itself changes. This makes democracy both uniquely responsive to the specific needs and parameters of its constituent members—its citizens—and unpredictable and unsettled in what form it will take. Such a community is uniquely empowered to take account of and address its own needs, and it is a regime unique in its ability to change and develop, that is, to *learn*, as its account of itself—our account of ourselves—develops; at the same time, it is a community capable of making very bad decisions—decisions based on the false opinions of its members—about all manner of issues, including especially about the nature of its own governance. Democracy is thus inherently ambiguous: the social self-responsibility that is its definition defines a *task*—an ongoing imperative rather than a settled accomplishment—and there is no guarantee that the governing of the community will in fact be in the interests of the community. When the opinions of the citizens are good and wisdom thus rules, the city of virtue and justice becomes possible for the first time, but when opinion is false and foolishness rules, this regime subjects itself to oppressive tyranny. We can see, then, that the inherent problem of the guardians remains, even when it is the people themselves who are responsible for guarding themselves.

Conclusion

The organization of a community is a form of social self-interpretation, and the structures of such regimes can thus be evaluated according to the quality of that interpretation. The analysis of regimes in Book VIII of the *Republic* shows how those regimes that are inadequate forms of social self-interpretation reveal through their own progressive development their implicitly vicious and oppressive dimensions.[67] It is with the emergence of democracy that the form of self-governance arises that is based on a true interpretation of our nature as human beings—as beings with *logos*. Such a regime, however, in empowering our *logos*, essentially empowers opinion, and the shape of government, subsequently, is determined by the vicissitudes of opinion. Our investigation has been into the distinctive character of the human world—the world of beings with *logos*—and this analysis of government has led us now to see that the distinction between true opinion and false opinion is ultimately the most decisive issue for the shape of the human world. We are thus brought to the two major analyses that make up the remainder of our study: how both true opinion and false opinion are possible. We turn, in chapter 3, to the image of the "divided line" in Book VI of the *Republic* and the study of knowledge; next, and finally, we turn, in chapter 4, to the "division of the soul," in Book IV of the *Republic*, and the study of persuasion.

Notes

1. On the stylistic complexity of Plato's presentation in Book VIII, see Roochnik, *Beautiful City*, pp. 101–102. See Newell, *Tyranny*, chap. 2, on the theme of what is concealed in describing the trajectory from timocracy through oligarchy and democracy to tyranny; in particular, Newell argues, this analysis ignores the "virtuous" tyranny of Cyrus.

2. For a basic statement of this situation that helpfully bears on the topic of this chapter, see Kurke, *The Traffic in Praise*, pp. 87–89. On the character of these oral-traditional poems, see Nagy, *The Best of the Achaeans*, and Herington, *Poetry into Drama*. On the culture that is portrayed in the epics, see Seaford, *Reciprocity and Ritual*, chap. 1.

3. Seaford, *Reciprocity and Ritual*, p. 6. For a precise study of the society implied in the Homeric epics, especially in relationship to the emerging *polis*, see Raaflaub, "Homer to Solon," especially pp. 43–45. Schaps, *The Invention of Coinage*, chap. 5, has a less subtle account of the relationship between the society portrayed in Homer and actual Greek history; Schaps also has a less sophisticated account of a "gift" economy than does Seaford, but his account is worth reading, especially alongside Seaford's fuller account of the Homeric economy in *Money and the Early Greek Mind*.

4. See Anthony, *The Horse, the Wheel and Language*, on the culture that produced the Indo-European languages and traditions.

5. Thomas and Conant, *Citadel to City-State*, pp. 10–12. Compare Schaps, *The Invention of Coinage*, pp. 117–118, on what a subordinate individual could expect from his "lord" [*basileus*]. For an attempt to reconstruct the organization of a hierarchically structured

Mycenean "state," especially focusing on the relationship between the different ruling positions of *wanax, lawageta,* and *basileus,* see Kelder, "A Great King at Mycenae." For an overview of the evidence of Mycenean culture, see Middleton, *The Collapse of Palatial Society,* pp. 1–17.

6. For the "heroic code," see *Iliad* XII; for the theme of hospitality, see *Odyssey* throughout. Compare Nietzsche's account of "master morality" in *The Genealogy of Morals* and *Beyond Good and Evil.*

7. My analysis here of the applicability of Socrates's argument to Homeric society and Spartan society thus challenges Annas's claim (*An Introduction to Plato's Republic,* p. 297) that timocracy "is unfamiliar to us as any kind of state, but some of its features are suggestive of what we call imperialism."

8. This is the cultural and experiential reality that lies behind the issue, frequently raised in the Platonic dialogues, of the apparent separability of courage from other virtues; this is most prominently a theme in the *Protagoras* and in the *Laws*. See Ibn Khaldûn, *The Muqaddimah,* Book I, chap. 2 (especially pp. 93–99), for a comparable cultural reality in the context of Muslim history. Compare Raaflaub, "Homer to Solon," p. 67.

9. Aristotle *Politics* I.2.1252a24–1253a1. The idea that the *polis* is at odds with the *oikos* is the general theme of the hyperbolic Book V of the *Republic*. See Raaflaub, "Homer and the Beginning of Political Thought," p. 35, on the emergence of the *polis*: "The polis developed into a tight unit in which the communal element was strengthened at the expense of the individual *oikos*, and power and political procedures were formalized and somewhat decentralized." The primacy of the *oikos* in Homeric and aristocratic settings is a central theme of Seaford, *Reciprocity and Ritual* and Kurke, *The Traffic in Praise.*

10. This gradual development is a theme running throughout Thomas and Conant, *Citadel to City-State*; the collective autonomy of the city-state is a central theme of Meiksins Wood, *Peasant-Citizen and Slave.* See Kurke, *The Traffic in Praise,* p. 89. The tension between the democratic culture of the *polis* and the aristocratic culture of the symposium is the central theme of Kurke, *Coins, Bodies, Games, and Gold*; see the closely related analysis in Morris, "Equality and the Origins of Greek Democracy."

11. *From Solon to Socrates,* pp. 7, 11. Compare Schaps, *The Invention of Coinage,* pp. 80–81: "If the post-Mycenean age had been one of geographic retrenchment, with local dynasts taking the place of regional palaces, the period that we call 'archaic,' from the eighth century to the sixth, was one of expansion.... The rise in population brought with it a new social organization. The old Mycenean citadels, long since abandoned, were once more brought into use, or new ones were established. Around these citadels, communities, at first simply groups of villages, grew into what the Greeks called poleis—not, by our standards, large cities, but unmistakable urban centers where people lived together, exploited the surrounding countryside, and managed their affairs with a greater or lesser degree of independence. A group of peasants and herders eking out a marginal living from the land had turned into an interconnected community."

12. Socrates explicitly identifies timocracy with Crete and Sparta at VIII.544c. The *Laws* is centrally focused on the critical assessment of this value system.

13. Munn, "*Erōs* and the *Laws* in Historical Context," p. 32, describes the Greek perception: "The cave of Zeus, which is the professed destination of this ambulating trio [in the *Laws*], is the place of origin of the most ancient laws known to the Greeks, the laws of Minos, first king of Knossos, received from Zeus, his father. The laws of Sparta represented by Megillus are another respected tradition, not so ancient as the Cretan laws, but also

expounded by a god, Apollo, to the revered Spartan lawgiver, Lycurgus." Compare Aristotle, *Nicomachean Ethics*, I.13.1102a9–10. On the historical reality of the emergence of the distinctive Spartan *polis*, see Raaflaub, "Homer to Solon," pp. 64–69.

14. For the idea that the city of the guardians in Book V of the *Republic* resembles Sparta, see Brann, "The Music of the *Republic*," pp. 22–23. The political regime in Sparta is explicitly discussed in some detail in *Laws*, Book IV. See also Lacey, *The Family in Classical Greece*, chap. VIII.

15. Indeed, it is the association of Socrates and his circle with such values that Xenophon identifies as the main reason for Socrates's prosecution and condemnation; this is the topic of *Memorabilia* Book I, chap. 2, and remains a guiding theme throughout the work.

16. For an analysis of Socrates's critique of Simonides and praise poetry, see Carson, "How Not to Read a Poem," an otherwise insightful piece that is marred by a disappointingly simple-minded interpretation of Platonic authorship. On the political economy of praise poetry, see Kurke, *The Traffic in Praise*, Part III, "Pindar's Political Economy."

17. See Kurke, *Coins, Bodies, Games, and Gold*, p. 142, on *areta* as generosity.

18. This argument is made in detail in Kurke, *The Traffic in Praise*. See especially p. 89 and n. 12 on the redirection of traditional structures through Pindar's poetry.

19. Aristotle, *Nicomachean Ethics* IV.2. On the historical reality of *megaloprepeia*, see Morris, *Death-Ritual and Social Structure*, chap. 4, "Taking It with You: Grave Goods and Athenian Democracy."

20. At II.357b–d, Glaucon distinguishes a good we choose for its own sake, and not for its consequences, from a good we choose both for its sake and for its consequences and a good we choose only for its consequences. Benardete, in *Socrates' Second Sailing*, pp. 39–40, complicates Glaucon's distinction.

21. On the criticism of Sparta, see Morrow, *Plato's Cretan City*, pp. 46–47 and pp. 299–300.

22. On the idea that it is the invisibility of one's wealth that is the violation of social convention, see Kurke, *The Traffic in Praise*, chap. 9.

23. Indeed, the word "timocracy" is commonly used—for example, by Aristotle in *Nicomachean Ethics* VIII.10—precisely to describe the regime Socrates calls "oligarchy," rather than, as he uses it, to describe the rule of honor.

24. The emergence of the Greek *polis* is studied through the lens of cultural anthropology in Seaford, *Reciprocity and Ritual* and *Money and the Early Greek Mind* and through the lens of archaeology in Morris, *Burial and Ancient Society* and Thomas and Conant, *Citadel to City-State*. For a helpful summary overview, see Raaflaub, "Homer to Solon." Compare Aristotle, *Politics* I.1–2.

25. For the emergence of the distinctive Athenian *polis*, see Raaflaub, "Homer to Solon," pp. 69–73, and Fornara and Samons, *Athens from Cleisthenes to Pericles*, chap. 2.

26. For Solon and his reforms, see Aristotle, *Constitution of Athens*, chaps. 5–13, especially chap. 7 on the property classes; with respect to the development of democracy in particular, Aristotle remarks in chap. 9, "There are three points in the constitution of Solon which appear to be its most *demotikotata* features: first and most important, the prohibition of loans on the security of the debtor's person; secondly, the right of every person who so willed to claim redress on behalf of any one to whom wrong was being done; and thirdly, the institution of the appeal to the jury-courts." Whereas the Oxford translation renders *demotikotata* "most democratic," Robinson (*The First Democracies*, p. 39, n. 20) notes that it should be translated "most populist." For a basic account of Solon's reforms, see Raaflaub, "Homer to Solon," pp. 70–73; Solon's reforms are also discussed prominently throughout

Seaford, *Money and the Early Greek Mind*. The system of four property classes employed by Solon had already been a part of the political system in Athens; see Aristotle, *The Constitution of Athens*, chap. 4. On the meaning of this property assessment, see Duplouy, "The So-Called Solonian Property Classes: Citizenship in Archaic Athens."

27. On the correlation of "the few" and "the wealthy" in oligarchy, see Aristotle, *Politics* IV.4. On the idea that the term "oligarchy" as a name for this regime is an invention of Plato, see Adam, *The Republic of Plato*, vol. I, p. 219.

28. Though these reforms are typically identified as the beginning of the democratic revolution in Athens, it is not clear how much this notion should properly be associated with Solon. Thus, for example, whether or not Solon actually admitted the "thetes" to the assembly, as Aristotle indicates in *Constitution of Athens*, chap. 7, is a matter of historical debate; see Stanton, *Athenian Politics*, pp. 66–67.

29. See Seaford, *Reciprocity and Ritual*, chap. 1, for a clear and concise account in relationship to Homeric epic. For the Mycenean economy, see Thomas and Conant, *Citadel to City-State*, pp. 10–12.

30. Compare Bourdieu's notion of "symbolic capital" in *Distinction*, p. 291.

31. Compare *Sophist* 223c, where the Eleatic Stranger asks, "Now shall we say there are two sorts of exchange, the one by gift, the other by sale?"

32. It is Solon's reform of weights and measures (noted in Aristotle, *Constitution of Athens*, chap. 10) that is typically associated with coinage; this correlation may, however, be anachronistic, as Kurke notes in *Coins, Bodies, Games, and Gold*, p. 317. The invention of coinage and the introduction of the money-economy is the central theme of Seaford, *Money and the Early Greek Mind* and Schaps, *The Invention of Coinage*.

33. On the "democratizing" character of money, compare Schaps, *The Invention of Coinage*, p. 120. The contestation between aristocratic and democratic systems of value is the central theme of Kurke, *Coins, Bodies, Games, and Gold*. The history of Lydia and its significance for classical Greek culture is a central theme of Munn, *The Mother of the Gods*.

34. The process by which this system of public trust emerged is the central theme of Seaford, *Money and the Early Greek Mind*.

35. See Seaford, *Reciprocity and Ritual*, pp. 13–25.

36. See Seaford, *Reciprocity and Ritual*, pp. 25–29.

37. Compare Schaps, *The Invention of Coinage*, pp. 116–117: "The items that Agamemnon offered to Achilles for his wounded pride were not things that he would have sold at any price, though he would give them away under appropriate circumstances. . . . Money did not work that way. An essential characteristic of money was that it was exchangeable for anything, great or small. . . . To the extent, then, that Homeric society had distinguished prestige goods from nonprestige goods, money subverted that distinction: money could buy anything and could be gotten in exchange for anything." See Adam Smith, *The Wealth of Nations*, Book I, for the attempt to determine the principles for correct or "natural" pricing.

38. See Aristotle, *Constitution of Athens*, chap. 1: "The whole country was in the hands of a few persons, and if the tenants failed to pay their rent they were liable to be haled into slavery, and their children with them." This is a structure not unlike that which resulted in the Medici bankers and other new "capitalists" gaining control over the lands of the traditional European aristocracy in early modern Europe. See Schevill, *Medieval and Renaissance Florence*, vol. II, p. 294.

39. Aristotle, *Metaphysics* Z.4, 16, and *On Generation and Corruption* I.10.

40. Compare Recco's discussion of oligarchy in *Athens Victorious*, pp. 114–115: "The situation of the city built around honoring wealth is 'abstract' in that it behaves as though it could value something separately from the conditions that bring it into being and from the situation that valuing it brings into being."

41. Like the discussion of the "division of the soul" in Book IV of the *Republic* (which we will consider in chap. 4), the discussion of the education of the guardians in Book V of the *Republic*, which we will not consider in detail in this book, presents the reader with a complex hermeneutical task, and reading it well requires careful attention to the "play" in Socrates's conversation. See Brann, "The Music of the *Republic*," pp. 22–23; Sallis, *Being and Logos*, pp. 371–396; and Freydberg, *The Play of the Platonic Dialogues*, pp. 118–122. Hyland, *Finitude and Transcendence*, chap. 3, is an attempt to show the intentional implausibility of the proposal of the "three waves" of Book V.

42. Compare *Laws* IX.875a, where the Athenian Stranger argues that we must recognize "that the true art of politics must not care for the private (individual), but for the common— for the common binds cities together, while the private separates—and that it is more preferable for both the individual and the community that the common be established." On this passage, see Zuckert, "On the Implications of Human Mortality," pp. 171–172.

43. The notion that what is "one's own" is already intrinsically a matter of what is "ours" is crucial to appreciating and assessing the sense of Socrates's repeated claim in the *Republic* that justice is to "mind one's own business" [*to ta hautou prattein*] (II.370a, IV.433a–d, 434c; compare III.406e), which is also one of the definitions that Charmides offers for *sōphrosunē* (*Charmides* 161b). For a thoughtful engagement with this theme in the *Republic*, see Hyland, *Finitude and Transcendence*, pp. 48–57.

44. On the distinctive formation of the emerging city-states in Attica and Euboia throughout the Greek Dark Ages, see Thomas and Conant, *Citadel to City-State*, pp. 60–84 and 85–114, respectively.

45. These transitions within the emergent money-economy are explored in detail in Seaford, *Money and the Early Greek Mind*.

46. Contra Annas, *An Introduction to Plato's Republic*, who claims that "Plato now gives a long, complicated and largely unconvincing account of how oligarchy becomes democracy" (p. 299).

47. On Solon's role as, essentially, that of a tyrant, see McGlew, *Tyranny and Political Culture in Ancient Greece*, chap. 3.

48. Aristotle, *Constitution of Athens*, chap. 5.

49. For a rigorous interpretation of both the facts and the meaning of the complicated history of these democratic reforms, see in particular Fornara and Samons, *Athens from Cleisthenes to Pericles*; see Robinson, *The First Democracies*, p. 41, n. 24, for a criticism of their assessment.

50. The empirical details of this process are discussed throughout Robinson, *Democracy Beyond Athens*. On the relationship between Athenian democracy and the emergence of other democracies, see chap. 4, especially pp. 188–200. For the reasons to believe that democracy developed in other Greek cities prior to its emergence in Athens, see Robinson, *The First Democracies*, p. xxx.

51. Recco helpfully lists eight characteristics that are identified with democracy by Socrates in Book VIII of the *Republic*; see *Athens Victorious*, p. 116.

52. Freedom is the topic of Recco, *Athens Victorious*, chap. 5; see especially pp. 155–156 for the basic meaning of *eleutheria* and pp. 162–163 on the rich sense of "freedom" in the

Republic; on p. 163 in particular, Recco helpfully identifies "license," "liberality," and "self-rule" as ascending senses of "freedom."

53. On slaves in democratic Athens, see Meiksins Wood, *Peasant-Citizen and Slave*, chap. 2, and Osborne, "The Economics and Politics of Slavery at Athens"; compare VIII.563b–d.

54. See Recco, *Athens Victorious*, p. 116: "Democracy, founded on the revolt against the rule of the rich, sets up freedom as its goal and produces a city whose most immediately salient characteristic is its variety"; and compare p. 180: "Lastly, and most importantly, political equality is justified by its special connection to *logos*. Through its institutions, a democratic city expresses a preference for persuasion over force, and thus for freedom, insofar as persuasion explicitly acknowledges the freedom of those to whom it is directed." The political terrain of persuasion will be our topic in chap. 4.

55. Meiksins Wood, *Peasant-Citizen and Slave*, chap. 3. Compare VIII.565a: Democracy is led by the people who "do their own work [or "work their own land" (Recco)—*autourgoi*] . . . and don't possess very much."

56. On the identification of democracy and philosophy, see Recco, *Athens Victorious*, chap. 3 and pp. 181 and 228–233. Compare Brann, "The Music of the *Republic*," pp. 28–29, on why democracy is the best place for Socrates.

57. Recco argues for this point in great detail; see, in particular, *Athens Victorious*, pp. 96 and 137–138.

58. On honoring as the fundamental function of *thumos*, see Recco, *Athens Victorious*, chap. 2, especially p. 137; *thumos* will be a theme in our study of persuasion in chap. 4.

59. See Recco, *Athens Victorious*, p. 137.

60. Compare Recco, *Athens Victorious*, p. 164: "Freedom is not another name for the good, but it provides the space in which alone what is best may thrive." Compare Benardete, *Socrates' Second Sailing*, p. 153, regarding the nature of the city in general.

61. Compare Recco, *Athens Victorious*, p. 183: "Opening the door to persuasion means making oneself vulnerable to deception"; and further, "Indeed, the possibility of deception is not a 'necessary evil' that is unfortunately connected with the truth-revealing powers of *logos*. It is *because* persuasion can become deception that *logos* has the power it does, and it is *through* being deceived that we come to learn."

62. This intrinsic vulnerability of democracy to tyranny is a central topic of Agamben, *State of Exception*.

63. On the rich history of tyranny in ancient Greece, see McGlew, *Tyranny and Political Culture in Ancient Greece*. McGlew specially emphasizes the ambivalence of the notion (and the reality) of tyranny; see especially p. 183: "The tyrant's role in the political language of the classical Athenian democracy was rich and complex: tyranny functioned not simply as a liminal construct providing graphic images of incorrect citizen behavior, but as a defining model of political freedom and as a bond between individual citizens." On tyranny in the context of the history of the Greek *polis*, see also Raaflaub, "Homer to Solon," pp. 73–75.

64. Aristotle, *Constitution of Athens*, 20. For the idea that Solon himself should be construed as a tyrant, see McGlew, *Tyranny and Political Culture in Ancient Greece*, chap. 3.

65. On the process of transformation of democracy into tyranny, see Recco, *Athens Victorious*, p. 120; for his analysis of the theme of desire as that is played out through Socrates's description of the transformations of oligarchy into democracy and democracy into tyranny, see pp. 135–136.

66. Compare *Laws* IX.853c: "We are not legislating, like the legislators of old, for heroes and sons of gods, when both the legislators and those for whom they gave laws were of divine descent; we are human beings legislating for human beings."

67. On the idea that these regimes undermine themselves by virtue of their one-sidedness, see Walsh, "Plato and the Philosophy of History." See also Dorter's discussion of this theme in *The Transformation of Plato's Republic*, pp. 274–279, which is rooted in his conception (p. 15) of the "Platonic view that opposites arise from each other."

B.
THE VICISSITUDES OF OPINION

3

TRUE OPINION

IN CHAPTER 1, WE SAW THE AMBIVALENCE THAT is intrinsic to the phenomenon of knowledge: at a personal level, knowledge is both a powerful transformation within our experience and a platform for alienation from our experience. But knowledge is also a cultural matter, and here too it is ambivalent. It is a specific kind of culture within which the ideal of "knowledge" is cultivated: specifically, it is the democracy with its money-economy that we studied in chapter 2. Indeed, like tragedy and comedy, philosophy and sophistry are themselves phenomena *of* the democratic *polis* in that it is precisely within democratic *poleis* that the realities we now understand as philosophy and sophistry came into being. And democracy itself—which amounts, as we have seen, to rule by opinion—is uniquely defined by this opposition inasmuch as it is the regime whose reality changes shape accordingly as the opinions that drive it range from wisdom to foolishness, which means, roughly, the extent to which it is primarily informed by philosophy or sophistry. In this chapter and the next, we will explore why, precisely, these two forms of experience arise together within the environment in which one is licensed to "think for oneself." In this chapter specifically, we will explore the conditions under which an opinion is true, and in our next, final chapter, we will consider how we become committed to false opinions.

The emergent intellectual culture within the Athenian *polis* is the defining context of the Platonic dialogues, and we will begin our study of knowledge here, in order to appreciate more fully why our nature as beings with *logos* implicates us simultaneously in the problems of philosophy and sophistry. The distinction between knowledge properly speaking and sophistry is a distinction in how we comport ourselves as beings with *logos*. For that reason, knowing is ultimately a matter of being self-responsible in our deployment of our *logos*-capacity. We will turn first to the *Apology* to clarify this notion of being self-responsible in *logos*, especially in relation to the culture of Athens in the time of Socrates.

We will then turn to the study of knowledge as such. The image that Socrates uses, in Book VI of the *Republic*, of knowledge as a "divided line" is a rich and powerful model for understanding what is involved in our experience of knowing, and the central study of this chapter will be the interpretation of this taking account of our taking account. Our study of this image (which will also involve us in reflections on the *Phaedo*, *Phaedrus*, and *Symposium*) will clarify both how knowledge is possible and also how this matter of being self-responsible in our *logos* ultimately requires a deeper kind of self-responsibility: knowing in its fullest development ultimately requires moral transformation.

This rich interpretation of the intrinsic demands of knowing—as calling for the wholesale commitment of the soul to the pursuit of the good—will also allow us to identify the distinctive character of sophistry: the various forms of sophistry are so many ways of dishonestly abstracting from the existential concreteness of knowing, a theme that will guide us in our fuller study of human psychology in chapter 4. Before turning to the detailed study of the "divided line," though, let us first return to the democratic *poleis* in which philosophy and sophistry arose.

I. Socrates and the New Intellectuals

As we noted in the introduction, a decisive feature of the ancient Greek cultural revolution was the emergence of "new intellectuals"—the "sophists." Reading Homer, for example, one will find chieftains, bards, and priests (among others), and one will certainly find (putatively) wise speakers (such as Nestor), but one will not find itinerant intellectuals. In the time corresponding with the rise of democracy in the late sixth and early fifth centuries BC, though, one does find such figures, and they precisely emerge within democratic cities.[1] Specifically, a movement grew up of thinkers who traveled between the Greek cities teaching the "art of speaking" [*rhētorikē technē*] and other related aspects of thinking and scientific learning.[2] This movement is generally believed to have been started by Protagoras (c. 490–420 BC) from Abdera, a democracy in Asia Minor, quickly followed by Gorgias (c. 485–373 BC) from Leontini, another democracy in Sicily.[3] Socrates himself (c. 469–399 BC), the central figure of the Platonic dialogues and the exemplar—both for Plato and for us—of the distinctive practice of "philosophy" proper, is effectively a second-generation figure within this movement, like Prodicus (c. 465–395 BC) from Ceos and Hippias (c. 460–399 BC) from Elis. These figures and this movement are a prominent theme throughout the Platonic dialogues, especially in the *Protagoras* and the *Gorgias*, dialogues that portray Socrates in conversation with the great sophists.[4]

The *Protagoras*, a dialogue that portrays a conversation between Socrates and Protagoras in about 432 BC (i.e., about a dozen years before the conversation in the *Republic*, at a time when Plato was not yet born, when Socrates was roughly forty years old, and when the Peloponnesian War was on the verge of starting), explores the emergence of this new intellectual culture in some detail, especially focusing on the nature of *logos* and its relation to wisdom.[5] The *Gorgias*, a dialogue that portrays a conversation of uncertain date between Socrates, Gorgias, and two younger men associated with Gorgias, explores the nature of rhetoric and its relationship to philosophy.[6] We have already had occasion to refer to aspects of each of these dialogues in exploring other themes raised by the *Republic*, but they themselves especially thematize the relationship between philosophy and sophistry. What they alert us to is that the very powers and skills that are deployed in the pursuit of wisdom—philosophy—seem also to be those deployed in dishonest manipulation—sophistry, a practice that Protagoras and Gorgias are often accused of, as, indeed, is Socrates himself.[7]

The reasons for the criticism of sophistry should be clear to us. Throughout our study, we have been guided by the theme of the ambivalence of *logos*. Our ability to take account can carry us to a comprehensive grasp of the inner nature of things, but it can also leave us self-satisfied with a superficial "theory" that is reflective of our ignorance of and detachment from things rather than of an intimate engagement with them. This potential problem is familiar to us in the common, contemporary, cultural criticism of academics: students or teachers are often thought of as people "with their heads in the clouds," more wrapped up in entertaining themselves with "mind-games" in their "ivory tower" than with a straightforward and sensible engagement with "the real world." This, indeed, is exactly the perspective pointedly examined in Aristophanes's *Clouds*.

The *Clouds* (initially produced in 423 BC) revolves around the figure of Socrates, and it portrays him as he appears in the eyes of ignorant and unsympathetic Athenians who experience the transformed world of the "new intellectuals" as a betrayal of traditional, down-to-earth values.[8] The play follows the adventures of Strepsiades, who, caught up in problems of debt brought about by his son, attends Socrates's *phrontisterion*—his "thinkery"—in order to learn argumentative tricks that he can take to the law-court in order to be absolved unjustly of the responsibility to pay his debts. At the *phrontisterion*, he finds Socrates and his students studying biology and meteorology (learning how the processes that produce flatulence are related to the processes that produce thunder), engaged in mathematical practices of measurement (calculating the distance a flea jumps), and studying the grammar and logic of language (contrasting masculine and feminine nouns with male and female animals). Strepsiades, who can see nothing in these studies except triviality and stupidity, nonetheless attends the school, hoping to learn logical tricks. Because of his complete failure at study and argument, he subsequently enrolls his son in the school. Though he then relies on the sophistical reasoning learned by his son to escape his debts, he nonetheless suffers from that very strategy as his son uses the same "new reasoning" to turn against Strepsiades himself. Ultimately, Strepsiades, blaming Socrates for his frustrations with his own situation, burns down the *phrontisterion*. Aristophanes's portrayal here of the Athenian public as an ignorant body that violently turns against Socrates, whom they construe as a teacher who engages in inappropriate and trivial investigations into the natural world and who teaches people how to use argument dishonestly so as to pervert justice in their own favor, is remarkably prescient, as is made clear in Plato's *Apology of Socrates*.

The *Apology*, Plato's portrayal of Socrates's defense before the court against charges of impiety in 399 BC, is both an autobiography of Socrates as a philosopher and a study of the nature of wisdom.[9] This connection between the story of Socrates and the story of wisdom emerges from the decisive event in his autobiography: Chaerophon, a friend of Socrates's, reportedly asked the Delphic oracle who was the wisest and received the answer that no one was wiser than Socrates (*Apology* 21a). According to Socrates, his subsequent life was spent grappling with this claim: specifically, it led him to test the wisdom of others whom one might have imagined to have a better claim than he to the title of "wisest."[10] His questioning of others characteristically revealed that they confidently held beliefs they could not justify, leading Socrates ultimately to conclude that his superiority in wisdom was his recognition of his own ignorance (*Apology* 23a–b). It was this practice of questioning others that ultimately led to Socrates's being accused of impiety: not recognizing the gods of Athens, introducing new gods, and corrupting the youth (*Apology* 24b). Socrates's story is important, both for what it reveals about the nature of wisdom and, indeed, for what it reveals about the nature of the city.

What is most distinctive about Socrates is his expectation that people should "think for themselves," so to speak. In his encounters with the putatively wise—politicians, poets, and expert craftsmen [*tous cheirotechnas*] are the groups he identifies (*Apology* 21b–22e)—Socrates first seeks to establish with each individual what that individual's view is, and then seeks, with that person, to determine whether that view is justified. He investigates, in other words, what reasons that individual has for holding the view that he has ("he" because, with the exception of his conversation with Diotima reported in the *Symposium*, there is no record in Plato's writings of Socrates holding these conversations with women, and in the case of Diotima it is she, not he, who does the questioning).[11] Through prompting that individual to defend his views, Socrates precisely challenges that individual to think for himself. This simple structure reveals quite a lot about our human nature.

Socrates's practice of questioning draws attention to a crucial, twofold aspect to our experience. First, we have "views," that is, we live within an interpretation of things: a "perspective," an "account" of things. In other words, as we have seen all along, it is our nature to "take account" of things. Unlike other natural beings, whose instinctive "take" on the world is part and parcel of their natural form, our perspective on things is not something that is given to us by nature, but is a function of how we, individually and collectively, have "made sense" of things. But, precisely because it is thus up to us to determine how we take account, we are accountable for our views; that is, we must also "take account" of this account. Socrates's questioning, then, is precisely an identification of our distinctive human nature as beings with *logos*, and the recognition of the demand for self-accountability intrinsically incumbent upon it.

In thus calling others to account through his questioning, Socrates refers to himself as a "gadfly" [*muōps*] (*Apology* 30e); that is, he functions like a constant irritant, waking people up to the ways in which they are irresponsibly taking things for granted.[12] His challenge to others is ultimately to call them honestly to address "what matters": people, he claims, generally treat "the good" as if it were money or immediate pleasure; he encourages them, on the contrary, to care for their souls, to care for their very powers of honoring, of taking account. In their practices, both individual and collective, each makes it clear that he has adopted an interpretation—an account of—the good, but each is taking this account for granted as if it were something obvious or natural. Socrates thus enjoins his fellow citizens to attend to the good as such, and thereby give an account of the account they have been presuming. In thus calling people to care for the good on its own terms, rather than thinking in terms of what seems to them to be—but ultimately is not actually—in their immediate self-interest, Socrates requires them to be self-critical. This practice makes him a "gadfly," because people find it challenging to be confronted with their own ignorance and to be called out of their comfortable habits of thinking and acting.[13]

We should notice that Socrates's philosophizing all takes place within *logos*—within the process of giving accounts. As Nikias says in the *Laches*,

> You don't seem to realize that whoever meets up with Socrates and enters into conversation with him will inevitably be shifted around by what the man says, no matter what topic the conversation started on, until he finds himself giving an account of himself [*to didonai peri hautou logon*]—the manner in which he is living now and how he lived his life in the past—and once he finds himself doing that, Socrates will not let him off until he puts the whole matter to a sure and thorough test. (*Laches* 187e–188a [translated by Gifford])

Socrates's questioning puts some issue into words—already a transformation of some aspect of our experience into an account—and then that questioning calls on another person to formulate in words his way of taking account of things—to give an account of how he takes account. When this account has been rendered, Socrates and his interlocutor now hold that answer to account. At every level—asking, answering, and evaluating—our resource for taking account—our *logos*—provides the medium for this philosophizing, and, indeed, this philosophizing takes place in the dialogue—the *logos*—enacted between the two interlocutors.

At none of these levels—asking, answering, evaluating, discussing—is taking account a simple or merely "mechanical" matter: at every level, taking account is an active matter in which our ability to assess can be better or worse. As Socrates makes clear throughout the dialogues, our immediate self-apprehension is not automatically authoritative as an account of our nature, and the process of inquisitive dialogue in which Socrates involves his interlocutor is precisely aimed at getting better at "knowing oneself." In his own self-description in the *Phaedrus*, Socrates makes clear this fact that we do not immediately apprehend our own nature: "I am still unable, as the Delphic inscription orders, to know myself. . . . Am I a beast more complicated and savage than Typhon, or am I a tamer, simpler animal with a share in a divine and gentle nature?" (*Phaedrus* 229e–230a). But this, one's own nature, is also not utterly alien to one, for one can take it is an object of investigation, as Socrates makes clear in the *Charmides* (another dialogue in which the Delphic inscription, "know thyself," figures prominently), when he asks Charmides whether he is moderate and, if so, what moderation is:

> It is necessary, I suppose, that if it really resides in you, it provides a sense of its presence, by means of which you would form an opinion not only that you have it but of what sort it is.... Since you know how to speak Greek... I suppose you could express this impression of yours in just the way it strikes you. (*Charmides* 158e–159a)

Those things that characterize our living experience are ipso facto manifest to us, and thus are objects of apprehension, but they, like any other realities, will be known only through our developed engagement with them. We can be better or worse at apprehending what is happening in our own experience, and we can be better or worse at putting it into words. And then, beyond this formulation in language, we can, again, be better or worse at reasoning about what we have thus articulated, both in the formal sense of being better or worse at grasping relationships of logic and in the substantive sense of being better or worse at assessing the weight and significance of what we are encountering. At every level, we must "take account"—there is no escape from this responsibility. In a profound way, Socrates's philosophizing is an embrace of the fact that *logos* is our medium: it affirms that this is the domain in which we must operate, and it also acknowledges that there is nowhere else we can turn to answer our questions.

Socrates further claims that this activity he engages in is a kind of service—divine service—and that, in performing this service, he is what is best for Athens (*Apology* 30d–31a). He is not acting out of self-interest but is acting out of his own best effort to make sense of what the good—what the god—demands of him. In calling people to account, he takes himself to be acting in service of their best interest as individuals, and in thus not allowing the citizens to bury themselves in prejudice, he aims to endorse and support the openness and integrity of the city. This, his self-interpretation, however, was ultimately not the judgment that Athens—the democracy—passed on him.

Athens, as embodied in the law-court, found Socrates guilty of impious and corrupting behavior. Socrates himself, according to his speech in Plato's *Apology*, believed this to be exactly the situation portrayed presciently by Aristophanes, namely, that he was in court because of the common, anti-intellectual perception that he "investigates things under the earth and things in the sky" and "makes the weaker argument stronger" (*Apology* 18b–c). In other words, though he took himself to be engaged in the rigorous, self-responsible practice of seeking wisdom, he was perceived to be a dishonest sophist. If we reflect again on his practice, we can see why in principle it could elicit just such a reaction from those who were not directly and personally involved with it.

The very meaning of "taking account" is that one is thinking for oneself, that is, one is personally accountable to the demands of grasping the sense of things. Thus, though it is *the sense of the thing* to which one is answerable, it is *up to oneself* to grasp that sense, to "make sense" of it, as we commonly say. Though it is the thing itself to which one is answerable, the "court of appeal," so to speak, is within oneself; that is, the very nature of the demand to think for oneself is that there is no one else to whom and nothing else to which one can turn for an authoritative confirmation that one is right.[14] Taking account of things, then—thinking for oneself—always puts one in the position that one is operating with *how things seem to one*. In thinking, one is necessarily grappling with one's own opinions and is necessarily reliant on one's own intellectual resources for assessing them. Consequently, it can be the case that what *one takes* to be a deep engagement with things is actually simply a matter of self-absorption, a matter of playing with thoughts and impressions whose significance is defined internally to one's experience, rather than being grounded in a transformative engagement with *ta pragmata*. Consequently, the realities of sophistry and skepticism necessarily emerge hand in hand with the reality of wisdom and philosophy, and we can see why those who do not know Socrates intimately cannot immediately recognize the difference between his practice and the practice of the sophists.[15]

This fact that we operate entirely within the domain of *logos* is what makes philosophy—wisdom—always a matter of questioning. There is no way out of the fact that we are taking account, and thus there can always be skepticism. We can also fall in love with our own accounting, rather than being rooted in the things themselves. How, then, does an account become reliable? This question, internal to the functioning of *logos*, is powerfully studied in Book VI of the *Republic* in Socrates's image of knowledge as a "divided line." In discussing this text, we will have to deal with many of the most fraught issues in the traditional debates about Plato—most notably the topics of the "soul" [*hē psuchē*] and the "forms" [*ta eidē*]. My own discussion will not engage directly with the history of interpretation of these notions; instead, I will remain exclusively focused on describing the distinctive character of our experience as beings with *logos*, and I will take up these notions not as any sort of "metaphysical theses" but only insofar as they illuminate aspects of our experience that any one of us can recognize through careful self-reflection; indeed, it is precisely my contention that what Socrates offers is a brilliantly insightful description of the fabric of experience—of the layers of meaning that are always already operative in our experience—and of its implications.[16] Before addressing the image of the "divided line" directly, though, we will discuss some other themes, especially as those are worked out in the *Phaedo*. As we subsequently examine the image, we will gradually find that our study of the nature of knowledge—of "true opinion"— draws us more and more deeply into the most intimate and important dimensions of our lives, dimensions that we will also explore through reflection on portions of the *Phaedrus*, *Symposium*, and *Phaedo*.[17]

II. Knowledge and the "Divided Line"

The Soul

The most important answer to the question, "What distinguishes a good account from a bad one?" has already been given in our earlier account of *technē*: a good account is rooted in *empeiria*, in actual, lived engagement with *ta pragmata*—the things of our everyday world. In contrast, one significant kind of bad account will be one in which one takes the developed *logos* of something—the "theory" of something—and embraces it *solely because it appeals to one's logos*. While it is true that a good account must appeal to one's *logos*, this characteristic alone is not what *makes it* true. To appeal to this feature alone is literally to treat oneself and one's perspective as the only relevant source of evidence. In knowledge proper, on the contrary, it is the thing itself that is the source of evidence. When one comes to grasp the *archē* of some state of affairs, it is true that that intelligible principle appeals to one's *logos*, but this grasp has the form of *seeing* that "this" is the character of "that": it is an apprehension *about* the worldly reality of which one has developed experience, not *about* one's own sense of what "seems rational." Things have a character of their own: that is, there is something there *to recognize*. Knowledge is precisely grasping *what it is to be* that thing, and that is a matter of fact, not a matter of imagination.

The first question pertaining to knowledge, then, is whether one is actually engaged with *to pragma* or is just imagining. In fact, we can be thus engaged, and we can learn—this was the point of our discussion of *technē*—and this fact that there is knowing reveals something metaphysically striking about us: we are so constituted as to be able to apprehend the forms of things. Aristotle describes this process of apprehension and what it reveals about our nature:

> [All animals] have a connate discriminatory capacity [*sumphuton dunamin kritikēn*], which is called perception [*aisthēsin*]. And if perception is present in them, in some animals retention of the percept comes about. . . . And when many such things come about, then a difference comes about, so that some come to have an account [*logon*] from the retention of such things. . . . So from perception there comes memory, as we call it, and from memory . . . experience [*empeiria*]. . . . And from experience, or from the whole universal that has come to rest in the soul (the one apart from the many, whatever is one and the same in all those things), there comes a principle of skill and of understanding [*technēs archē kai epistēmē*]. . . . Thus the states [of familiarity with first principles—*tas prōtas archas* <99b20–21>] neither belong to us in a determinate form, nor come about from other states that are more cognitive; but they come about from perception—as in a battle when a rout occurs, if one man makes a stand another does and then another, until the original position [*archē*] is reached. And the soul [*psuchē*] is such as to be capable of undergoing this. (*Posterior Analytics* II.19. 99b35–100a14 [translation modified])

Other organisms can interact meaningfully with their environments, and thus "know" things within the terms of their capacities for practical engagement, but we are the kind of being that asks the question "What is it?"[18] We can, in other words, ask about the *being* of things—ask about them absolutely or intrinsically, rather than just relative to the terms of our own interests. As Aristotle says, "The soul [*psuchē*] is such as to be capable of undergoing this." It is this definitive characteristic of the human *psuchē* that is the central focus of the *Phaedo*.

In the *Phaedo*, Phaedo's report of the conversation that Socrates had immediately before his death, Socrates offers a rich and subtle description of the unique characteristics of the human soul. He initially describes a phenomenon that he refers to as "separating the soul from the body." Discussing the attitude that the philosopher has toward the pleasures of food, drink, and sex, Socrates asks his interlocutors,

> All in all, doesn't it seem to you . . . that the business of such a man is not with the body; instead, he stands apart [*aphestanai*] from it and keeps turned toward [*pros . . . tetraphthai*] the soul as much as he can? . . . In such matters,

> isn't the philosopher clearly beyond other human beings in releasing the soul from communion with the body [*apoluōn . . . tēn psuchēn apo tēs tou sōmatos koinōnias*] as much as possible? . . . And I suppose the soul reasons most beautifully when . . . bidding farewell to the body, she comes to be herself all by herself [*autē kath' hautēn*] as much as possible and when, doing everything she can to avoid communing with or even being in touch with the body, she strives for what is. (*Phaedo* 64e–65a, 65c)

Socrates's Pythagorean interlocutors Simmias and Cebes can hear in these lines only their own simple-minded cartoons about the soul and the afterlife; consequently, they miss what is in fact a profound and compelling description of what is truly distinctive of our experience. Apparently unlike any other animal (though that, of course, is an empirical question), we have an "inner" life: we have the capacity to draw ourselves away from our involvement with the world—"loosen the intentional threads," as Maurice Merleau-Ponty describes it[19]—and to turn our attention to our own awareness as such. In so doing, we open up for ourselves a unique domain of experience. This reality, the reality of the soul [*hē psuchē*], "herself all by herself," is certainly nowhere "else" than right here in our bodily involvement with the world, but it is not reducible to that reality. Instead, it is a reality with which we engage precisely by "putting in brackets [*Einklammerung*]," as Edmund Husserl says, the terms of our bodily and worldly experience.[20] This is the distinct phenomenon of self-reflection, with which we are all, presumably, quite familiar.

As Socrates makes clear, though, our self-reflection—our "separating of the soul from the body"—is not a simple "once and for all" ability that we all possess equally. Instead, like the effort at self-description that Socrates points to in the *Charmides*, this effort at self-reflection is something we can be better or worse at accomplishing. In gathering itself from the myriad specific details of everyday engagement and concentrating itself in this act of self-focus, "the soul"—the reality that is the very capacity we have for engagement with other worldly realities—is engaged with the unique reality that it itself is. This reality is a unique terrain whose character must be learned like any other: like any other reality, the reality of the soul is one with which one must develop *empeiria* if one is to know it. It is just such self-reflection that Socrates encourages in his interlocutors and that provides the fundamental domain for philosophical investigation; indeed, as Socrates asks in the passage quoted above, "Isn't the philosopher clearly beyond other human beings in releasing the soul from communion with the body as much as possible?"

This quotation, like Socrates's dialogic practice in general, makes a crucial point about (philosophical) inquiry into human nature: in the investigation of human nature, we are not "innocent bystanders"; that is, the investigation cannot be conducted by one who is indifferent. On the contrary, the very field of investigation is open only to one who has undergone or is undergoing a radical, personal transformation. One must, as Socrates remarks in Book VII of the *Republic*, "turn around [*periagein*]," gathering one's soul—oneself as an experiencer—together in this act of self-reflection (VII.518c–d).[21] The existential drama of this turn is captured in the image of "the cave."

Book VII of the *Republic* opens with Socrates giving an image to illustrate "the effect of education and of the lack of it on our nature" (VII.514a). According to the image, we are prisoners in a cave, looking only at shadows projected on a wall by puppets and a light behind us that we cannot see. For these prisoners (us), knowledge seems to be only their (our) guesses about the behavior of the puppets, guesses that in fact are only expressions of their (our) misunderstanding of what is happening. It is when one of them (us) is dragged out of the cave, past the puppetry and out into the daylight, that that one will recognize the ignorance and, indeed, the absurdity of the perspective he or she formerly imagined to be knowledge (VII.514a–d). The image of the cave portrays the way that in our everyday life we are prisoners to a world we do not understand, in which we take pride in ourselves or honor others as wise when we are in fact dwelling in claims that have no meaningful purchase on reality.[22] Our education into the true causes of things necessarily involves developing a critical orientation toward this, our normal perspective on things; as Socrates asks,

> And if in that time there were among them any honors, praises, and prizes for the man who is sharpest at making out the things that go by, and most remembers which of them are accustomed to pass before, which after, and which at the same time as others, and who is thereby most able to divine what is going to come, in your opinion would he be desirous of them and envy those who are honored and hold power among these men? Or, rather, would he . . . want very much . . . to undergo anything whatsoever rather than to opine those things and live that way? (VII.516c–d)

The transformation in one's perspective necessarily thus inherently includes a recognition of what was wrong in the way one formerly "took account" of things. This is a change that is not accomplished easily, however. As Socrates indicates in the image, this process of education is emotionally and behaviorally demanding, and it involves one in a process of radical disorientation in relationship to the norms of everyday experience:

> And if [someone] compelled him to look at the light itself, would his eyes hurt and would he flee, turning away to those things that he is able to make out and hold them to be really clearer than what is being shown? ... And if ... someone dragged him away from there by force along the rough, steep, upward way and didn't let him go before he had dragged him out into the light of the sun, wouldn't he be distressed and annoyed at being so dragged? (VII.515d–e)

Education is disorienting and challenging, and ultimately it requires that one change one's ways. In short, the process of self-reflection—the process of grasping our own nature as beings who "take account"—is as much a radical transformation in how we *live* as it is the acquisition of new "information" about the factual character of the human soul. Holding on to both of these dimensions—the "practical" and the "theoretical," so to speak—is crucial for understanding what is involved in philosophy.

We have noted already the apparently unique character of the human soul in this, its ability to reflect on itself—its ability to take account of its own taking account. Socrates's conversation in the *Phaedo* focuses on the distinctive *capacities* of the human soul, the capacities that enable and are intrinsically involved in this self-reflective capacity. The conversation in the *Phaedo* especially draws attention to our definitive ability to entertain the sense of something "as such" or absolutely. In our engagement with something, though we no doubt only actually engage with it according to our own interests, we can ask the question *what it is in itself*, that is, we can entertain the sense of its own reality, absolutely. Indeed, just as we can ask what *it* "is," we can ask about "is" itself as such: we can ask what it is *to be*, absolutely—we can ask about "being qua being" [*to on hēi on*, as Aristotle says], describing the definitive project of metaphysics.[23] The human soul "is so constituted as to be able" to ask this question: what is distinctive of the human soul is that we are "metaphysical" beings by nature.

"Recollection" [Anamnēsis]

Our everyday experience is constitutively alive with the themes of "what" and "is," which roughly amounts to saying that we recognize our world *as real*, as something *in its own right*, not relative to our perspective. Socrates's conversation in the *Phaedo* focuses on these terms and on other such "absolute" terms that we are alive to, such as "one," "beautiful," "good," and "equality."[24] As human beings, we are all alive to the meaning of these terms, but these terms also each announce a meaning that, paradoxically, cannot be met with *as such* in our experience: consequently, these are not notions that we can *learn*. That such absolute terms cannot be learned is a point Socrates makes most directly in his discussion of the notion of "equality."

We regularly wonder whether "this" is equal to "that." We ask and answer this question of particular things, with respect to particular properties: this is equal (or unequal) to that in weight ("two pounds"), this is equal (or unequal) to that in length ("two feet"), and, especially relevant to our earlier reflections, this is equal (or unequal) to that in value ("two dollars"). Being equal merely "with respect to," though, is precisely *not* being equal as such, inasmuch as the starting premise of our question is that the two items being compared are different from each other: with any of these equals that we equate in a relative way, we could ask the question of equality at a deeper level, at which point we would recognize them to be unequals, which reflects the fact that the *question* of equality does not accept to be limited to the relative, but inherently invokes an absolute significance. As Socrates says in Book VI of the *Republic*, "nothing incomplete is a measure of anything" (VI.504c). Socrates makes this point in his conversation with Cebes:

> We claim, I suppose, that there's some "equal." I don't mean stick equal to stick or stone to stone or anything else like that, but something other, beyond all these things—the equal itself. . . . [Isn't it that] we've seen sticks or stones or some other things that are equal, and from these we've noticed [*enenoēsamen*] the equal itself, although it's other than these? (*Phaedo* 74a,b)

We engage with this absolute significance of equality when we think mathematically: "1" really is *equal to* "1" and "2 + 2" really is *equal to* "4." Here, though, the terms of the equation—the equals—are themselves absolute: that is, it is not one stick or two stones or four people, but "1" *as such* and "2" and "4" *as such* that we are considering. In Book VI of the *Republic*, Socrates makes this same point with respect to geometrical figures:

> [Geometers] make the arguments for the sake of the square itself and the diagonal itself, not for the sake of the diagonal they draw, and likewise with the rest. These things that they mold and draw, of which there are shadows and images in water, they now use as images, seeking to see those things themselves, that one can see in no other way than with thought [*tēi dianoiai*]. (VI.510d–e)

In short, "equality" and "square" are terms whose meaning is inherently absolute; we draw on these terms in relative contexts all the time, when we compare the weights of stones or carefully "square" the boards we are using to construct a wall, but we engage with them absolutely only when we take them up in relation to other absolute terms in thought.

But notice that what this means is that we do not encounter—and we never could encounter—anything in our experience that lives up to the meaning of such a term: the very nature of these "absolute" meanings is that they can never be met with "as such" in any particular experience. This entails that we could never pose the question of equality or oneness simply *on the basis of* the things of empirical life, for they on their own are insufficient to give rise to this meaning. In recognizing particular (unequal) things to be equal, we are taking account of those things in terms that those things themselves cannot account for: the very sense of those things is their pointing to a meaning that they are themselves inadequate to realize. But we do "take account of" our experience in terms of "equality," "one," "square," and so on when nothing in our experience is sufficient to give rise to the meanings of these terms. For that reason, this sense must be something we are already able to bring to our experience of those things, rather than something we acquire from them. Socrates draws Cebes's attention to exactly this point:

> Therefore, before we began to see and hear and use the other senses, I suppose we must have had occasion to grasp the knowledge of the equal itself, the equal that *is*, if we were ever to refer there the equals that came from our senses and to think that all such things are putting their heart into being the sort of thing the equal is but are inferior to it. (*Phaedo* 74e–75a, 75b)

The absolute notion "equality" cannot be "learned" from its finite realizations because, if we did not *already* recognize particular things as "trying to be" equals, we would never be able to make the relevant comparison of them from which we would draw the absolute notion as a conclusion. The notion of equality is thus something the soul necessarily possesses "before" its experience of anything particular, for it is already present in that experience of the particular, and not something it derives—learns—from that experience.[25] Likewise, the arithmetical notion of "1," the notion of "2," or again the geometrical notion of "square" or of "triangle," is in each case a notion whose absolute character is such that it could never be met with in any experiential realization of it, and each is thus not a meaning we "learn" from experience but is a meaning we "recollect [*anamimnēskomai*]," in the language of the *Phaedo*: we "discover" these meanings that we find are already available to us by virtue of being the kinds of beings that we are.

The recognition of equality, and, similarly, the recognitions of "1," "2," and "square," are clear examples of the way in which we operate in our experience with significances we could not have learned from experience, but the domain of such significances is not exhausted by, or even primarily about, mathematics. As Socrates says to Cebes,

> Our present argument isn't about the equal any more than it's about the beautiful itself and the good itself and the just and the holy and, as I say, about all those things upon which we set the seal "the what it is itself" [*to auto ho esti*] in the questions we ask as well as in the answers we give. (*Phaedo* 75c–d)

Any absolute notion is such that it could not be "learned," but is instead a matter of *anamnēsis* or "recollection."

This issue of the apprehension of absolute meanings that are already involved in our everyday perception of things is also the focus of the exchange between Socrates and Glaucon at the end of Book V of the *Republic* that inaugurates the discussion of "the philosopher," which is the central theme of Books VI and VII:

> [SOCRATES:] "Since fair [*kalon*] is the opposite of ugly [*aischron*], they are two."
>
> [GLAUCON:] "Of course."
>
> "Since they are two, isn't each also one?"
>
> "That is so as well."
>
> "The same argument also applies then to justice and injustice, good and bad, and all the forms [*pantōn tōn eidōn*]; each is itself one, but, by showing up [*phantazomena*] everywhere in a community [*tēi koinoniai*] with actions, bodies, and one another, each is an apparitional many [*polla phainesthai*]."
>
> "What you say," he said, "is right." . . .
>
> "The lovers of hearing and the lovers of sights, on the one hand," I said, "surely delight in fair sounds and colors and shapes and all that craft makes from such things, but their thought is unable to see [*idein*] and delight in the fair itself [*auto to kalon*]."
>
> "That," he said, "is certainly so."
>
> "Wouldn't, on the other hand, those who are able to approach the fair itself [*auto to kalon*] and see it by itself [*horan kath' hauto*] be rare?"
>
> "Indeed they would."
>
> "Is the man who holds that there are fair things but doesn't hold that there is beauty itself and who, if someone leads him to the knowledge of it, isn't able to follow—is he, in your opinion, living in a dream or is he awake? Consider it. Doesn't dreaming, whether one is asleep or awake, consist in

> believing a likeness of something to be not a likeness, but rather the thing itself which it is like?"
>
> "I, at least," he said, "would say that a man who does that dreams."
>
> "And what about the man who, contrary to this, believes that there is something fair itself and is able to catch sight [*kathoran*] both of it and of what participates [*ta metechonta*] in it, and doesn't believe that what participates is it itself, nor that it itself is what participates—is he, in your opinion, living in a dream or is he awake?"
>
> "He's quite awake," he said. (V.475e–476d)

The *eidē* or "looks" to which Socrates refers at V.476a—*kalon, aischron, dikaion, adikon, agathon, kakon*, and all the others—are precisely the lenses through which we apprehend the things of our experience: we see things *as* fair, or *as* good. Those who love sounds and sights [*hoi philēkooi* and *hoi philotheamones*] delight in the sounds and sights seen as fair, but they are not able to see—*idein*—the fair itself in the same way, for the fair itself is not itself one of the things of everyday life, not one object of perception among others. And yet, one is able to see—*horan*—the fair itself in roughly the same sense that one can see another person: at no point does the personhood—the soul—of the other display itself as one thing in the world among others, but one can see another person *through* the myriad behaviors in and by which the soul presents herself. Analogously, one can recognize the fair as such or the good as such *through* the myriad fair and good things of the world.

Socrates's use of verbs is meaningful here: *idein*, the verb translated as "to see" when discussing the lover of sights, is an aorist infinitive and hence implies a momentary or discrete action, whereas *horan*, the verb translated as "to see" when discussing the one who recognizes the *eidos* as such, is a present infinitive and hence implies an ongoing action. This resonates with the sense that recognizing the *eidos* is not a discrete perceptual activity but is an ongoing activity that takes place within the activity of recognizing fair things. And, indeed, Socrates says as much a few lines later, when he refers to the man who is able to "catch sight both of it and what participates in it": it is a matter of distinguishing different aspects *within* a single experience, and this apprehension—which Bloom translates as "catch sight of"—is a matter of *kathoran*, an intensified version of the simple verb "*horan*," which is typically rendered "see clearly," or something similar.[26] The point is that here one is seeing better what one already took oneself to be seeing.

This point—of "seeing through"—is made clear in the ensuing exchange. Socrates describes seeing and hearing as powers [*dunamai*], and he describes how we recognize their existence:

> We will assert that powers are a certain class of beings [*genos ti tōn ontōn*] by means of which we are capable of what we are capable, and also everything else is capable of whatever it is capable. For example, I say sight and hearing are powers, if perchance you understand the form [*to eidos*] of which I wish to speak. (V.477c)

Socrates goes on to note that a power has none of the sensory features that

> I see [*horō*] in many other things towards which I look [*pros ha apoblepōn*] when I distinguish one thing from another for myself [*diorizomai par' emautōi*].... With a power I look [*blepō*] only to this—on what it depends and what it accomplishes [*eph' hōi te esti kai hō apergazetai*]. (V.477c–d)

It is a regular—immediate and nonreflective—part of our experience to recognize powers: this is true in the case Socrates notes, when we recognize someone as able to see or hear us, but it is also true more broadly, such as when we recognize a plant as "alive" or (in the case of a more passive "potentiality") when we see a glass as "fragile." This power is not another discrete object of perception, separate from the sensibly apparent body to which we impute the power. In each case, rather, as Socrates observes, the power *as such* is not an object of sensory apprehension but is instead something that is recognized *through* the sensory presentation of its material conditions and its material accomplishments.

As we have seen in relationship to number and so on, to see any individual thing as fair or good requires one to recognize it *in terms of* a meaning to which it itself is not adequate; hence the description of the one who cannot recognize *auto to kalon* or *auto to agathon* as "believing a likeness of something to be not a likeness, but rather the thing itself to which it is like" (V.476c). Below, we will have reason to consider beauty and the good on their own terms. For the moment, let us consider the most pervasive of all of these absolute notions: the very notion of "is" or being itself.

Like other animals, we are aware of our surroundings. We, however, precisely notice our surrounding *as* "real things"—as "beings." In other words, in noticing anything, we implicitly notice *that it is*. Because this is pervasive and "obvious" to us, we do not imagine ourselves to be doing anything other than simply apprehending "what is there." And yet, this very significance—"is," the fact that we recognize *of each and all* that it and they "are"—is, like equality, a significance that cannot be learned perceptually.

Of anything, we say that it "is": if we cannot say this, it is not something—it is not.²⁷ When we say of something that it is, we are naming it, in its specificity, as participating in the real. In this sense, we name what is most intimate to it—indeed, precisely what is most "real" about it. In that sense, the "being"—the "is"—of something is not a property of the thing, but is its very substance, its very "what it is." A thing is, we might say, how it "reals." No thing, however, exhausts what it is to be. While "is" is said most intimately of each thing, it is also said of all things, and its meaning thus exceeds the meaning of any particular thing that is and, indeed, it exceeds the meaning of all. "Is" names "the all" [*to pan*], but its meaning nonetheless exceeds that all *as* that one and only seamless unity [*to hen*] to which all necessarily belong; and, as Parmenides famously noted in his poem, this one and only "is" that is the real as such necessarily will be the same "is" tomorrow that was "is" yesterday, for precisely inasmuch as time "is," it is necessarily a participant in one and the same reality that is being itself. It is this aspect of its significance to which Socrates draws Cebes's attention:

> "Does being itself [*autē hē ousia*]—whose being we give an account of in our questioning and answering—always keep to the self-same condition, or does it vary from one moment to another? (*Phaedo* 78d)

Precisely what we mean by "is" is that anything about which we say "it is" is a participant in the one and only context that now and always defines the domain of the real, which is thus that which "always keep[s] to the self-same condition, [and] does [not] vary from one moment to another," as Socrates said in the above quotation. Anything we encounter in the world is a finite being that "is" a temporally and spatially extended process of realizing itself; indeed, even "equality" as such and "one" as such, though not spatially or temporally extended, are still finite inasmuch as they are specific notions; in this sense, then, neither the worldly beings that exist as finite processes of coming into being and passing out of being nor the inescapable and absolute realities that we find ourselves already to be engaged with in our experience with the things of our world are strictly identifiable with or exhaustive of what it is to be: as existents, all of these enact and realize the meaning of "is" without exhausting it:²⁸ "is" is precisely a significance specific to each but never exhausted in any or all of these, its realizations. Precisely what we mean, then, whenever we say of anything that it is, is something that we could never have learned from those existent things.²⁹

Further, the apprehension of being itself—that "whose being we give an account of in our questioning and answering," as Socrates remarks in the above quotation—is not just one contingent feature of our nature, but is at the heart of our distinctive human reality. This perception of things as "beings," that is, experiencing *ta pragmata in terms of* the issue of what it is to be, is integral to our experience as beings with *logos*: our "taking account" of things is precisely a matter of asking of things, "What is this?" and, in general, construing things in the intelligible, "categorial" way that is expressed in our implicitly and explicitly formulating articulations of this world in propositional form: "S is P."[30] Indeed, the similarly pervasive presence of such notions as "equality" and "one" in our account-taking is ultimately a refinement of the recognition of things in terms of "is"; that is, these further notions are, so to speak, the "how" of something's "is": "This *is* a 'one,' and this 'one' *is* 'equal to' that 'one.'" Our apprehension of things, then, is simultaneously both a grasp of those things in their unique specificities—the size, shape, and behavior of this dog now—and a grasp of those things *as* they fit within the absolute parameters according to which "is"—being itself—is articulated. Reflecting on ourselves and grasping the nature of our own reality as beings who take account, then, involves the recognition that we (already) are participants in a world that answers to absolutes, which are themselves not learnable.

We have now recognized about ourselves as beings with *logos* that we operate in a unique domain—the inherently self-reflexive domain we have called *psuchē* or "soul"—and we have discovered further that that domain is itself intrinsically characterized by being *already definitively in relation* to absolute meanings—indeed, to the meaning of "the absolute." With this background in place, we are now prepared to discuss the further articulation of this domain that is encapsulated in the image of the "divided line."

Shadows

Earlier, we asked what makes an account good or bad, and we noted that, most fundamentally, a good account is rooted in *empeiria* of *to pragma*. By investigating our own reality as beings who take account, we have now also seen that *ta pragmata*—the things of our everyday experience—are embedded in a reality that, qua reality, has its own articulations, articulations to which our accounting is inherently answerable. We can thus assess the quality of an account *in fact* by its responsiveness to *to pragma* and also assess it *in principle* by its responsiveness to these absolute parameters of the real. These absolutes—being and its articulations—are thus like the rules of "logic," as those are typically construed, but they are in fact broader and richer, for this "logic" of sentences—"S is P"—is, as we have seen, no less the very substance of the things themselves.

This giving an account of that to which we are answerable in our accounts is the subject of Socrates's and Glaucon's discussion at the end of Book VI of the *Republic*, at which point Socrates invokes the image of a "divided line" to put on display the relationships we have just been analyzing (VI.509d–511e, revisited at VII.533e–534a).[31] According to the image, our experience can be understood as a kind of embedded hierarchy in which the most immediate, contingent, and relative dimensions of our experience implicitly rely on—are "mediated by"—a sequence of more necessary and absolute aspects of experience, such that the more immediate and relative is in each case a kind of "shadow" of the more mediated and absolute. Let us turn now to exploring the four progressively more fundamental segments of the line—which are characterized, respectively, as imagination [*eikasia*] of images, trust [*pistis*] in things, the "figuring out" [*dianoia*] of things through "mathematicals," and insight [*noēsis*] into form (VII.533d), all ultimately contextualized by relationship to "the good" as such—beginning with a most familiar aspect of our immediate experience, namely, the recognition of shadows.

We are all familiar with the experience of seeing a shadow or recognizing a reflection in water (VI.509d–510a). When one sees a shadow, what one is encountering is a pattern of light and darkness on a surface, but one experiences it *as* the shadow *of* a person or dog and so on—without this recognition, it is not seen *as* a shadow.[32] To see the play of light and darkness as a shadow is immediately to recognize what we see as an *effect* of the cause—the shadow is an *image* of the thing. Yet, the sensory information offered to us in our experience is incapable in principle of communicating to us the meaning that is perceptually immediate to us.[33] *In* the play of light and darkness, that is, we see the presence of a dog or a tomato plant or a house, but in reality the "dog" or "tomato plant" or "house"—a substantial living being or a human-made artifact—exceeds ontologically the reality of light and its absence.[34] This experiential character of making something present to us that in principle could never actually *be* present in the experience in question is the focus of our further study of the "divided line."

If we turn from the shadow to that which it makes present—the dog or tomato plant or house—we typically take ourselves now to be directly encountering a present reality. Yet here, too, we face an analogous situation of something being made present to us that in principle cannot be realized in what is present. To recognize a tomato plant *as* a tomato plant, for example, is to experience what one encounters as a unitary living being, the same individual one saw yesterday and will see tomorrow, and one destined to produce large, red, tasty globes (tomatoes) at the end of the growing season. Yet none of these features that are definitive of our perception—the individual unity, the temporal sameness, or the "destiny"—can ever be strictly "present" to us as such: what is present, rather, is merely a finite and specific distribution of green plant fiber. Just as being "of a dog" exceeds in principle the reality of the present light and darkness that we call "a shadow," so does being "of a self-same individual realizing its natural potential" exceed in principle the reality of the present green fiber that we call "a thing." In seeing what is present *as* a tomato plant, we are seeing the fiber as the effect and image of a cause that is not itself actually present, just as seeing a shadow is seeing the light and darkness as the effect and image of a cause that it is not itself actually present (VI.510a). But, whereas we typically recognize that the shadow is only the image of a deeper reality, in our everyday perception we typically believe the present things to *be* the realities we are encountering; we are not acknowledging that, like shadows, they are really the presentations to us of realities that are not thus immediately present.[35] In both cases, there is a "taking account" happening: one thing is being seen in terms of another. "This is that"—but, as we noted earlier, we mistake our own account-taking for a neutral and innocent perception of the obvious.

Our whole world of immediate perception, in other words, is, as we have seen already in our discussion of the *Phaedo*, subtended and pervaded by structures of reality that themselves are not—in principle, could not be—the objects of perceptual experience as such. Our grasp of the shadow *as* a shadow is perceptually immediate, not a discursive process, and similarly our grasp of a dog *as* a dog is perceptually immediate, not a discursive process. And just as, in recognizing the shadow *as* the shadow of a dog, it is clear that we have *already* recognized the reality that it is the image of, in thus grasping the dog as a dog, we have *already* recognized *what it is to be a dog*, that is, the distinctive form of life—the "species" [*eidos*]—that explains the unity, enduring sameness, and destiny that can never be "present," and indeed, as we noted above, we have *already* recognized "being," "one," "equal," "square," and so on, all of which are necessarily implicit in this recognition.[36] When we shift from the recognition of the shadow to recognition of the thing of which it is an image, we turn from an everyday perception of sensory displays that we explicitly see as images of things to an everyday perception of things that we believe to be the immediate presence of reality itself. When we shift from the perceptual recognition of the thing to that which is implicitly reflected in the thing, however, we turn away from everyday perception and enter a different *kind* of cognitive domain.

The explicit recognition of the species "dog" or of "being," "one," "equality," "square," and so on—those realities we have implicitly recognized in our perception of the dog—is a matter of turning to what is intrinsic to our perception, simultaneously grasping the deeper reality of the things perceived and the deeper reality of our experience. First, as we have seen above in our discussion of the *Phaedo*, in studying these founding parameters of things we are engaged with a kind of "object," a kind of reality that is different from that of the objects of our everyday perception. Second, though, as our discussion of the *Phaedo* also showed, in studying these real parameters of things we are also engaged with the nature of the soul itself, in that we have entered the domain of that with which the soul is inherently engaged. And, in recognizing this exact simultaneity, that is, in noticing that studying these realities is inseparable from studying the nature of the soul, we are precisely noticing a relationship between soul and reality that does not take the form of everyday empirical life; that is, we are required to recognize a different *kind* of relationship between the soul and the reality with which it is engaged than we typically presume to be the case. The discovery of this realm, then, is a revolutionary transformation in our experience of the nature of things, of the nature of ourselves, and of the relationship between ourselves and reality. In each case, this recognition challenges the terms in which we grasp these things in our ordinary experience of the world.

The relationship we find between the soul and its object when we reflect on our knowledge of the parameters of being is different from our everyday experience of *ta pragmata* in a number of important ways. Broadly, we are talking about what we would normally call matters of "intelligence" rather than matters of "perception." In our empirical perception, we encounter independent members of a natural world, each in the process of coming to be and passing away, and each marked by its own distinct set of sensible characteristics that we can know only by engaging in the empirical, temporal process of taking stock of them. With "matters of intelligence," the situation is quite different. Here, as we worked out in our discussion of the *Phaedo* above, we are still engaged in knowing the things of our everyday world, but we use *our own abilities* of intelligent apprehension to know them. In other words, when we know things in terms of their "parameters of being," we do not empirically investigate a different set of independent members of the natural world; instead we turn to our own *understanding* of what it is for anything to be. Our knowledge of "one," "equality," "is," and so on is nonetheless not a product of our creative imagination but is an application of insights we experience ourselves as having *already* acquired—not "already" in the sense of "at a different moment of natural time," but "already" in the sense of "always already there whenever we perceive." Our knowledge is a matter of intrinsic insight [*nous*] into the nature of being, which, again unlike empirical perception, is an apprehension of truths that are pervasively, permanently, and definitively true of all beings rather than being specific, contingent matters that come into being and pass away. That this insight into the nature of being is intrinsic to the soul and not a matter of empirical study is the point Socrates makes in the *Phaedo*:

> "Now haven't we also been saying from way back that the soul, whenever she makes use of the body for investigating something, whether through seeing or through hearing or through any other sense (for that's what investigating through the body is—investigating something through sensing), then she's dragged by the body into things that never keep to the self-same condition, and she herself wanders and is shaken up and gets dizzy, just as if she were drunk, because she's had contact with such things?"
>
> "Of course."
>
> "But whenever, herself by herself, she investigates, she goes off there [*ekeise*], to what's pure and *is* always and is deathless and keeps to the same condition, and since she's akin to this, continually comes to be with it—whenever, that is, she's come to be herself all by herself and this is possible for her—and then she's stopped her wandering and, around those things, always keeps to the self-same condition, because she's had contact with such things; and this state of hers is called thoughtfulness [*phronēsis*]—isn't all this so?" (*Phaedo* 79c–d)

We *find ourselves* occupying an absolute standpoint that affords us the capacity of "figuring out" or "taking account of" [*dianoein, logizein*] situations.[37] We can, however, shift from *employing* these capacities in our apprehension of everyday things, and instead turn our attention "there," as Socrates puts it, and notice this absolute standpoint itself:

And when, in this way, we are pure and free of the thoughtlessness of the body, we shall, as is likely, be in the company of things that are pure as well and, through our own selves, shall recognize everything unadulterated—and this, no doubt, is the true. (*Phaedo* 67a–b)

As we noted when we first considered the reality of the soul, though, this world "there" is not some other natural place: it is, rather, immanent to our experience "here," without being reducible to it.[38] In short, matters of intelligence differ from matters of perception in that they rely on the soul's intrinsic grasp of the ultimate nature of things.

We can indeed "turn around" and focus our attention "there"—we can turn, that is, from the "visible" segment of the line to the "intelligible" segment of the line (VI.509d)—but, as Socrates emphasizes in the image of the cave, this turn is an existential transformation, and not one we easily or automatically undergo.[39] Before completing our discussion of the "divided line," we need first to look more carefully at this experience of turning. In particular, we must consider more carefully what is involved in mathematical experience and in the experience of beauty.

Turning Around [Periagōgē]: Mathematics and Beauty

In Book VII of the *Republic*, Socrates argues for the particular pedagogical value of mathematics. "[The ability to calculate and to number] probably is one of the things," Socrates says, "that we are seeking that by nature leads to intellection [*pros tēn noēsin*]; but no one uses it rightly, as a thing that in every way is apt to draw men toward being" (VII.522e–523a). The experience of mathematics, as we shall see, is especially cognitively privileged in our apprehension of the ultimate nature of things, not for its empirical role of allowing us to assess the quantity of *ta pragmata*, but for its heuristic role is enabling our transformed "metaphysical" grasp of reality and our relationship to it.[40]

In our perception of an individual organism (a theme to which we will return later), we might very well think that our recognition of the organism as a member of a natural species like "dog" or "tomato" is just a matter of a developed, habitual expectation rather than the apprehension of any unique "reality." Indeed, in *On the Origin of Species*, Darwin, contrary to Aristotle, precisely argued that the apparent reality of species is reducible to contingent, historical process and thus does not represent any "deeper" reality than the reality of individual organisms.[41] This uncertainty about the empirical or nonempirical reality of natural species means that we do not automatically see the force of the claim that *ta pragmata* are "shadows" in the sense we discussed above. Mathematical realities, though, like the examples of "equality," "square," and "one" that we reflected on above, are not thus ambivalent. As we noted Socrates saying earlier,

> Geometers make the arguments for the sake of the square itself and the diagonal itself, not for the sake of the diagonal they draw, and likewise with the rest. These things themselves that they mold and draw, of which there are shadows and images in water, they now use as images, seeking to see the things themselves, that one can see in no other way than with thought. (VI.510d)

When we engage in mathematics, we recognize that the very meaning of those mathematical realities is that they are nonempirical realities that are universally and necessarily true of all empirical situations without being reducible to or defined in terms of those situations. Further, we precisely recognize that our grasp of these realities is innate, that *we are rational*. Our experience of mathematics is privileged for inaugurating us unambiguously into the domain of "absolute" cognition, in which the soul is intrinsically related to the objects of its knowledge. To put it another way, we find here an experience in which the soul, in giving an account, is answerable to a norm, even though it does not step out of its own experience of account-giving.

Though mathematics is thus heuristically privileged in revealing to us the intelligible domain, it is not itself the most powerful exponent of that domain.[42] Let us remember, again, Socrates's remark from the *Phaedo*, which we quoted above:

> Our present argument isn't about the equal any more than it's about the beautiful itself and the good itself and the just and the holy and, as I say, about all those things upon which we set the seal "the what it is itself" [*to auto ho esti*] in the questions we ask as well as in the answers we give. (*Phaedo* 75c–d)

Mathematical experience reveals to us the intelligible domain, but there are other experiences that have the same characteristics we have just been describing; that is, they too display a relationship of the soul with its object that is radically different from the form of our everyday engagement with *ta pragmata*.[43] Particularly relevant for our purposes, beauty *as such*, and the good *as such*, like the mathematical realities of number and equality as such, have a character that is radically different from the character of the objects of our everyday experience. Socrates describes this in the *Phaedo* in relation to beauty:

> "The equal itself, the beautiful itself, each thing itself that is [*auto hekaston ho estin*]—in short, that which *is*—do these ever admit of any sort of change whatsoever? Or does each thing that *is*, being of a single form [*monoeides*] when taken all by itself, always keep to the self-same condition and never ever in any way whatsoever admit of any alteration at all?"
>
> "It's necessarily in the self-same condition, Socrates," said Cebes.
>
> "But what about the many beautiful things, such as human beings or horses or cloaks or any other such things of this sort, or equal things or anything else having the same names as those other things we mentioned? Do they keep to the self-same condition? Or, in complete contrast to those other things, are they, so to speak, never in any way self-same, either in relation to themselves or to each other?"
>
> "That's how it is," said Cebes. "These in turn never keep to the same condition." (*Phaedo* 78d–e)

Whereas beautiful things, like equal things, are multiform and changing, the reality of what it is to be beautiful, like the reality of what it is to be equal, is uniform and unchanging. Further, our engagement with these realities is very different from our everyday engagement with *ta pragmata*, as Socrates notes in the discussion in the *Phaedo* (to which we referred above) in which Socrates draws the attention of Simmias and Cebes to our definitive capacity to "gather" ourselves in an experience of self-reflection. There, Socrates asks,

> "And what about this sort of thing, Simmias: Do we claim that there is some just itself—or no such thing?"
>
> "We do claim it, by Zeus!"
>
> "And also some beautiful and good?"
>
> "Why, certainly."
>
> "Well, ever see anything of that sort with your eyes?"
>
> "In no way," said he.
>
> "But did you lay hold of them by any other sense that comes through the body? And I'm speaking about the being [*tēs ousias*] of all such things, about bigness and health and strength, and, in a word, all the rest—whatever happens to be. Is what's truest about them beheld through the body? Or does it work this way: ... using unadulterated thought itself all by itself [*autēi kath' hautēn eilikrinei tēi dianoiai*], [someone] attempts to hunt down each of the beings that's unadulterated and itself all by itself, and once he's freed himself as far as possible from eyes and ears and, so to speak, from his whole body, ... isn't this the man, Simmias, if anyone, who will hit upon what *is*?" (*Phaedo* 65d–66a)

In each case, the "as such"—beauty or good "itself," that is, "what it is to be" beautiful or good—is not itself a sensible matter. These are realities with which we operate, but the very character of the "as such" is such that, in principle, it could not be sensible as such. Our engagement with these realities informs and illuminates our experience of *ta pragmata*, but it is not derived from that engagement; instead, engagement with these realities is constitutive of the very nature of the soul. Consequently, our explicit apprehension of them is a matter of "turning" the soul to reflect on itself rather than a matter of investigating natural beings. We have already seen how this is the case with our mathematical experience. Let us now consider how this is so in our experience of beauty. Though our experience of quantitative relationships is our most immediately apparent engagement with the "absolute" standpoint, it is not our deepest engagement with it, and our deeper engagements with the "intelligible"—specifically, our recognitions of beauty, goodness, and, indeed, being—reveal further aspects of the character of this domain that are not apparent in mathematical knowing.

Whereas the experience of mathematics is cognitively primary for its heuristic role in revealing to us the intelligible domain, our experience of beauty is affectively primary for this same purpose. When we experience something as beautiful, we notice something about it that is more than the list of sensory features. It is blue, yes, and it is cubical, yes, but in having these features, *it is beautiful*. This beauty, furthermore, is not simply something *I like* but is something *it has*. And, though this beauty is not merely something I like, it is nonetheless something to which I cannot be affectively indifferent: I am drawn by it. Like quantity, beauty is supersensible, objective, and compelling. One thing that is striking about the experience of beauty, though, and what differentiates it from the experience of quantity, is the twofold intimacy of beauty.

First, whereas we experience quantity as something indifferent to the concreteness and particularity of the thing, we experience beauty as uniquely immanent in the particularities of the thing. In other words, a thing would still be a "one" if its features were to change, but a thing would not be beautiful if its features were to change. We really experience *this particular thing itself* as beautiful. This ontological intimacy of beauty to the thing in its specificity thus has the character of revealing the apparent *absoluteness* of the contingent thing.

Second, the compulsion we feel to acknowledge the beauty of something is not an intellectual observation but is an emotional *attraction*: though we apprehend the beauty *through* our theoretical powers—our powers of observing a separate object—we experience these observable features in a way that is more practical than theoretical in that we feel an urge to *respond*. The beauty of something touches us in our own intimate core—it *matters* to us that *we* have this experience of it. In other words, just as the beauty is not indifferent to the thing itself in its particularity, so is it not indifferent to us in our particularity: in experiencing the beauty of the thing, we experience ourselves as being addressed directly by a reality that cannot be contained within the narrow cognitive parameters of our experience. In this sense, beauty, like mathematics, is normative for our experience.

In the experience of beauty, we find that we ourselves are "already" involved with the thing "itself": though I might have no chronologically prior knowledge of or involvement with the thing, I feel my care for it. I am "already" in relation to it, in the sense that my being moved by it is not an optional matter for me, but is a way in which I feel it compelling my interests prior to any decision on my part. This sense of being "already" touched by the beautiful thing can itself take varying forms of intensity, though. In its most immediate form—the visually pleasing character of an appearance—this care for the thing is only a hint, an intimation of something deeper than our everyday pragmatic engagement. For that reason, this experience can actually seem more superficial than intimate. Though the experience of beauty offers me an experience of things beyond the terms of the "practicality" of our everyday affairs, I can nonetheless adopt an instrumental relationship to this new reality I discover. This is the attitude especially illustrated in the first speeches about *erōs* in the *Phaedrus*.

We have a range of different experiences of beauty, but the most immediately compelling is our experience of beautiful bodies that excite in us erotic desire. There is more than one way that we can respond to this desire, and, indeed, for many people, teenage life is defined by the struggle to determine how to deal with this.[44] Typically, we try to satisfy this desire with the sensual pleasures of bodily coupling. Even more, it is common for people to interpret these sensual pleasures as the goal, and to see in beautiful bodies only the opportunity for obtaining this goal. This is the attitude that lies behind the speech of Lysias that Phaedrus repeats and that Socrates rearticulates in his own subsequent speech in the *Phaedrus*. In each of these two speeches, the narrator makes an argument to convince the addressee—a beautiful boy—that it is better to be a means of sensual pleasure to someone without emotional attachment than to someone in love. In other words, both speeches seek to detach sex from love, as we express it in our rough-and-ready everyday parlance, and both speeches, further, seem themselves to be part of the narrator's effort to act instrumentally on the soul of the addressee precisely to get that beautiful boy to make himself available for the narrator's pleasure. The attitude expressed here is surely familiar to us all as the foundation of our usual sense of the nature of sex—the attitude we ourselves adopt and especially the attitude that is presumed in the myriad portrayals of sexuality that we are confronted with in advertising and entertainment.

Indeed, this attitude is so familiar that we commonly take it for granted as simply a factual representation of the nature of sexual desire. What is important to recognize here, though, is that this attitude is an *interpretation* of our own feelings: it is a *taking account* (even if not reflectively cognitive) of our experience of attraction. And the central point of Socrates's discourses in both the *Phaedrus* and the *Symposium* is that this taking account is a fundamental *misinterpretation* of our experience, a misinterpretation of the nature of *erōs*. Beauty, in fact, according to Socrates's "palinode" in the *Phaedrus*, is precisely the immediate showing—the "shine" [*pheggos*] (*Phaedrus* 250b)—of "there" here: it is, in other words, the way in which the insufficiency of the prosaic world appears in and as the intimation of that intelligible reality that both informs *ta pragmata* and is native to our own reality as souls.[45] The desire we feel in its presence is a feeling of recognition, the sense that our own most intimate reality is being addressed, and the desire is ultimately the desire for inhabiting a world in which that intimate inner nature is fulfilled.[46] The desire, then, is ultimately a desire to *leave* the world of instrumental calculation, and for that reason the "slavish economizing" (*Phaedrus* 256e) in which we subordinate this experience of beauty to the pursuit of sensual pleasure is thus precisely the opposite of its fulfillment.

Two especially important aspects of our experience are revealed in this analysis of sexual desire. First, our feelings are themselves not transparent in their meaning, but themselves need interpretation: our behavior, in other words, is not a straightforward reaction to a stimulus or a neutral calculation of how to answer to our desires, but is itself a *taking account* of ourselves, and one in which we can do well or badly, just as in any other matter of accounting. Second—and this is perhaps the most prominent aspect of Socrates's discourses about *erōs*—the experience of beauty *is itself educative*; that is, our own relationship to beauty naturally encourages us to develop the very insight that Socrates articulates in his speeches. This latter point is especially the theme of his speech in the *Symposium*, a speech in which he reports a dialogue he had with Diotima.

Diotima begins by defining the nature of *erōs*. We use the word "love" or the word "desire" broadly to name the way we seek to be happy through any one of a number of different means. When we talk about "erotic desire," though, we mean something different from the desire to be happy through possessing money or knowledge or through playing sports (*Symposium* 205d). This form of desire, with which presumably all of us (or at least most of us) are familiar, is the particular kind of excitement that arises in the presence of a beautiful body. Socrates himself offers a definition of this at the beginning of his first speech in the *Phaedrus*:

> Everyone knows that *erōs* is a form of desire [*epithumia tis*], and we know that even those who are not in love [*mē erōntes*] desire beautiful things. How then shall we distinguish the one who loves [*ton erōnta*] from the one who doesn't? . . . When passion without reason rules over straight-minded opinion and is itself driven toward the pleasure of beauty, and further, when this passion is violently moved [*errōmenōs rhōstheisa*] by kindred desires toward the beauty of the body and is victorious, it takes its name from that very force [*autēs tēs rhōmēs*] and is called love [*erōs*]." (*Phaedrus* 237c, 238b–c)

Socrates gives a further description of this familiar experience in Book V of the *Republic*:[47]

> But it isn't appropriate for an erotically inclined man to forget that all boys in the bloom of youth pique the interest of a lover of boys and arouse him and that all seem worthy of his care and pleasure. Or isn't that the way you people behave to fine and beautiful boys? You praise a snub-nosed one as cute, a hook-nosed one you say is regal, one in between is well proportioned, dark ones look manly, and pale ones are children of the gods. And as for a honey-colored boy, do you think that this very term is anything but the euphemistic coinage of a lover who found it easy to tolerate sallowness, provided it was accompanied by the bloom of youth? In a word, you find all kinds of terms and excuses so as not to reject anyone whose flower is in bloom. (V.474d–475a)

Our familiar sense of sexual desire, as we noted above, is the charge we feel in our very bodies in the presence of beautiful bodies that motivates us to pursue sensual pleasure with them. The remarks from Book V of the *Republic* remind us that the presence of beautiful bodies is the occasion for the experience, and the definition from Socrates's first speech in the *Phaedrus* reminds us that the form in which we encounter it is this charge that touches us at our most intimate bodily level;[48] as we indicated in our discussion of Socrates's palinode in the *Phaedrus*, though, the *nature* or *meaning* of this desire is not immediately obvious. It is this that Diotima defines in the *Symposium*. The specific and definitive character of *erōs*, she says, is the desire for "giving birth in beauty [*tokos en kalōi*]" (*Symposium* 206b). Given the occasion of the (objective) presence of a beautiful body, then, and this (subjective) feeling of charge, what will actually *satisfy* that desire (as opposed to simply discharging it) is to create something that expresses the reality—the recognition—that these two (objective and subjective) different sides intimate. The satisfaction of our erotic desire, in other words, is not a matter simply of offering us fleeting sensual pleasure, but is a matter of allowing the blossoming of an intrinsic fertility or being "pregnant" [*egkumōn*], as she puts it. Erotic fulfillment is thus fundamentally a matter of *creativity*, of bringing something new into being; in this situation beauty *inspires* us.[49]

The inspired creativity of true erotic fulfillment can take different forms. "All of us," Diotima says, "are pregnant, Socrates, both in body and in soul" (*Symposium* 206c), and these different forms of "pregnancy" point to different fulfillments. The erotic desire inspired in us in the company of someone beautiful can be, for example, beyond the pursuit of immediate pleasure, the exuberant desire to bring into being another person—a child. This is the "pregnancy in body" that Diotima speaks of: "Now, some people are pregnant in body, and for this reason turn more to women and pursue love in that way, providing themselves through childbirth with immortality and remembrance and happiness, as they think, for all time to come" (*Symposium* 208e–209a). Beyond this, though, "there surely are those who are even more pregnant in their souls than in their bodies, and these are pregnant with what is fitting for a soul to bear and bring to birth" (*Symposium* 209a). In its richest fulfillment, our erotic desire impels us precisely to discover our own nature through expressing it: it is a matter of releasing from the soul its natural strivings.

What are these natural strivings—the "pregnancy"—of the soul? "Wisdom and the rest of virtue, which all poets beget, as well as all the craftsmen who are said to be creative," Diotima says (*Symposium* 209a). When we feel erotic passion, in other words, what is stirring in us is the excitement to realize our human possibilities. The beauty of another inspires us to desire, and this desire is ultimately a desire to grow. Diotima offers a description of a typical human situation:

> When someone has been pregnant [*egkumōn*] with these in his soul from early youth, while he is still a virgin, and, having arrived at the proper age, desires to beget and give birth, he too will certainly go about seeking the beauty in which he would beget.... He is much more drawn to bodies that are beautiful

than to those that are ugly; and if he has the luck to find a soul that is beautiful and noble and well-formed, he is even more drawn to this combination; such a man makes him instantly teem with *logoi* about virtue. . . . In my view, you see, when he makes contact with someone beautiful and keeps company with him, he conceives and gives birth to what he has been carrying inside him for ages [*ha palai ekuei*]. (*Symposium* 209b–c)

This description reminds us of the complex response we have to situations of erotic involvement with another person. It is true that the sensibly apparent beauty of the body of another person can generate this charge in us, but we can be similarly affected by the other's soul, and the enthusiasm of such an experience ushers in quite different forms of behavior: behaviors that themselves reflect the engagement of *persons*—beings with *logos*—with each other. With the appropriate other, we can be inspired to strive for moral and intellectual fulfillment, a striving that redefines for us our sense of what our desire is, and thus intrinsically involves the recognition of the limited and insufficient character of our own earlier "interpretation" of that desire.[50]

If we follow Diotima and describe accurately what happens in real erotic situations, then, we must acknowledge first that what we commonly differentiate as sex and love are not so clearly distinguished, in that it is a *person* to whom we are attracted, and this means a bond of souls is being developed in and through the bond of bodies. Second, we must recognize that erotic desire is not itself static but is something that can develop: the erotic impulse, initially "made sense of" in terms of relatively immediate ends of bodily interaction for the sake of sensual pleasure, itself takes on different parameters, not through deliberate decision but simply through its continued enactment in an appropriately supportive context. We are actually led, by the inspiring beauty, to recognize more deeply the sorts of fulfillment we might seek.[51] In this sense, the experience of beauty is inherently educative.[52]

According to the accounts given by Diotima in the *Symposium* and by Socrates in the *Phaedrus*, we human beings are analogous to other natural beings in that we have a natural trajectory of development that will unfold if properly nurtured. In our case, though, it is beauty that offers us the nutrition we need: if we allow ourselves to follow our attraction to beauty, that experience will itself unfold, in appropriately supportive contexts, into our ever-richer engagement with the distinctive character of our human reality—the reality of beings with *logos*. Through the experience of beauty, we precisely have an intimation of our involvement in a reality that exceeds the parameters of the prosaic demands of everyday life, and, if we are open to it, that experience will precisely allow us to recognize ever more fully exactly the nature of this involvement: the very involvement in the "intelligible" that we have been investigating through our studies of "recollection" in the *Phaedo* and our studies of the "divided line" in the *Republic*. And what is specially significant about the way in which beauty intimates our home "there" is that that "extramundane" reality is one that we precisely find *in* the singularity of the beauty to which we are attracted and in the singularity of our own engagement with it. The experience of beauty reveals our home "there," but it also reveals that "there" is precisely found "here": it is the very reality of the "here," and it is what summons us to care about it.[53]

Mathematical understanding is integral to our ability to deal with *ta pragmata* intelligently, but it also puts on display for us—if we turn and attend to it—the fact that our experience of *ta pragmata* does not exhaust reality. The appreciation of beauty is similarly a dimension of our involvement with the things of our everyday life that puts on display for us—if we turn and attend to it—the irreducibility of reality to the terms of everyday life. What is most striking of all about the experience of beauty is that *it itself encourages us to perform this turning of the soul*. And, whereas the mathematical experience encourages us to imagine the ultimate nature of reality in abstraction from the things of everyday life, the experience of beauty impresses on us the irreducible worth of the singular things of our everyday world; in other words, the real as such is not something that exists in separation from our everyday world but is enacted only in and as that world.[54] Recognizing reality is not a matter of looking elsewhere: it is a matter of grasping truly the real substance of *ta pragmata*.

Mathematics and the experience of beauty are familiar experiences we have—experiences of forms of necessity that impinge on us—that are especially well-suited to triggering in us the recognition that our everyday involvement with *ta pragmata* does not exhaust reality: that the things of everyday life, which we typically presume to be "the real," are in fact "shadows" that exist as the revelation of a deeper reality of which they are an inherently insufficient realization. We can take up on its own terms this deeper reality, the "really" real [*to ontōs on*] of which *ta pragmata* are the enactment [*mimēsis*]; that is, we can turn our intelligence away from *ta pragmata* as such to the articulation of the parameters of *what it is to be* as such. Having now investigated these distinctive ways in which mathematical experience and the experience of beauty both intrinsically reveal the nature of intelligible reality and impel us toward recognizing that revelation, we are in a position to investigate the final theme in Socrates's image of the "divided line," namely, our experience of the good.

The Good

We recognize equals, dogs, squares, and beauties, and we similarly recognize goods. And just as those other recognitions are possible only because the soul is *already* intimately cognizant of the normative force of the notion of equality as such or beauty as such, so is our recognition of goods dependent on our recognition of the normative force of good as such; as Socrates says, "This is what every soul pursues and for the sake of which it does anything" (VI.505d–e).[55] Whenever we think about something, "I like that" or "That's better," we are recognizing a good: these judgments—whether explicitly cognitive or unreflectively perceptual—are all premised on our grasp of the independent sense of "good" itself, a sense, like "equal" or "beautiful," that is not reducible to, derivable from, or learnable from the finite things of everyday life—*ta pragmata*. These finite things, though in some sense good, better, or even best, are never themselves *the* good, never good absolutely, and thus they are equally in some sense not good (bad), not better (worse), not the best. Beyond these explicit judgments of comparative evaluation, though, there is an even more pervasive recognition of the good operative in our experience. Socrates draws our attention to this more basic recognition in the *Phaedo*.

Describing his own philosophical development, Socrates remarks that he "as a young man was wondrously desirous of that wisdom they call 'inquiry into nature' [*tēs sophias hēn dē kalousi peri phuseōs historian*]" (*Phaedo* 96a). He was interested, that is, in understanding those things that come into being and pass away—studying the things that populate our everyday experience of the natural world. He describes a typical aspect of this attitude—an attitude that masquerades as a neutral stance, but that in fact brings its own interpretive prejudices:

> I used to think this was clear to everyone: that a human being grows because of eating and drinking. For when, from the food he eats, amounts of flesh are attached to flesh and amounts of bone to bones . . . then the bulk that's little has later become a lot and in this way the small human being becomes big. (*Phaedo* 96c–d)

What Socrates is describing here is the merely additive or quantitative interpretation of growth: the growth of the human being, on the account he used to hold, is to be explained by the addition of material. This interpretation, as Socrates goes on to make clear, is importantly insufficient.[56]

When human beings—or just about any natural organism—grow, they grow according to the terms set by their own nature: at a certain point, for example, people reach their maximum, mature height, and no amount of eating will increase that. Indeed, even though further eating will quantitatively increase the size of the body, that increase will, after a certain point, generally be only an increase in fat, not a continued enlargement of the functioning members of the body. And indeed, different organisms, for example a human and a dog, can eat the same meals, and yet the human will grow into a human form and the dog into a dog form. What all of these points reveal is that growth is not simply quantitative or additive: it is qualitative, and indeed it is more fundamentally qualitative than quantitative. The materials "added" to the organism in the form of food are the *conditio sine qua non* of growth—they are the occasioning circumstance without which the growth could not happen—but they are not the *source* of that growth. Socrates describes this difference: "It's one thing to be genuinely the cause, and another to be that without which the cause wouldn't be a cause" (*Phaedo* 99b). The reason *why* the person or the dog grows is *because that being is a person* or *because it is a dog*: it is this reality of "human" or "dog" to which we must appeal if we are to understand the transformations of the organism's coming to be and passing away.

This recognition of the human or the dog as the true "cause" of the growth of the organism is the same point we made earlier in our discussion of the divided line: the individual human being and the individual dog are not arbitrary assemblages of matter that simply happened arbitrarily to take on the particular material configuration that each has; on the contrary, the living process of each is an enactment of *form*, that is, each has developed the way it has because of its *species*-identity. Its development has taken the form it has *because that is how a human or a dog develops.*

This insight that the life-process of the organism is a *development*, that it is the realization *of a life-form*, is the key to Socrates's account of the change his attitude took in the course of his own philosophical development. Correcting his earlier assessment of the "additive" interpretation of growth, Socrates says,

> If someone should want to discover the cause concerning any such thing—in what way it comes into being or perishes or is—he'd have to discover this concerning it: in what way it's best for it either to be or to undergo and do anything whatsoever. (*Phaedo* 97c)

Within the very world of nature that was the object of his investigations, in other words, Socrates recognized the need to see organisms as answering *in their very process as material beings* to a goal: there is *for the organism* a "better" and a "worse," an *immanent* norm that we acknowledge in recognizing the realities of health and illness, or of injury and healing. These notions of good are not dependent on our recognition—are not simply matters of explicit comparative evaluation—but are intrinsic to the very reality of the organism, and, for that reason, our recognition of these goods as goods is intrinsic to our recognition of these organisms as organisms. In other words, the very notion of "nature" is inconceivable—unrecognizable—except to a being (a soul) that *can* recognize "good."

Our recognition of "goods," then, is not just a matter of our positing our own subjective preferences. More fundamentally, our recognition of the good is integral to our very ability to recognize the *things* of our everyday world; indeed, this was the focus of our initial discussion of *technē* as the ability to care for its object. As we saw there, "good," far from being a merely "subjective" matter, is integral to the very fabric of being. There are further consequences to the fact that, as we do with "equal" and "beautiful," we find our experience already illuminated by the good.

Like equality and beauty—indeed, like all the realities that populate the realm of intelligibility—good has imperative force. We have already seen, in the context of the organism, that the good of the organism is the cause of its development. In that sense, just as we noted earlier that "being" ultimately names what is most intimate to a thing, so is the good what is ultimately most substantial about the thing, the material reality being the realization of this defining reality. As thus immanent to the very being of the thing, the imperative force of the good is ontological, that is, it is what dictates how the organism will develop. What is even more striking about the good, however, is that it is subjectively imperative. The very *meaning* of "good" is that it is what *should* be, and to recognize the good—to *have recognized* the good *already*—is to have our experience illuminated by the compelling force of "should." Socrates's portrayal of the good through the metaphor of the sun in Books VI and VII of the *Republic* precisely emphasizes this subjective notion of "illumination" and its coordination with the objective, ontological sense of the good:

> When sight is in the eyes and the man possessing them tries to make use of it, and color is present in what is to be seen, in the absence of a third class of thing whose nature is specifically directed to this very purpose, you know that sight will see nothing and the colors will be unseen.... Doesn't [sight] get the power it has as a sort of overflow from the sun's treasury? ... As the good is in the intelligible region with respect to intelligence and what is intellected, so the sun is in the visible region with respect to sight and what is seen.... The sun not only provides what is seen with the power of being seen, but also with generation, growth, and nourishment although it itself isn't generation.... Analogously, not only being known is present in the things known as a consequence of the good, but also existence and being are in them as a result of it, although the good isn't being but is still beyond being, exceeding it in dignity and power. (VI.507d–e, 508b–c, 509b)

In empirical life, we recognize the sun to be simultaneously the source of the heat that allows natural growth and the light that allows our ability to see it; analogously, the good is both the substantial source of the good that is intimately integral to each thing *and* it is what fundamentally illuminates our apprehension of those realities as such. But to see in terms of the good is to see in terms of what should be and, inasmuch as this perceptual aperture is constitutive of our perspective and not an optional attitude we might turn on or off, this perception of "should," like our perception of beauty, is intimately gripping to us. We are not capable, in other words, of *not* caring about the good.

"How things should be" is thus the most basic form of how things appear to us. This means that it is the very nature of our experience to present us with a challenge, with an imperative, and the ongoing enactment of our perspective will be a matter of how we do or do not measure up to this pervading, defining sense: this, ultimately, is the core sense of what it means to "take account." In other words, whereas the good for anything qua organism is the form that is constitutive of its *bodily development*, for the human being—the being that can "take account" of things—this answering to the good is constitutive of its *experience*.

It is constitutive of our experience always to be answering the question "Is this as it should be?" In other words, we see things as answering to the norm of the good. Typically, this perception is implicit: to see a tomato plant as a tomato plant is to see the specific state of the green fiber in terms of the intrinsic norm that is definitive of the tomato plant but, as we saw above, we do not typically notice this "intelligent" character of our perception. Similarly, we see things—*ta pragmata*—in terms of how they sit with respect to our own values, and our actions with respect to them are always answering to what we have thus already taken to be the good; though this endorsement of what we take "the good" to be in our behavior is an interpretation—a "taking account" of the good as such—we again typically take it as "natural" or perceptually obvious, rather than acknowledging it as an interpretive judgment on our parts, a judgment *that itself needs to be evaluated*. "Turning around" and owning up to the imperatives intrinsic to the "given" powers we inherit as beings with *logos* thus ultimately requires us to subject our own already-established account of the good to scrutiny: the imperative, intrinsic to our nature as beings with *logos*, is that we ask about this, our own prejudice, "Is this presumption about the good correct?" And this is not a detached question, but it is precisely a challenge that touches us in the most intimate way possible—a challenge to the very way we live.

Our everyday sense of value infuses the very fabric of things. Our values guide our action, which is always specific: our values are what turn us toward "here"—they are *how* we see the good (or bad) in things. Changing our sense of good, then, is changing our sense of how we see things here. It is changing how we recognize the good or bad in *ta pragmata*. The "turning of the soul" that amounts to holding ourselves answerable to the good thus amounts to assessing in *ta pragmata* how they are occasions for turning to the good, or, in other words, how they can be turned to the good as opposed to being turned to the bad. Ultimately, then, "turning the soul around" amounts to a living commitment to the pervasive turning of the things of this world—*ta pragmata*—to the good.

Our taking account, then, is not simply a matter of being cognitively correct in our detached apprehension of the things of our world. It is also a matter of behaving appropriately, a matter of the practice of *being* good, and this amounts to discerning within things, which are never the good as such but are thus always ambivalently good and bad, how they can be good.[57] As Socrates says in the *Euthydemus*,

> So, to sum up, Clinias, I said, it seems likely that with respect to all the things we called good in the beginning, the correct account is not that in themselves they are good by nature, but rather as follows: if ignorance controls them, they are greater evils than their opposites, to that extent that they are more capable of complying with a bad master; but if good sense and wisdom are in control,

they are greater goods. In themselves, though, neither sort is of any value. (*Euthydemus* 281d–e)[58]

Things are by nature ambivalent—simultaneously good and not good—and to be turned to the good oneself is to be pervasively engaged in working to turn these always-ambivalent things of the world—*ta pragmata*—toward the good. For the being with *logos*, the natural trajectory and fulfillment is simultaneously moral and cognitive: indeed, knowing oneself is ultimately a matter of recognizing—"knowing"—the good, and that is ultimately a matter of practice.

III. Sophistry

We began this chapter by reflecting on the familiar pairing of philosophy (wisdom) and "sophistry." We noted this initially in the historical emergence of the cultural practice that gave rise to both of these opposed practices. We then saw why, because knowledge necessarily takes place *in logos*, the threat of sophistry always lurks within the philosophical project. It is this last point in particular that required us to explore "taking account" as such, in order to determine what it is that makes an account true. We noted that, beyond answerability to the empirical specificities that we encounter perceptually and factually—an answerability that is only adequately addressed through developing *empeiria* with *ta pragmata*—our accounts are answerable *in principle* to the intelligible parameters of being—matters of logic that are, indeed, matters of metaphysics. What our study of the "divided line" has now revealed is that the unique relationship the soul has to intelligibility entails further that adequately answering to intelligibility is not simply a matter of detached cognition, but has an inherently behavioral dimension as well: the nature of intelligibility cannot adequately be grasped except through the practicing of "turning around," which is to say, taking account of oneself—of one's own unique role within the experience of *ta pragmata*. These reflections on the experience of turning around revealed ultimately that this answerability to intelligibility cannot be separated from answerability to the good. Competently taking account, then, is an existential matter: it is a matter of how one lives one's life in and through the process of dealing with the empirical specificities of the everyday world. In short, competently taking account ultimately requires that one embrace the very stance—philosophy—advocated and practiced by Socrates himself. Because of the intimate and intense demands of "turning around" that such philosophy requires, though, it is not surprising that (as we shall see in greater detail in chapter 4) we more commonly rest content with attitudes that are not truthful—we settle, that is, for false opinion. Such false opinion amounts to excuses not to hold ourselves answerable to the rigorous cognitive and behavioral demands of requiring our opinions to be comprehensively answerable to the good. Grasping the complex range of demands that competent knowing involves allows us now to recognize the various forms that these sophisms can take.

The powers that allow us to grasp the nature of things are powers we *find ourselves* able to deploy, without being able to claim credit for those powers: this is the meaning, as we have seen, of the notion of *anamnēsis*, "recollection." These powers are "gifts": they are powers we "inherit," so to speak, not powers we have earned. We have not studied these powers systematically, but the powers we have noted include (a) our ability to calculate the quantity of things; (b) our very capacity to recognize things as "beings," as *real*; (c) our capacity to recognize things as natural, as organisms; (d) our ability to recognize the beauty in things; and (e) our ability to recognize the worth—the good—of things. Further, though we have not studied the relationships between these powers systematically, we have nonetheless seen that these abilities are not an unrelated set of different powers, but are themselves "nested"; that is, there is no recognition of nature, for example, without recognition of "is" and good. In any taking account, then, we are *in the debt* of these powers—powers to which we are *answerable*—and the adequacy of our accounting depends on our acknowledging this debt, on our avowing our answerability. Sophistry in general is the disavowal of this debt, and the specific forms of sophistry are specific forms of disavowal—disavowals, that is, of one or another of the specific powers that are our "gifts." Here, again, I will not aim at a systematic account of all the possible forms of sophistry, but the nonsystematic outline of our "gifts/debts" allows us nonetheless to articulate roughly the range of the types of sophistry. I will identify three basic types, and a few subtypes.

There is first the dishonest disavowal of the intelligible domain entirely. A version of this disavowal is seen culturally in the anti-intellectualism that Aristophanes imputes to the Athenian public in *Clouds* and that seems responsible for the condemnation of Socrates in the *Apology*. In both the ancient world and the contemporary world, this attitude is seen in a reductive "empiricism" that dogmatically asserts the exclusive reality of the things of everyday perceptual life even while drawing on the powers of intelligibility that exceed that domain. It is some version of this attitude that Socrates has in mind in the quotation we noted in which he rejects the attitude of the natural scientists—"the wisdom they call 'inquiry into nature'"—that he had formerly embraced (*Phaedo* 96a), and this similarly seems to be the perspective, which the Eleatic Stranger names in the *Sophist*, of those who "drag everything down to earth from the heavenly region of the invisible, actually clutching rocks and trees with their hands ... insist[ing] that only what offers tangible contact is" (*Sophist* 246a). Such an attitude, rather than "sophistry," might better be construed as a "vice" of knowing in that it rightly, but one-sidedly, appreciates the irreducible ultimacy of *ta pragmata*—of "here"—as the only site where reality is happening, but it is dishonest in its failure to acknowledge its intrinsic reliance on participation in a kind of reality—the grasp of being as such—that exceeds the terms it is prepared to realize.

The second form of sophistry is the one discussed earlier in this chapter that imagines knowledge to be simply a matter of whatever appeals to one's own sense of *logos*. One form of this might again be better construed as a vice of knowing, and this is the attitude we discussed in some detail in chapter 1 when we considered the problem of "theoretical" knowledge detached from experience. More strictly sophistical is the pretense that facility in argumentation is the equivalent of knowledge. This, the attitude that truly imagines it can "make the weaker argument the stronger," is powerfully displayed by the brothers Euthydemus and Dionysodorus in the *Euthydemus*.[59]

The third, and most significant, form of sophistry, though, is the "relativism" that denies truth altogether. This is a more extreme version of the second type, which imagines truth to be whatever appeals to one's own *logos*, in that it takes the fact of *logos* to be sufficient evidence that truth is impossible. It is this normlessness that especially seems to mark Gorgias and his world (though scholars have challenged the idea that this is true of the historical Gorgias); it is also associated with Protagoras's notion that "man is the measure of all things" (though the discussion of Protagoras's position in both the *Protagoras* and the *Theaetetus* in fact suggests that Protagoras is himself more subtle and properly philosophical than this caricature allows). This denial of norms can take place at a number of levels that we have considered: it can deny the force of logic, it can deny the reality of being, it can deny the integrity of beauty, and it can deny the commandment of the good. The dishonesty in this view is that it does not acknowledge that our very openness to these domains of reality comes only in an experience of answerability; that is, we are *already* in relation to the norms of truth, beauty, and goodness.

We could, of course, explore the phenomena of sophistry—and, indeed, of knowledge—in much greater detail, but what we have established so far is sufficient to allow us to reiterate the theme that has guided our study from the start, namely, the problematic temptation to abstraction that is "endemic," so to speak, to *logos*. Each of these forms of sophistry operates in denial of the realities with which it is actually confronted; more specifically, these forms of sophistry all rely on powers—powers to recognize aspects of reality—without acknowledging their debt to these powers. Such attitudes are possible—and, indeed, are capable of being superficially persuasive—precisely because our intellectual abilities are "gifts," that is, *we did not earn them*. Like the son who inherits wealth, whom Socrates invokes in his conversation with Cephalus (I.330b–c), we "spend" our "birthright," so to speak, without grasping what is involved just in having it.[60]

What is strikingly lacking in all of these attitudes is the humility and submission that characterize the unqualified commitment to the good that philosophy calls for: a commitment that must be enacted behaviorally as well as cognitively.[61] And, as I suggested in the introduction, it is just these attitudes that typically pass for "proper" philosophy. Indeed, it is not surprising that, in the contemporary academy, such attitudes of "detached" intellectualism and skepticism would be institutionally welcome, for the comfortable separation they allow of theory from practice and teacher from student equally allows the institution to deliver an impersonal educational "product" on a large scale and to be free of risk. But what is free of risk for the institution is not, for that reason, free of risk for the student; as Socrates warns Hippocrates in the *Protagoras*, "You cannot carry teachings away in a separate container. You put down your money and take the teaching away in your soul by having learned it, and off you go, either helped or injured" (*Protagoras* 314b). There is thus an important sense in which the goals of the contemporary institutions of education precisely substitute impersonal, disengaged sophistry for the rigorous, singular engagement with the specific and personal "here" that is philosophy proper, and this should be a matter of significant concern for us.

Conclusion

Our *logos* is what makes knowledge possible for us, but it also makes falsehood and dishonesty possible. Navigating our *logos* properly is a matter of using the powers it makes available to us to become competently answerable to its demands, and this is a matter of the most rigorous and demanding existential challenge: a matter of "turning" the soul. The very nature of *logos*, though, is that it immediately offers us the possibility—and, indeed, the temptation—to be superficially self-satisfied, to live within the world it makes available to us without living up to the demands it puts on us. Philosophy is the practice of using our *logos* to own up to our answerability. Sophistry is the use of *logos* to justify ourselves in avoiding our answerability.

As beings possessing *logos*, it is fitting that we live in a world of government and, specifically, a world of democratic government. The democratic political world precisely empowers us to live *as* beings with *logos*—it empowers us to "take account"—but the health of that political world—of the distinctly human environment—depends on our taking account well: it depends, that is, on philosophy. The demands of philosophy are extreme, however, and we are strongly tempted to pacify ourselves with the sophisms that excuse us from embracing the full responsibility of "turning around." Indeed, as we will now see in chapter 4, the very nature of our existence as beings with *logos* is such that we are prone to false opinion—prone to being persuaded by "the weaker argument."

Notes

1. See Robinson, *Democracy Beyond Athens*, pp. 210–216: "The idea that the older sophists and Greek democracy were in some way connected is not entirely new, of course. Scholars have often seen links between the two. The most common approaches, however, have been either to sift through what little we know about the opinions of the sophists to see how well they accord with a democratic ideology, or to discuss the conditions in fifth-century Athens (where many of them spent time) to gauge what effect the democratic constitution there had in attracting them to the city or in nourishing their practice once they arrived.... However, in concentrating solely on trying to recover the ill-attested political positions of the sophists, or on Athens' role in providing a congenial setting for them, we pass over a potentially more fundamental democratic connection.... When we consider the cases of the older sophists, of whom any canonical list would include Protagoras, Gorgias, Prodicus, Hippias, Thrasymachus, and perhaps Antiphon, we immediately notice that all of the men came from states which certainly or probably practiced *demokratia* during the time of their early careers.... The evidence is weaker for Prodicus and Thrasymachus than for Protagoras, Gorgias, Hippias, and Antiphon, but the overall pattern is impossible to miss." Compare also McCoy, *Plato on the Rhetoric of Philosophers and Sophists*, who notes (p. 118) that there is no philosopher in Socrates's first, "true," city in *Republic* II. See Taylor and Lee, "The Sophists," for the idea that these figures were a development within the tradition of itinerant rhapsodes.

2. Guthrie, *A History of Greek Philosophy*, Vol. III, *The Fifth Century Enlightenment*, offers a rich discussion of the historical reality of this movement.

3. On the democratic nature of these cities, see Robinson, *Democracy Beyond Athens*, pp. 103–105, 140–145. For the idea that Socrates needs a democratic environment for his philosophical practice, see Brann, "The Music of the *Republic*," pp. 28–29.

4. Socrates's engagement with later-generation sophists is portrayed in *Hippias (Major)* and *Hippias (Minor)*, which both portray conversations of uncertain date between Socrates and Hippias of Elis. (Because the *Hippias [Major]* is not mentioned in ancient sources, its authenticity has sometimes been doubted, though scholars have not generally been persuaded by this doubt; it is in fact an extremely rich discussion of *to kalon*—"the beautiful"—that should be read in conjunction with the *Symposium* and the *Phaedrus*.) Unlike Protagoras and Gorgias, who are portrayed in the dialogues as quite powerful and even wise figures, and Prodicus, about whom Socrates speaks positively, Hippias is portrayed in these dialogues as vain and manifestly dull-witted. Later-generation sophistry is also a central theme in the *Euthydemus*, in which Socrates engages with the fallacious reasoning of the brothers Euthydemus and Dionysodorus from Chios and Thurii. On whether Gorgias is rightly called a "sophist," see Corey, *The Sophists in Plato's Dialogues*, chap. 2: while acknowledging that Gorgias is at times referred to in the dialogues as a sophist, Corey plausibly argues that nonetheless the dialogues operate with a precise distinction between sophists and orators, and that Gorgias (and Thrasymachus and Callicles) should be classed only among the latter; for my purposes here, this distinction is not important, and so I follow the broader cultural convention that uses the term *sophist* generically. Like me, and unlike most interpreters of Plato, Corey emphasizes that the Platonic portrayal of the sophists is generally quite sympathetic, emphasizing the close and constructive relationship between this tradition and Socrates's practice. On the relationship between sophistry and rhetoric in Plato's dialogues, see also McCoy, *Plato on the Rhetoric of Philosophers and Sophists*, pp. 12–13; as McCoy writes (p. 19): "*Rhetorician, philosopher, sophist,* and *poet* are not merely terms that describe a set practice like *doctor* or *painter*. Instead, these terms are still in development, words being fought over in a battle about what *logos* can or should do."

5. On some complexities in determining the dramatic date of the *Protagoras*, see Walsh, "The Dramatic Dates of Plato's *Protagoras*."

6. The uncertainty of the dramatic date of the conversation derives from the inclusion of details in the conversation that seem to imply different dates. On the complexity of setting of the *Gorgias* overall, see Fussi, "Why Is the *Gorgias* So Bitter?"; see p. 42 on the specific problem of the inconsistency in dramatic date.

7. In the *Protagoras*, Socrates denies that he is a sophist after he is identified as one by Callias's doorman (*Protagoras* 314d–e). In that same work, Socrates defines the *sophist* as "a kind of merchant who peddles provisions upon which the soul is nourished," and, on the basis of this definition, he is correct to deny this title for himself, since he does not teach for pay. In the *Sophist*, the meaning of sophistry is investigated in detail by a stranger from Elea (and philosophy is implicitly identified as one form of the genus "sophistry"). Corey's *The Sophists in Plato's Dialogues* is an excellent and compelling interpretation of the precise meaning of the term *sophist* and of the major sophistical figures as they appear in the dialogues. On the original (fluid) meaning of the term *sophistes*, see McCoy, *Plato on the Rhetoric of Philosophers and Sophists*, pp. 7–8.

8. Interpretations of Aristophanes are typically as simplistic as are typical interpretations of Plato, with the result that the works of Aristophanes are in need of a methodologically rigorous rereading. In relation to the *Clouds*, it is virtually universal to portray Aristophanes as if he shared the perspective of his characters, imagining

Aristophanes to be a conservative critic of philosophy, rather than a critic of Athenian popular culture (as he is in every other comedy). For a textually subtle and philosophically astute approach to interpreting Aristophanes, see Freydberg, *Philosophy and Comedy*. The *Clouds* is the subject of chap. 1 of Freydberg's book; see especially p. 19: "Those who condemn Aristophanes for an unjust and damaging caricature of Socrates therefore have a *prima facie* case: to an 'everyday' audience that cannot distinguish satire from documentary, this apparent mockery of Socrates might indeed serve to prejudice many of them against him. But much evidence to the contrary can be drawn from the Platonic dialogues, in which Aristophanes appears sympathetically, and also from parts of the historical record, which indicate that Socrates was present and acknowledged the play in a friendly manner. In my view, however, the strongest evidence for the 'innocence' of Aristophanes can be found within the *Clouds* itself, where the very same practices that come in for censure in the dialogues come in for ridicule in this comedy."

9. In many ways, the *Apology of Socrates* seems the most obvious starting point for the study of Plato, for it is precisely the "definition"—the autobiography—of Socrates, who is himself the defining figure in most Platonic writings. On the theme of why the *Apology* should be the first Platonic text that one studies, see Sallis, *Being and Logos*, pp. 25–26; Sallis points out that, in the *Apology*, Socrates's speech is directed to "the men of Athens" rather than to any single interlocutor, and thus offers the most immediately and publicly accessible presentation of his perspective. See also Kirkland, *The Ontology of Socratic Questioning*, p. xxiii, on the significance of Socrates bringing himself before "the many" in the *Apology*. On the rhetorical dimensions of Socrates's speech in the *Apology*, see McCoy, *Plato on the Rhetoric of Philosophers and Sophists*, chap. 2.

10. On Socrates's relation to the oracle, see Russon and Fagan, "Introduction: Socrates Examined," pp. xiii–xiv, and Freydberg, "'Oracles and Dreams' Commanding Socrates."

11. This situation is reflective of Athenian society, in which women were secluded. There are other examples of Socrates engaging with women: in Xenophon, *Memorabilia*, III.10, Socrates talks with Theodote; in the *Menexenus*, Socrates claims to be reporting a speech of Aspasia.

12. I have discussed the nature of this Socratic practice in "The (Childish) Nature of the Soul in Plato's *Apology*."

13. Compare Corey, *The Sophists in Plato's Dialogues*, p. 37: "It is true, as Aristotle would later write, that 'all men by nature desire to know.' Yet, for the most part, people live not in quest of knowledge but in the belief that they already possess it. When puzzles emerge, we tend to suppress them." On the existential meaning of the gadfly's sting, see Kirkland, *The Ontology of Socratic Questioning*, p. 94.

14. See Sallis, *Being and Logos*, p. 376, on the related theme of the inherent "privacy" of the soul.

15. See Baracchi, "The 'Inconceivable Happiness' of 'Men and Women,'" for the idea that philosophy, because it is an inaugural and transformative discourse, must always risk appearing as sophistry. See McCoy, *Plato on the Rhetoric of Philosophers and Sophists*, pp. 87–92, for a rich and illuminating discussion of the nature of *logos* and the significance of this for the difficulties in distinguishing philosophy from rhetoric in the context of the *Gorgias*.

16. Thus, I do not believe that there is any "Platonic Theory of the Forms": this notion relies on taking the dialogues as presentations of doctrine rather than as dramas, an approach I criticized in the introduction, and it depends on simplifying, decontextualizing,

and hypostatizing concepts taken from the many complex and insightful discussions of form, unity, and universality as they exist in experience and nature.

17. Of course, as the *Theaetetus* makes clear, knowledge is more than simply "true opinion," but that designation is sufficient for our purposes here; for a provocative interpretation of the complex arguments about knowledge in the *Theaetetus*, see Kirk, *The Pedagogy of Wisdom*. Compare III.414b.

18. On organisms interacting meaningfully with their environments, and the relevance of this for what "truth" is, see Barnes, "An Aristotelian Way with Scepticism."

19. Merleau-Ponty, *Phenomenology of Perception*, p. viii.

20. Husserl, *Ideas*, pp. 60–61. On the relevance of phenomenology to the interpretation of Plato, see Russon, "To Account for the Appearances."

21. On the idea that Socrates's engagement with his interlocutors aims to address the soul of the interlocutor rather than simply the content of the interlocutor's claims, see Metcalf, *Philosophy as Agōn*, pp. 74–79.

22. For an insightful analysis of the cave image, see Aygün, "An *Apology* in the Cave Light." Rothleder, *Fraught Decisions in Plato and Shakespeare* (prologue to part III), provocatively interprets the cave image in light of the theme of debt, which is the orienting theme in her interpretation of the *Republic*. Baracchi also has a rich interpretation of the cave image in the "Proleptikón" of *Of Myth, Life, and War in Plato's Republic*, pp. 18–35; see especially p. 19 for the insightful discussion of the sense in which Glaucon's self-reflection is rooted in an image. Brann analyzes the cave image in "The Music of the *Republic*," pp. 72–78. See also Sallis, *Being and Logos*, pp. 444–454, and Recco, *Athens Victorious*, pp. 196–207.

23. *Metaphysics* Γ(IV).1.1003a21.

24. Particularly helpful aspects of this issue are developed in the medieval notion of "transcendentals"; see especially Ibn Sīnā, *Metaphysics* I.5, on "being," "thing," and "one" as primary conceptions of the intellect, and Thomas Aquinas, *On Truth* I.1.

25. I have taken up the argument about equality in another context in "We Sense that They Strive."

26. Compare the use of the same verb [*katidein*] at *Republic* IV.434e, where Socrates talks about "catching sight" of justice in an individual man by first seeing it in a city, and the companion discussion at II.368e, where Adeimantus asks Socrates what he "notices in" [*kathorais*] this comparative approach that is relevant to justice; compare II.368c on the idea that this is an investigation for "one who sees sharply [*oxu blepontos*]." Socrates similarly uses the verb at IV.432d.

27. See *Sophist* 237c–e. Logical and sophistical discussions of "what is not" are the primary subject of the *Sophist*, and it is outside the scope of this project to address them directly. See also note 29, below.

28. Compare the parallel analysis at VI.509d, where Socrates, introducing the discussion of the divided line, draws this fundamental distinction between the sensible and the intelligible: "Conceive that, as we say, these two things *are*, and that the one is king of the intelligible class and region, while the other is king of the visible."

29. In this sense, what "is" is thus also what, in another sense, "is not," if we take beings as our model for reality.

30. See Brann, "The Music of the *Republic*," p. 53, and Sallis, *Being and Logos*, p. 393, on the intimate correlation of the distinctness of things and our articulations in language.

31. The heart of Sallis's interpretation is a rigorous and brilliant analysis of the "divided line"; see *Being and Logos*, pp. 413–443. Brann also has a compelling analysis; see "The Music

of the *Republic*," pp. 47–60. Benardete has a careful interpretation of the interrelation of the images of the sun, the divided line, and the cave in *Socrates' Second Sailing*, pp. 157–177.

32. McCoy, *Image and Argument in Plato's Republic*, pp. 44 and 214, makes a similar point.

33. This is the fundamental epistemological point made by Hume, famous for waking Kant "from his dogmatic slumbers," namely, that the relationship of necessary connection—causality—cannot itself be a one of the simple sensory data; see *A Treatise of Human Nature*, Book I, pt. III, sec. II.

34. See Sallis, *Being and Logos*, p. 419, for the idea that the shadow is a way in which the thing appears.

35. See Sallis, *Being and Logos*, p. 429, for the idea of things as images, and pp. 421–428, especially p. 428, for the idea that we typically come to rest in the visible and do not recognize the intelligible.

36. See Sallis, *Being and Logos*, p. 407, for the idea that we can grasp the visible only by grasping the intelligible. Compare Brann, "The Music of the *Republic*," pp. 49–50.

37. Compare Brann, "The Music of the *Republic*," p. 52, on *dianoia* as "thinking things through." Sallis has a very rich discussion of *dianoia* in the *Republic* in *Being and Logos*, pp. 424–443.

38. See Sallis, *Being and Logos*, pp. 416–417, n. 58, for the idea that the divisions on the line are four modes of one reality showing itself. See Recco, *Athens Victorious*, pp. 206 and 222, for the corresponding idea that "turning around" is not a matter of seeing something new but of seeing the same things differently. On the related notion of the "placelessness" of philosophy—it is "of" a place, but not defined by it—that is implied by the inseparability of the "there" from the "here" while being irreducible to it, see Baracchi, "The 'Inconceivable Happiness' of 'Men and Women.'"

39. Socrates describes the need for a "turning around" [*periagōgē*] at VII.518c–d. See Brann, "The Music of the *Republic*," pp. 78–79, for discussion of the place of this "turning" in education. Compare *Gorgias* 487a on the idea that good inquiry is about one's soul and not just one's ideas; on this point, see McCoy, *Plato on the Rhetoric of Philosophers and Sophists*, p. 103 and passim.

40. The role of mathematics in "turning around" is carefully discussed by Recco, *Athens Victorious*, pp. 207–218.

41. No doubt Darwin's account of the origin of species is a necessary corrective to Aristotle's apparent presumption of the eternity of species. But though this is pertinent to assessing the ultimate metaphysical character of natural species, it is largely irrelevant to the metaphysical issue of natural individuals as that is raised here. Even within the context of the critique of the eternity of species, it remains true that individual organisms live a life "larger" than themselves, rather as a "German" lives a reality larger than herself, inasmuch as she carries forward and is defined by a historical, cultural, and linguistic reality that exceeds the causality of her individual self; and, most importantly, that reality, enacted as a kind of immanent teleology, is not "present" in the moment. For contemporary discussions of the notion of species, see the essays in Wilson, *Species*, and compare Oyama, "The Lure of Immateriality."

42. The limitations of mathematics as a model for intelligibility are the central principle behind Roochnik's interpretation of the *Republic* in *Beautiful City*; see especially pp. 30–40.

43. See VII.523a–c and the discussion that follows on the experiences of "summoners"; for the analysis of these passages, see Sallis, *Being and Logos*, pp. 429–431; Recco, *Athens*

Victorious, pp. 211–213; and Brann, "The Music of the *Republic*," p. 82. On "dialectic" as the study beyond mathematics that "turns the soul," see Recco, *Athens Victorious*, pp. 218–233.

44. See Russon, "Why Sexuality Matters."

45. *Phaedrus* 245c–257b. On the interpretation of this speech, see especially Nicholson, "The Discourses of the Phaedrus."

46. This interpretation of *erōs* and beauty is essentially of a piece with Gordon's interpretation of *anamnēsis* in the *Phaedo* in chap. 6 of *Plato's Erotic World*.

47. On the presence and absence of *erōs* in the *Republic*, see Sallis, *Being and Logos*, pp. 376–378, 452. Broadly, Sallis's point (which builds on Brann's recognition in "The Music of the *Republic*," p. 16, that the "first city" has no birth) is that the realities of *erōs* are pointedly ignored in much of the discussion of the city, and, as he writes, discussing the "comedy" of Book V of the *Republic*, "What the comedy brings to light is that it is *eros* that disrupts the city—that because the city is not able to incorporate *eros*, hence, human birth, the body, and privacy, it is something either more or less than a human city. But, a city which excludes *eros* thereby excludes also the philosopher. We begin to see how really paradoxical the paradox of the philosopher-king is. How is a city whose entire character involves the exclusion of *eros* supposed to admit the highest kind of *eros*: philosophy?" That the presence or absence of *erōs* is what defines the different portions of the discussion in the *Republic* is the organizing theme of Roochnik, *Beautiful City*; see especially pp. 55–57, 77.

48. For a challenge to the way Socrates describes *erōs* in Book V of the *Republic*, see Benardete, *Socrates' Second Sailing*, pp. 131–132.

49. The powerful distinction between discharging and expressing is central to Dewey's account of art in *Art as Experience*; Hegel draws a closely related distinction in his account of mood in the *Encyclopaedia of the Philosophical Sciences*. For discussion of these distinctions, see Russon, "Expressing Dwelling," and "Emotional Subjects."

50. The interpretation of *erōs* as simply a pursuit of sensual pleasure is thus a belittling of sexuality—one that denies the intrinsic relevance of sexuality to our concern for the good. It is for this reason that Socrates is "ashamed before this man, and in fear of Eros himself" as he begins his "palinode" as a corrective to the earlier speech in which he articulated an instrumental interpretation of *erōs* (*Phaedrus* 243d). The idea that our *erōs* is ultimately for a *person*—that is, as much a matter of soul as of body—is thematized in Book III of the *Republic* (III.402d–403c), where, after having discussed the virtues of courage, moderation, liberality, and magnificence, Socrates asks Glaucon, "If the fine dispositions that are in the soul and those that agree and accord with them in the form should ever coincide in anyone, with both partaking of the same model, wouldn't that be the fairest sight for him who is able to see?" Socrates then asks whether one who lacks this harmony should equally solicit our love [*erōs*], and Glaucon answers, "No he wouldn't, . . . at least if there were some defect in the soul. If, however, there were some bodily defect, he'd be patient and would willingly take delight in him." In response to Socrates's further questioning, Glaucon affirms, at III.403a, that the correct way to handle this *erōs* is with moderation (whereas Socrates, in the *Phaedrus*, emphasizes on the contrary the importance of *erōs* as *mania*, "madness").

51. Compare Achtenberg, *Essential Vulnerabilities*, p. 31 (discussing Socrates' palinode in the *Phaedrus*): "Vulnerable to the boy's beauty, the soul opens to the very idea of that beauty and shares it, non-violently, with the boy."

52. Diotima describes this process further at *Symposium* 209e–210c. It is because *erōs* educates us into an experience that is not defined by the instrumental parameters of everyday

practicality that Socrates describes erotic experience as a kind of "madness" [*mania*] throughout his "Great Speech."

53. Compare Brann, "The Music of the *Republic*," p. 25, on Socrates as a person "who is here and now doing the business of the just city."

54. On the abstraction of mathematics, see Recco, *Athens Victorious*, pp. 195 and 213–218; compare his discussion on p. 65 of the fact that the power of calculation is indifferent to virtue.

55. The analysis of "The Good" is the core of Brann, "The Music of the *Republic*"; see pp. 46–72. See Sallis, *Being and Logos*, pp. 402–412, for a discussion of the use of the sun as an analogy for the good in Book VI of the *Republic*.

56. For a rich and provocative interpretation of the larger interpretive context of this remark by Socrates, see Benardete, *Socrates' Second Sailing*, pp. 1–2.

57. Compare Recco, *Athens Victorious*, pp. 222–228, on the idea that "dialectic"—the "science of the free" (*Sophist* 253c) or the stance of philosophy itself—is a form of knowing that inherently involves "taking a stand." See also McCoy, *Plato on the Rhetoric of Philosophers and Sophists*, who argues throughout chap. 5 that, more than a matter of detached knowledge, "philosophy is described [in the *Republic*] as a *love* of what is" (p. 122, my italics); as she concludes, "Love, more than knowledge, defines the soul of the philosopher in the *Republic*" (p. 137).

58. Compare *Protagoras* 333e–334c.

59. For a rich study of Socrates's engagement with these figures, see Jaklic, *But Socrates, What Is It That You Do?*

60. Compare the parable of "the prodigal son," *Luke* 15:11–32.

61. On this issue, compare McCoy, *Plato on the Rhetoric of Philosophers and Sophists*, pp. 103–106; McCoy here offers an illuminating analysis of Socrates's conversation with Callicles in the *Gorgias* regarding the goodwill [*eunoia*], frankness [*parrhēsia*], and knowledge [*epistēmē*] that are involved in good inquiry.

4

PERSUASION

WE HAVE SEEN THAT OUR NATURE AS BEINGS who take account is such that this, our native capacity, has an intrinsic trajectory of development in which our taking account is adequately accomplished only in the comprehensive embrace of answerability that is philosophy itself, an endeavor that is moral as well as cognitive. Measuring up to the intrinsic demands of taking account, though, is not something we can automatically or easily do, and adopting the philosophical stance thus essentially involves education. The child who "learns" to walk does not "invent" walking, and walking is thus a matter of *anamnēsis*—of awakening an ability and answering to an imperative that is intrinsic to the child's nature—and not strictly something "learned." Still, while "to walk" is not learned in the sense of being information gleaned without motivation through empirical investigation of evidence, it is learned in the sense that children must gradually accustom themselves to exercising this capacity, and thus learn through familiarity what this, their given ability, involves: in short, children must learn *how* to appropriate their own powers. The structure is the same with our capacity for taking account. As we have seen in chapter 3, the ability to take account weaves together a powerful variety of insights—insights into quantity, being, the good, and so on—and thus taking account, like walking, is not so much something "learned" as it is something that is "recollected." That said, however, taking account well is a developed ability that comes only through our learning *how* to deploy these rich resources that we are "given" just by virtue of being human. In order to walk, children must develop and exercise their skills at holding the neck and torso straight, their skills at moving hands, arms, knees, and hips, their skills at balance, and so on. In order to take account well, the range of skills that must be developed and exercised involves all of the most important sectors of human life.

Socrates discusses this development—this education of the philosopher—in Book VI of the *Republic*.

Initially at VI.485b–487a and then again at VI.490a–c, Socrates and Adeimantus describe the philosopher. For the one who is fine and good [*ton kalon te kagathon*], Socrates says, "Truth guide[s] him, and he ha[s] to pursue it entirely and in every way or else be a boaster who in no way partakes of true philosophy" (VI.490a). Socrates then emphasizes, as we have seen in chapter 3, that the pursuit of truth is not merely a cognitive matter but a moral one as well:

> If truth led the way, we wouldn't, I suppose, ever assert a chorus of evils could follow it . . . but a healthy and just disposition, which is also accompanied by moderation. . . . Why, then, must I also force the rest of the philosophic nature's chorus into order all over again from the beginning? You surely remember that, appropriate to these, courage, magnificence, facility at learning, and memory went along with them. (VI.490c)

Carrying out the philosophical commitment to truth requires cognitive developments, such as cultivating one's memory and facility at learning, but it also cannot be separated from the cultivation of virtues of character, such as moderation and courage. In short, as we have seen in chapter 3 in our analysis of what is involved in "taking account," philosophy is the consummate development of our nature as beings with *logos*.

In fact, our popular culture, like that of Socrates's Athens, would not commonly associate the name "philosophy" with the notion of consummate human development; instead, like the Socrates portrayed in Aristophanes's *Clouds* and Plato's *Apology*, philosophers are popularly slandered either as dangerous individuals who "make the weaker argument the stronger" or as useless individuals with their heads in the clouds. Socrates and Adeimantus discuss why the consummate development that is philosophy in fact occurs rarely and, indeed, why what is called "philosophy" is typically something either vicious or useless. It is in this discussion of the corruption of the would-be philosopher that Socrates, echoing the quotation from the *Euthydemus* that we noted in the last chapter, makes an especially important point:

> Now consider how many great sources of ruin there are for these few. . . . What is most surprising of all to hear is that each one of the elements we have praised in that nature has a part in destroying the soul that has them and tearing it away from philosophy. I mean courage, moderation, and everything we went through. . . . And what's more . . . besides these, all the things said to be goods

corrupt it and tear it away—beauty, wealth, strength of body, relatives who are powerful in the city, and everything akin to these. (VI.491b–c)

The particularly interesting point that Socrates makes here is that the very elements of an education into virtue are precisely temptations to vice.

A natural organism that is well-endowed with healthy natural capacities will typically develop well: its strength of natural endowment is an advantage that betokens a better and easier fulfillment of its natural potential than would be likely for a weaker specimen. It is thus striking that, as Socrates notes in the above quotation, a strong endowment is as much a liability for human development as it is an advantage. The development of philosophy is indeed what is most "natural" to us—it is precisely the fulfillment of our "nature"—but it does not come about by nature; on the contrary, it relies on our own activities, which themselves require to be molded by an appropriate education. Because we must thus take responsibility for our own development, our education, both at an individual level and at a social level, is always mediated by our own limited perspective: our development, in other words, is vulnerable to the weaknesses in our perspective. What is at stake in our development is our character as beings with *logos*, and it is precisely our [*ex hypothesi*] underdeveloped *logos*—our taking account—that is the aperture through which this development can occur.

The final aspect of our study, then, will be the investigation of the vulnerabilities of our *logos* as they pertain to our development. To carry out this investigation, I will turn primarily to Socrates's proposal, in Book IV of the *Republic*, of a tripartite "division of the soul," which, I will argue, quite powerfully and effectively illuminates the various dimensions of human motivation. This analysis, in turn, will allow us to grasp both what is required for healthy psychological development and what role our social and political culture plays in encouraging or inhibiting this development. In order to appreciate the force of the "division of the soul," particularly as it pertains to our healthy development as beings with *logos*, we will begin by reflecting on how we come to hold the views that we hold: we will reflect, in other words, on the phenomenon of persuasion.

I. Persuasion

Argument

Logos, the ability to take account or to "make sense," is also our possibility to *be persuaded*. In other words, in being our ability to make sense, *logos* is also our openness to being swayed by the ways of making sense that are presented to us by others. Indeed, it is this ability to be *shown* the sense of a situation that is why education is possible at all. At the same time, however, this ability to be swayed by the accounts—the *logoi*—offered by others is also our vulnerability to poor argumentation: to sophistry and rhetoric. Whether at the level of making sense of the world directly or at the level of recognizing or rejecting other *logoi*, we are vulnerable to the mistake of believing what immediately appeals to our *logos*—what "seems to us" to be convincing—rather than actually being educated by the engagement with the inherent sense of *ta pragmata* that is revealed only in the *empeiria* that comes from extensive engagement. Indeed, our education precisely is a reliance on *logoi* in place of *empeiria*—that is, it is our great advantage that we can learn about the world without having to reenact all the educative experiences through which human culture has gradually learned about the world. And so, being able to discriminate well about (putatively persuasive) *logoi*, to take account of accounts, is the crucial skill that shapes our education in general and our personal (moral) development in particular.[1]

Being able to take account of accounts well, though, is itself a highly developed ability. This point is dramatized by Glaucon's behavior at the beginning of Book II of the *Republic*. In his conversation with Thrasymachus in Book I of the *Republic* (I.336b–354c), Socrates argued that injustice is never more profitable than justice.[2] Book II begins with Glaucon asking Socrates to revisit this argument since he, Glaucon, is unconvinced by it.[3] Socrates's response to Glaucon's request makes an important point:

> [Glaucon] didn't accept Thrasymachus' giving up but said, "Socrates, do you want to seem to have persuaded us, or truly to persuade us, that it is in every way better to be just than unjust?"
>
> "I would choose to persuade you truly," I said, "if it were up to me." (II.357a–b)

As Socrates's response makes clear, persuasion is not something one does alone: whether or not one's *logos* persuades another depends on whether the listener is or is not persuaded by it. This is why an account that is sophistical can sway an ignorant listener, but it is also, as is putatively (and, I believe, in fact) the case here, why an argument that is intrinsically compelling can fail to win the assent of a listener. In other words, the fact that Glaucon is not persuaded does not entail that Socrates's account was not inherently persuasive (i.e., inherently attuned to the demands of *logos* as such), but it may simply indicate the weakness of Glaucon's ability to follow an argument.[4]

Another important aspect of *logos* is revealed in Glaucon's conversation with Socrates. In order to set up the conversation he wants to have with Socrates, Glaucon restates the aspect of Thrasymachus's position that he wants Socrates to address again. He explains his motivation to Socrates:

> For, Socrates, though that's not at all my own opinion, I am at a loss [*aporō*]; I've been talked deaf by Thrasymachus and countless others, while the argument on behalf of justice—that it is better than injustice—I've yet to hear from anyone as I want it.... That's the reason why I'll speak in vehement praise of the unjust life, and in speaking I'll point out to you how I want to hear you, in your turn, blame injustice and praise justice. (II.358c–d)

The important point to notice here is that Glaucon *does not believe* that Thrasymachus is right, but he also *cannot find anything wrong with* Thrasymachus's argument. This situation—one that is presumably quite familiar to all of us—demonstrates that one's perspective—the human *psuchē*—is not a single, monolithic fabric. On the one hand, Glaucon can "calculate," as it were, the force of Thrasymachus's argument: he can assess, in other words, the ways Thrasymachus's account "makes sense," rather as a juror might listen to the conflicting arguments in a law-court in order subsequently to assess their relative merit. On the other hand, though, there is something else within him that moves his actual belief: something in him that responds to something other than the calculated sense of argument, and because of this he has not *been persuaded*. I emphasize the passive form of the verb here to highlight the fact that persuasion is something that we undergo; that is, we *find* something to be in fact compelling to us or not, whether we like it or not. Argument as such, then, though no doubt compelling in its own right (for Glaucon cannot say no to Thrasymachus's argument, though he would like to), is not the only thing that moves the soul.

In this case of Glaucon's *aporia*—his being at a loss for how to proceed—we can imagine different possibilities for what the conflict in his soul is. It could be the case, for example, that he simply *wants* Socrates's view to be correct (for any one of a number of reasons), and this conflicts with his feeling argumentatively compelled by Thrasymachus's *logos*. Alternatively, it could be that he has an inarticulate sense that the logic of Thrasymachus's argument involves some "sleight-of-hand," but he, Glaucon, simply does not have the logical acumen to sort out where the problem lies. Yet again, he may be swayed by the very sort of claim we have been making since chapter 1, having a lived sense from his *empeiria* that justice is not being adequately captured in Thrasymachus's "theory." Whatever the actual case is with Glaucon, we can certainly recognize that all of these sorts of conflict are possible and, indeed, common in our experience.[5]

More specifically, Glaucon's internal conflict reminds us of some of the different registers in which we are engaged with things, and it shows us the ambivalent place of argument within that field. We can have a deep existential sense that something is true without being able to defend it argumentatively, with the result that the arguments of others can pull us to endorse views that do not otherwise "feel right." On the other hand, we can merely "pay lip service" to an argument, affirming it to be compelling but treating it as only so many words without inhabiting the world that it articulates, and instead taking up residence, so to speak, in our preconceived attitudes. Argument, as we have seen above, is simultaneously and ambivalently a relationship of words that operate according to their own internal rules (of logic/metaphysics) and an expression of the nature of things; consequently, we can mistake mere words for substance or substance for mere words.

Glaucon's situation thus also reminds us that we can live with an easy duplicity. It is common for us to accept words that work well together, even though they do not adequately articulate the reality of our experience. We can accept words on formal grounds without being existentially swayed. On the positive side, this can be a recognition of the independent weight of *logos*, that is, the recognition that we are pulled otherwise, and that it is important to recognize the weight of argument to establish the truth, even though it does not "feel" right. On the other, negative side, though, it can mean that we do not expect *logos* to answer to experience. Let us think about these other sides of our experience that can pull us in different directions than argument does.

Motivation

We ended chapter 3 with the recognition that, as agents, we are always grappling with the issue of what "should" be the case. Let us now explore what in fact compels our action, leading us to believe that this or that is what we should do in this or that situation. We will see that, prior to any explicit, rational reflection about the good on our part, there are two essential ways in which our recognition of what "should" be—our sense of value—has already been shaped: Socrates calls these two "desire" [*epithumia*] and "spirit" [*thumos*].

We can notice first that, very obviously, we are commonly drawn by pleasure. Indeed, we have already reflected in chapter 3 on our attraction to beauty and our orientation toward sensual pleasure. It is in terms of pleasure that we are *immediately* struck by the compelling character of something. The very meaning of what attracts our desire is that it is perceived (immediately) as "to-be-pursued"—we experience it as drawing us to it. Socrates discusses this aspect of the experience of desire with Glaucon in Book IV of the *Republic*:

> Would you set down all such things as opposites to one another, . . . acceptance to refusal, longing to take something to rejecting it, embracing to thrusting away, whether they are actions or affections? . . . For example, won't you say that the soul of a man who desires either longs for what it desires or embraces that which it wants to become its own; or again, that, insofar as the soul wills that something be supplied to it, it nods assent to itself as though someone had posed a question and reaches toward the fulfillment of what it wills? . . . Won't we class not-wanting, and not-willing and not-desiring with the soul's thrusting away from itself and driving out of itself and along with all the opposites of the previously mentioned acts? (IV.437b–c)

Desiring, as Socrates remarks, is an assenting to something.[6] It is not, however, a reflective act of pondering something and deciding explicitly in its favor; instead, desiring *is already* an assenting, a turning-toward that has already happened. Similarly, to find something not desirable is not to think reflectively about removing something but is already a thrusting-away. Desire, then, is incipient motion: it is the feeling of experiencing something *as* turning toward or away from it—or, more exactly, inasmuch as this is a matter of being struck prior to reflection and thus prior to one's sense of avowed agency, desire is an experience of *being turned* toward or away from it; indeed, we often describe ourselves as "moved" when we speak of our feelings—our *pathē*, or "undergoings," as the Greeks call them.

Furthermore, if there is no desire, there is no motion. Though desire is an experience of passivity, it is nonetheless *I* who desire, *I* who move—and, indeed, I will never act, never move, unless I have some desire, some motivation. The desires that actually motivate one's action are, as we shall see, open to shaping and development, but the immediacy of actually desiring something is nonetheless the condition without which no action ever takes place. Our action, then, always and necessarily has its beginning in the passivity of an immediate experience of compulsion.

We are beings who act—free beings who are accountable for what we do—but at its most basic and immediate level, our action is *drawn from us* by things: experientially speaking, "will" or "choice"—our freedom, our "taking account" as it is enacted in practice—at its root is not something we do, but something we undergo. Our motivation does not begin, in other words, in our self-conscious reflection; such reflection is a force we super-add to the already-immediate fabric of incipient motion. Thus, "sometimes there are some men who are thirsty but not willing to drink" (II.438c); that is, their reflective calculation [*logismos*] about what it is best to do must resist a motivation within them that has already been persuaded, so to speak, by the goodness of the water: it must resist their own *already being drawn* to it. Desire, then, is the most immediately "persuasive" aspect of our experience: it is the way we experience things as already "under our skin," so to speak. Let us look further, though, at our "lived" experiences of persuasion.

The immediacy of our experience is not simply the encounter of the things of the world that are attractive or unattractive; our experience is also the ongoing reality of our own perspective—of ourselves as engaged with *ta pragmata*. Our immediate motivations can be "outward-looking" and acquisitive, so to speak, focusing on our desires with respect to the things of our world, but they can also be "inward-looking" and assertive, focusing on our attitude with respect to our own place in the world—this is the experience of "spirit (*thumos*)."[7] We feel the immediacy of anger, for example, when we feel ourselves wronged or slighted: there is an offense against ourselves that has been committed.[8] Or, again, we feel pride *in ourselves* or we feel ashamed *of ourselves* when we have a sense that our relationship to things is either appropriate or inappropriate.[9] These—our immediate experiences of "self-consciousness"—are initially "practical," an asserting of ourselves. Like desire, these experiences are immediately felt—they are "undergoings" or *pathē*—but, because they pertain to our soul as it relates to *ta pragmata* rather than to any particular thing in the world, they are more like attitudes than specific actions, but nonetheless they are impulsions to action: to be angry is to desire "to return pain for pain," to be ashamed is "to shrink from disgrace," and so on, as Aristotle puts it.[10] The action, though, is an expression of our attitude toward ourselves, rather than immediately an expression of our reaction to the thing: it is a reaction to the thing *as that* reflects an attitude toward oneself. Thus, an otherwise desirable thing—a gift, for example—can be offensive when it is used to taunt or to humiliate. There can, therefore, be a conflict of these two distinct sorts of motivation. This point is illustrated in Socrates's story of Leontius, son of Aglaion.

While discussing the character of the soul with Glaucon in Book IV of the *Republic*, Socrates reports the experience of Leontius when he encountered the corpses of men who had been publicly executed:

> He desired to look, but at the same time he was disgusted [*duscherainoi*] and made himself turn away; and for a while he struggled and covered his face. But finally, overpowered by the desire, he opened his eyes wide, ran toward the corpses and said: "Look, you damned wretches, take your fill of the fair sight." . . . This speech . . . indicates that anger sometimes makes war against the desires as one thing against something else. . . . And in many other places, don't we . . . notice that, when desires force [*biazōntai*] someone contrary to calculation [*logismon*], he reproaches [*loidorounta*] himself and his spirit is roused [*thumoumenon*] against that in him which is doing the forcing [*tōi biazomenōi*]. (IV.439e–440b)

In this situation, Leontius has a considered view [*logismos* or "calculation"] that there are things that one should not look at—in this case, dead bodies.[11] In addition to this *reflective* view, however, he has two *immediate* experiences. On the one hand, he encounters the immediacy of desire that we discussed above: the attraction of the spectacle is something he experiences as *drawing* him—it is experienced, as Socrates says in the quotation, as a "force." On the other hand, he has a similarly immediate sense of disgust.[12] But, unlike desire, with its orientation to the attractiveness of pleasurable *things*, disgust is an immediate sense about *how one should relate to* things. Disgust engages, in other words, with one's *values*, with what one *honors*. Consequently, when Leontius, through his behavior, pays homage to the dishonorable thing, his "spirit is roused" [*thumoumenon*] *against himself* for it is not the things as such but his way of dealing with them that is immediately repellent to him.[13] He is angry with himself for being more powerfully motivated by his immediate desire to take pleasure in looking at the dead bodies than by his sense of propriety.

The conflict with himself that is experienced by Leontius is of a type that should be familiar to all of us. It is perhaps most famously articulated by Paul in his Epistle to the Romans:

> We know that the law is spiritual; but I am unspiritual, sold as a slave to sin. I do not understand what I do. For what I want to do I do not do, but what I hate I do. And if I do what I do not want to do, I agree that the law is good. As it is, it is no longer I myself who do it, but it is sin living in me. (Rom. 7:14–17)

Paul's description reminds us of what we saw above, namely, that desire compels immediately—we experience it as a force—but it is nonetheless we ourselves who desire. Consequently, we can experience our desire as a kind of alien within ourselves who moves us despite the values we avow. In this way, we find that we are not immediately in control of our own selves, and this, perhaps, explains the reason for the affective intensity of our self-reproach, namely, we have a sense that we *should* be in control of ourselves, we should be *free*, when in fact we are "slaves" to (ourselves as) desire and thus not living up to our own nature, not adequately holding ourselves accountable to what, on our accounting, we take to be the good.

This experience of Leontius (and Paul) thus helps us to differentiate the range of ways in which we are "persuaded." Of course, persuasion takes place at the level of argument. This discussion of "desire" [*epithumia*] and "spirit" [*thumos*] demonstrates, however, that persuasion also takes place both before and, so to speak, below reflection.[14] Our reflective views—such as that "one should not look at certain spectacles" or perhaps that "one should not quench one's thirst with whiskey"—are *intelligent* views, that is, they are a matter of "taking account" of things at the level of *principle*, and that means they take the form of universal claims and hence of impersonal claims. Such impersonal, universal reflection, however, is always undertaken by someone who is *already* a desiring, spirited "animal with *logos*" engaged with *ta pragmata*. It is our desires and the forms of our "spirit" that *are* our determinate modes of involvement with things, and our taking account will thus always be superimposed on a rich world that is already determinate, not just in terms of the "objective" features of things but in terms of our "subjective" forms of involvement: the world of our immediate experience, in other words, is already shot through with "value," with a kind of interpretation or "taking account" of things that has not yet gone through the formative "filter" of explicit reflection. In this sense, then, even before we engage our reflection, we are already being persuaded.[15]

When we take it upon ourselves to answer to a situation—to choose how to act—our reflective "account-taking" (our *logismos* or *dianoia*) is always grappling with and against these other "given" forms of "taking account." "I" am not any single one of these: I am all of them. Talking about the body in Book V, Socrates notes that "when one of us wounds a finger, . . . we say that *this* human being *has* a pain *in* his finger (V.462c–d, italics added), and, analogously (but contra Socrates's misleading claim in his exchange with Glaucon), it is "the same himself" (IV.431a) who simultaneously feels desire, lives from an affective sense of himself, and is weighed upon by argument.[16] This is why, as we saw above, Glaucon's "calculation" can leave him cold and "unpersuaded": the argument, though it appeals to his ability to calculate, has not spoken to the existential grip that the issues actually have on him, a grip that is not simply a matter of reasoning. Insofar as we are beings with *logos*, we are beings who have a relationship with ourselves—we are always "toward" ourselves and never just "one with" ourselves either in the sense of being an immediate being that just "is" or in the sense of being a comprehensive coalescence with ourselves; rather, we diverge from ourselves and unite with ourselves.

As we noted in the discussion of democracy, we are free—this is what it fundamentally means to be a being who can take account, rather than to be simply a being that has its form of undergoing a situation given by nature. But being thus free does not mean we are immediately or totally in control of ourselves; it means, rather, that we have the capacity for shaping how we respond to situations, a capacity that itself we can do more or less to develop. Our development of such a self-possessed account-taking comes by way of our explicitly reflective affirmation of principles—our coming to be persuaded of certain ultimate truths "on principle"—and having this persuasion reflected in the full range of our engagement with *ta pragmata*, in our *living*. But this reflective persuasion is always contextualized by the two forms of prereflective "persuasion": our "already being persuaded" about the inherent value—the attractiveness—of things and our already being persuaded about the inherent value—the boundaries—of oneself.

Education

Both our sense of "it is" and our sense of "I am" are prereflectively established with this infusion of turning toward or turning away, in the case of "it is," and of defense against transgression in the case of "I am." Further, as we noted in chapter 3, one may be better or worse at the skill of "calculation" [*logismos, dianoia*]. Our intelligence allows us to reflect critically on ourselves and to recognize that our desires and our attitudes need reforming, but our intelligent grasp of principles itself requires cultivation and development. Thus all three of these domains of our persuasion—pleasure, "ego," and thinking—require education, and the education of these dimensions of our experience is the domain of virtue [*aretē*].

And though our cognition is no doubt improved by intellectual study, our education is not simply a cognitive one, for it is not simply at a cognitive level that we are persuaded.[17] It is this rich domain of the intersection between cognition and the persuasion of the noncognitive dimensions of our experience—the *pathē*—that we shall explore now, as we reflect further on these virtues that are the goal of education. And we will eventually go on to see that these different domains of psychological persuasion, in addition to being what needs education, also present obstacles to the very project of education, personal obstacles that are intimately connected with fundamental structures of cultural and political life.

II. Virtue

One of the distinctive realities of being a being with *logos* is that, unlike other natural beings, we humans do not have our development preordained: neither its path nor its unfolding. Provided that a tree is supplied with its appropriate, natural conditions, it will, on its own, carry out the process by which it achieves its own mature, arboreal state. Similarly, a dog, provided that its appropriate, natural conditions are met, will, on its own, grow to canine maturity. In the case of human beings, however, the situation is different. Though human beings in their strictly organic development will similarly reach biological maturity naturally, provided they have an appropriately supportive environment, with respect to their taking account—their definitively human characteristic—they themselves must ascertain the proper goal of their own development and then determine the means for achieving it. Our healthy development requires education, and we alone have the responsibility for bringing that education into being. Consequently, the successful enactment of our education is not guaranteed.

Life-forms are characteristically marked by a kind of multiplicity: the oak tree and the greyhound both gather together in unity a multiplicity of functions and a multiplicity of parts. This unity-as-integration is evident in the organic parts themselves. The ear, for example, is simultaneously the ability to hear and the precise, organized configuration of pinna, ear canal, ear drum, cochlea, and so on: hearing is, quite literally, the power *of that bodily system* (itself integrated with the rest of the body, of course), and, similarly, that bodily system exists as a unity only in hearing and as hearing. Likewise, the unity that defines the identity of each life-form exists only as such an integration-in-action. What is distinctive of the human being, again, is that the accomplishment of such an integration in our case requires our own involvement: we must actually use our *logos*—our taking account—to fulfill our *logos*. Consequently, a distinctive and definitive human problem—an ontological problem, so to speak—is that our intrinsic multiplicity can exist in a state of disintegration, such that the human individual can be "one" in a formal sense without being "one" in substance. Again, we recognize analogous maladies in other animals in organic conditions of disease, such that the body, in some sense, fights itself and does not achieve its natural state of unified functioning. With the human being, though, this disintegration is *at the level of our sense-making, as that is manifest in our behavior*: this distinctively human disintegration is a malady of soul, not as the principle of unity of the organic body but as that reality of the "inner life" in its autonomy that we encountered initially in our discussion of the *Phaedo*.

Our ability to take account is the same as our ability to be persuaded and, as we have seen above, our being persuaded happens at a number of different levels: the nonreflective levels of *epithumia* and *thumos* as well as the reflective level of *logismos*. Consequently, the education of our *logos* and the integration of our constitutive functions necessarily are a matter of the education and integration of *epithumia*, *thumos*, and *logismos*. We can thus contrast the character of the functioning of each of these dimensions of our experience as that character exists outside a state of effective integration with the rest and the character of its integrated functioning: we can, for example, as we already anticipated in chapter 3, distinguish between how our desire functions in our experience when it is or is not "persuaded by" our *logos*, as Aristotle puts it.[18] The situations of conflict we considered above—the cases of Glaucon, Leontius, and Paul—all attest to the way in which the "taking account" by these individuals is not consistent across the different registers of its operation. The excellent form of our behavior qua humans will be, on the contrary, precisely the cultivation of these different dimensions of our experience to the state in which they do function, each independently, in support of the others. For each of the different dimensions of our behavior—of our persuasion—we can recognize an excellence—the *aretē* or "virtue"—that is its development to a state of integration with our defining capacity for *logos*. Socrates discusses these virtues especially in Books III and IV of the *Republic*.[19]

Wisdom, Courage, and Moderation

Our fulfillment depends on the integrated development of our different capacities, but, as we have seen from the beginning, the fact that we are beings with *logos* means that we are beings who can abstract, that is, who can engage meaningfully with realities independently, in isolation from the substantial conditions of their realization. The coherent development of our *logos*-functioning depends on our using our *logos* to organize and orchestrate the cooperative development of the various dimensions of our capacity for being persuaded. But these various capacities for being persuaded—pleasure, "ego," and argument, roughly—though they "belong" together in our integrated pursuit of the good, can each be a capacity that we cultivate in its own right, without regard for its relation to the others and to the good. We can notice this initially about our distinctive ability to argue—*logismos*—which is, essentially, our ability to "take account" in the abstract.

That our account-taking capacities can be developed "abstractly" has been our theme throughout this study. Though, as we saw in detail in our study of knowledge in chapter 3, the proper fulfillment of our ability to think is found in the rigorous submission to the pursuit of the good, we have also seen that our basic ability to "calculate" reflectively or to "argue"—*logismos*—can be developed as a detached skill that disavows any ties to substance. This skill is undeniably important—without the ability to handle argument well on its own terms, neither the possession of appropriate *empeiria* nor the intention to be good will be sufficient to grant one access to the truth—but this skill on its own remains normless and empty; indeed, this detached "rationality" is precisely the vehicle for sophistry. But, though it is insufficient as an end in itself, it thus remains the case that the autonomous cultivation of our ability to use well our ability to "think things through" is an essential dimension of the cultivation of our *logos*, of our ability to be persuaded. Though the virtue of "wisdom" [*sophia* or *phronēsis*] is richly defined in the *Republic* as being "of good counsel" (IV.428b), the analysis of wisdom actually focuses on the abstract excellence of the "calculative part [*logismos*]."[20] Indeed, this abstract cultivation of our thinking is what typically passes in contemporary contexts for "philosophy," which, as I argued in the introduction and as we saw at the end of chapter 3, is often indistinguishable from sophistry. Our fulfillment as beings with *logos* does indeed require the independent cultivation, the "virtue," of our ability to think, but if this capacity is cultivated *as* independent—that is, if it is imagined to be self-sufficient in independence of other practical aspects of our experience and in independence of submission to the good—it actually becomes a "vice," a force of disintegration. In this sense, then, there is what I will call a "relative" virtue of wisdom, which is the perfection of the capacity for abstract reasoning, which has nonetheless to be distinguished from an "absolute" virtue of wisdom, which requires the concrete embrace of the good and which was essentially our topic in chapter 3.

We similarly need to *develop* our unreflective sense of "ego"—that which motivates outrage in those situations in which we feel our own reality is not given due weight and which motivates feelings of pride or shame when our own actions do or do not seem to conform adequately to our avowed values.[21] Our *thumos* registers the threshold where we feel challenged, not so much in the externally measurable sense of threats to our life, but in the internal, lived sense of where we experience our boundaries.[22] These boundaries, too, are not so much matters of space (though they can, of course, involve that, when, for example, we feel our personal space violated), but matters of our values, and whether our sense of honor—what we honor—is being given adequate play in our treatment by others (or by ourselves). Our *thumos* responds to our sense of being threatened, and so we need to develop an appropriate sense of what is and what is not actually threatening. Describing this "virtue," this excellence of *thumos*, Socrates says, "This kind of power and preservation, through everything, of the right and lawful opinion about what is terrible and what not, I call courage [*andreia*]" (IV.430b).[23] The virtue of courage is thus a matter of *educating* our *thumos*: bringing our immediate and unreflective sense of when we are threatened into line with what our reflective assessment—our *logismos*—would recognize. In other words, it is a matter of "taking account" of our situation well.

The virtue of courage is basically the introduction of "objectivity" into our emotional life. The everyday observation of people reveals how easy it for us to fly into a rage over our sense of being violated: people constantly swear at each other in rush-hour traffic, take offense at perceived slights by their intimate companions, and complain about how they are treated on public transit or in stores, but the eagerness of people to show outrage under virtually any circumstances attests to the fact that this automatic sense of moral righteousness does not reflect a careful assessment of situations—does not give situations "their due." In these familiar instances of self-righteousness, rather, individuals rely simply on their "own sense" of violation to determine whether or not "returning pain for pain" is justified; the standard, in other words, is simply subjective. In an attitude of courage, on the contrary, one takes a stand because one has, to the best of one's ability, assessed the situation and determined what is right, and one subsequently stands by that reflective assessment *even if one is subjectively uncomfortable.* Figures like Thrasymachus and Callicles are ready to fly into a rage simply because they cannot "have their way"; they are, as we say, remarkably "thin-skinned." There is, on the contrary, some courage displayed by figures such as Theaetetus and even the young Charmides, for example, who accept to subject themselves to possible humiliation under Socrates's scrutiny because they believe that it is the right thing to do.[24] These individuals choose to accept threatening situations because they assess those threats to be unworthy of flight and because they believe the threats should thus be endured in order to pursue what those individuals have assessed to be a greater good. In this case, their *thumos* has been cultivated such that they would be ashamed to act on their "subjective" distress and not stand up for the good.

Of course, as we have noted, our reflective assessment can itself be faulty, so, while "persuading" *thumos* by our *logismos* is the proper *form* for the healthy development of our soul, the simple fact that our sense of ego conforms to the terms of our reflective assessment of things does not automatically entail that our emotional assessment of things is appropriate. For example, we typically think of the battlefield as the paradigmatic domain of courage.[25] Here, soldiers display courage by their willingness to die—to face the *absolute* threat—"for their country." We are familiar with many situations, though, in which individuals challenge the propriety of their countries' actions, and in these cases their courage is shown precisely in their refusal to die on the battlefield. Indeed, Socrates's own biography gives us a good example of this: though Alcibiades in the *Symposium*, for example, notes Socrates's striking bravery in battle, what is more striking is Socrates's willingness to refuse to carry out the orders of "the Thirty," whose rule he deemed illegitimate, and perhaps more striking still is his willingness to die for his "faith," as documented in the *Apology* and *Crito*. Thus, even though one may have educated one's soul to the point that one unhesitatingly stands up for what one believes to be good, such courage is in fact a hindrance to the good if one's beliefs are faulty. Indeed, this may be the case with the moral outrage that Anytus feels toward Socrates.[26] There is a sense, then, in which courage is itself truly realized only if it is coordinated with real wisdom, with a true grasp of the nature of things. As with wisdom, then, with courage we can recognize both a relative virtue and an absolute virtue: the relative virtue of courage is having persuaded one's *thumos* to answer to one's ("objective") belief about what is good rather than simply taking a stand against any challenges to one's ego, while the absolute virtue of courage requires that one actually hold oneself answerable to the good as such, whatever it might prove itself to be.

Our unreflective experience of desire, too, requires development. Like our immediate sense of ego, our immediate sense of desire feels to us as if it were simply imposed on us: not something we are doing, but something we undergo. Our desires, though, like our sense of ego, are already a form of "taking account": though in the moment they seem to us simply to be "objective," our experience over time makes it clear that our desires are expressive of a perspective. To a young child, for example, eating onions, drinking wine, listening to jazz music, or sitting still through a performance can seem to be obviously unpleasant and undesirable, whereas that same child, once grown up, may relish all of these things while finding it obviously undesirable to play with dolls, eat peanut butter and jelly, or sing "The Farmer in the Dell."[27] This experience that characteristically accompanies aging also characteristically accompanies education, and this is true both of more practical disciplines and of more theoretical ones. Bodily exercise, for example, typically seems like an undesirable burden to the person who is "out of shape" and who would, indeed, most benefit from the exercise, whereas it is quite common for the "fit" person who exercises regularly to look forward to the exercise; for the former individual, it is typically a matter of considerable "conflict within the soul" to actually engage in exercise, whereas the latter individual typically finds it easy and "natural" to do so. Again, for the child first encountering addition and subtraction, or for the adult who feels alienated from mathematics, working through the basic operations of arithmetic can be difficult and unpleasant, whereas for someone who has effectively learned these skills, employing them can be a deliberately pursued pastime in, for example, the solution of mathematical puzzles (such as Sudoku). In general, the experience of learning involves the change in one's experience of some domain such that an engagement that was once difficult and unpleasant becomes easy and pleasant. Our desires, thus, rather than simply reflecting an "objective" truth about objects that we undergo, reflect how we have already been "persuaded" that something is desirable or not, and thus reflect a perspective—a perspective that could be oriented otherwise.

That our desires characteristically change as our perspective changes shows that our desires are not simply facts imposed on us from just one side; at the same time, however, it also shows that our desires are not one-sidedly subjective or arbitrary. That we characteristically come to take pleasure in what we learn shows that desire *makes sense*. It also shows that in fundamental ways our desires are themselves reflective of *the sense of* our situation—of the relationship, that is, between who we are and what we are encountering. Consequently, our desires, just as they are neither objective nor arbitrary, are also not "innocent": beyond simple matters of "personal preference," they are a fundamental barometer of how we have established our relation to the world.

As in the case of Leontius, therefore, we can easily find ourselves in situations in which, at the level of our unreflective desires, we find ourselves behaving—responding immediately to the world (which is already incipient action)—in a way that reflects values that are different from those either that equally immediately define our sense of ourselves—"ego"—or that we reflectively embrace. In other words, we can find ourselves in conflict with ourselves; indeed, to some degree such a situation is surely the norm for everyday life, in that most of us, most of the time, will not have our desires, our sense of ego, and our reflective calculation perfectly aligned with each other. This, indeed, is where the discussion in the *Laws* really begins:

> ATHENIAN STRANGER: For the person in relation to himself, should the relationship be understood to be one of enemy to enemy? . . .
>
> KLEINIAS: . . . Why, right here, stranger, is the first and best of all victories, the victory of oneself over oneself; and being defeated by oneself is the most shameful and at the same time the worst of all defeats. These things indicate that there is a war going on in us, ourselves against ourselves. (*Laws* I.626d–e)

This self-conflict can operate at a relatively minor level: for example, when one feels excessively drawn to eating desserts, despite one's reflective interest in being a healthier eater, or when one feels excessively drawn to eating hot dogs, despite the lived demand of one's sense of ego that one be elegant and refined. Such conflict is a matter of more major significance, though, when one's sexual appetite runs in conflict with one's reflective commitment to marital fidelity or when one's desire for intoxicating drink repeatedly leads one to behave in ways that one subsequently finds embarrassing. This characteristic human condition entails two intrinsic goals that define our human condition: more immediately, it is important that we learn to control the conflicting forces within us; ultimately, it would be best if the conflict itself were overcome, if, that is, we were to change ourselves such that the various dimensions of our motivation are reconciled with each other.[28] These norms—self-control and self-coherence—are not externally devised objectives projected on desire: they are norms intrinsic to our condition, objectives implied in our own experiences of self-conflict.

Though our desires are a way of "taking account," and in that sense reflect something that the soul is "doing," we experience them as something we undergo and therefore not as matters over which we have immediate control. Consequently, when we endeavor to bring our behavior into line with our reflectively avowed values, our desires commonly confront us, to a greater or lesser degree, as an alien force. Most commonly, our ability to function as self-possessed, self-responsible individuals will take the form of "mastering" these "alien" desires: we generally evaluate ourselves and others by this issue of whether we can stay committed to our avowed values despite the temptations we experience to do otherwise. We have seen all along that our condition as beings with *logos* is such that we must take our own formation and development in our own hands, and this taking control of ourselves in the typically occurring condition of "self-conflict" with respect to our desires is what is typically required of us: this—"a certain kind of order and mastery of certain kinds of pleasures and desires" (IV.430e)—is the fundamental sense of "moderation" or "temperance" [*sōphrosunē*] by which we define the condition of the healthy, well-developed individual.[29] Precisely because moderation in this sense is a matter of self-*control*, it is clear that this is a situation in which one is precisely *not* in control of oneself: one desires differently than one would like, and thus, at the level of desire, one is run by—controlled by—something other than one's (reflective) self. Moderation as "self-mastery" is thus secondary to what we would recognize as the healthier state in which one actually desires "properly." Moderation in the sense of controlling one's desires is, as we noted above, what is typically required first if one is in process of education: when one begins to change, one normally has to struggle with one's older habits. As we noted above, though, a change in our desires themselves is fundamental to education, and so moderation in the sense of desiring well is thus the superior state that should emerge from a successful project of self-control.[30]

As with wisdom and courage, though, so with moderation: the reeducation of our desires will be as good or as bad as is the fundamental sense of good that defines the reeducation. One can indeed get beyond mastery to a new form of desire that coheres with one's avowed values, but those values can still be misguided. One can, for example, believe theoretically in the values of a money-economy and come to embrace the value of competition at every level so that, beyond one's calculative sense and beyond one's sense of ego, one actually *wants* and *finds pleasurable* participation in agonistic social environments; equally, one can believe theoretically in the value of the family and come to embrace the value of honor at every level so that, beyond one's calculative sense and beyond one's sense of ego, one actually *wants* and *finds pleasurable* participation in rigorously hierarchical social environments. In either case, moderation in the primary sense is *formally* realized, in the sense that one's soul is a coherent unity, reflective at every level of one's commitment to the good; nonetheless, it does not follow that either of these states of desire is true moderation, for, as we have already seen, each of these is a compromised commitment to the good—it is a commitment to *a* good, rather than a commitment to the good as such. As with wisdom and courage, then, so with moderation: we must distinguish the relative virtue from the absolute virtue.

With each of the domains of persuasion then—*logismos, thumos,* and *epithumia*—we can see that there is a real skill—an excellence, a "virtue"—to be developed with respect to that aspect of our soul taken in the abstract, and there is deeper development of virtue, which is the orientation of soul as a whole toward the good as such; this is a "virtue" the accomplishment of which depends on these other skills as its conditions without itself being reducible to them. The moral importance of this distinction between the "absolute" form of the virtue and its "relative" form—why the relative virtue can actually be a vice—is particularly well illustrated in the *Charmides*.

Sōphrosunē *in the* Charmides

When we think of what the problem is that moderation is meant to address, we generally think of two possible situations. In the extreme—which mostly means in our dramatic imaginings—we think of pathological situations of wanton hedonism, which, again, we typically associate with figures of crime, whether in the form of violent outlaws or in the form of powerful tyrants (and for which our criticism is not always easily differentiated from envy). In normal situations—which means in our everyday practicality—we typically think of "sloppy" behavior, and this, again, typically in two forms: (1) we think of moderation as a desirable corrective for individuals who seem "to let their desires get the better of them," individuals we notice because their behavior typically violates our sense of propriety and causes socially awkward situations; and (2) we think of moderation as a developmental norm for our children, who must precisely learn how to handle their desiring behaviors "properly" and develop "good manners." The discussion of moderation in the *Charmides* addresses just these concerns.

The *Charmides* is set around 429 BC, when Socrates has just returned to Athens after a long absence spent serving in a military activity that would subsequently prove to be the beginning of the Peloponnesian War (and roughly at the time of Plato's birth).[31] In the dialogue, he converses primarily with Charmides and Critias, who were to become notorious twenty-five years later, at the end of the Peloponnesian War, for their behavior during the regime of the Thirty Tyrants, (and who happen to be Plato's cousin and uncle, respectively). *Sōphrosunē*—moderation—is the central topic of the conversation, in which Charmides first proposes three different definitions of *sōphrosunē* to Socrates and Critias subsequently proposes a number of further definitions. The interpretations that Charmides and Critias offer demonstrate well the problems of the "virtue" of moderation when it is not rooted in a commitment to the good as such.

The initial definitions proposed by Charmides thematize our everyday concern with moderation. Charmides, himself described (competitively) by Critias as the most moderate young man around, demonstrates that moderation by showing deference to Socrates, initially in the form of a reluctance to present himself as having anything important to say and, in general, a reluctance to speak (specifically on the ground that he wants neither to make Critias look bad nor to appear boastful himself).[32] Correspondingly, when he is finally coaxed into talking, he first proposes that *sōphrosunē* means "quietness" [*hēsuchia*].

> At first, he shied away and was rather unwilling to answer. Finally, however, he said that in his opinion *sōphrosunē* was doing everything in an orderly and quiet way—things like walking in the street, and talking, and doing everything else in a similar fashion. "So I think," he said, "taking it all together, that what you ask about is quietness." (*Charmides* 159a–b)

The value Charmides presents, both in word and in deed, is one that, as we noted above, we typically rely on in thinking about the upbringing of children: one of the major values we impress on children is that they must learn to hold themselves still—a very important skill, especially given their original nature, which is vividly described in the *Laws*:

> Each young thing is incapable of remaining calm in body or in voice, but always seeks to move and cry: young things leap and jump as if they were dancing with pleasure and playing together, and emit all sorts of cries. (*Laws* II.653d–3; see also 664e–665a, 672a–d, and 673c–d)[33]

As adults, we are (generally speaking) able patiently to sit still, quietly, for long periods of time without getting upset; we are able to keep quiet while others speak and, indeed, to "hold our tongues" when what we have to say would be inappropriate in a situation. In these and similar ways, we adults have learned to be governed by our reflective, "calculated" sense of what a situation calls for, and not to be distracted by whatever immediate desires we might have that would work against this "quietness," and our ability— our everyday sense of *sōphrosunē*—is rooted in our having been brought up to "be quiet." The second definition Charmides proposes, following Socrates's questioning of his initial answer, goes further in this same direction: "Well, *sōphrosunē* seems to me to make people ashamed and bashful, and so I think modesty [*aidōs*] must be what *sōphrosunē* really is" (*Charmides* 160e). The "quietness" of *sōphrosunē* is not just any quietness, but the quietness of "knowing one's place" in the shared social world, and holding one's behavior bound by a sense of propriety—the very sort of propriety that Charmides initially feared he would offend by answering Socrates's question—and this is what we call "modesty."[34] Charmides's first two definitions, therefore, reflect very well our everyday sense of this "virtue."

The older Critias, in fact, shows himself to have trouble "keeping quiet." Socrates shifts to talking with him precisely because Critias makes it clear, initially through his body language and subsequently through his verbal intervention in the conversation between Socrates and Charmides, that he is dissatisfied with the way Socrates's conversation with Charmides is going.[35] This happens after Charmides shies away from taking up Socrates's probing of his own [Charmides's] view and instead proposes to discuss a view "he has heard" about what *sōphronsunē* is (*Charmides* 161b); Critias is dissatisfied with Charmides's defense of this view:

> It was clear that Critias had been agitated for some time and also that he was eager to impress Charmides and the rest who were there. He had held himself in with difficulty earlier, but now he could do so no longer.... Critias couldn't put up with this [conversation] ... so he gave [Charmides] a look and said, "Do you suppose, Charmides, that just because you don't understand what in the world the man meant, ... the man himself doesn't understand either?" (*Charmides* 162b–d)

In the ensuing conversation (which makes up the bulk of the *Charmides*), Critias offers a number of definitions of *sōphrosunē*, all of which revolve around the notion of "knowing oneself"; more specifically, Critias interprets *sōphrosunē* as knowing one's limits, in the sense of knowing the point at which one is no longer in control. In general, Critias is oriented toward something like the value of "focus," or the idea that one should know what one is after and should know how to get it. *Sōphrosunē* in this sense is something like not allowing oneself to be distracted—"keeping one's eyes on the prize," as we sometimes say. Like Charmides, Critias in fact presents one of our very familiar understandings of *sōphrosunē*.

Just as we instill in our children the value and practice of quiet, so do we typically imagine that something like single-minded drive is a mark of success. In both cases—"moderation" in its childhood form and in its adult form—we, quite reasonably, treat successful development as a matter of learning not to be dominated by distracting desires, in order to stay focused on the demands of one's situation. Here, in both its childhood form and its adult form, moderation is understood in it "proper" form; that is, it is understood to mean that one is developing oneself to a point where one's desires are not something with which one must "struggle," and indeed, it seems true that, in practice, this virtue is demonstrated by both Charmides and Critias: for each of them, desire is precisely "not an issue," as each seems to have become a person who easily does "what he should" (even though Critias reveals some of his limits in losing his temper in conversation with Socrates). Charmides, that is, seems to demonstrate well that he has embraced the value of "quietness" and does not struggle with desires to act otherwise; Critias, in turn, seems to be a powerful, effective adult, able to take on responsibility and accomplish what he intends (as is indicated by his apparent role of mentoring Charmides, and by his subsequent historical behavior). The insufficiency of this conception of *sōphrosunē* is made clear in the *Phaedo*, however, in a way that is confirmed by the historical realities of Charmides and Critias.

In his discussion of the virtues in the *Phaedo*, Socrates distinguishes, as we have done above, between a more "formal" understanding of virtue and a more substantial understanding. We can distinguish, in other words, the cultivating of the relevant "skill"—something quite important in its own right—and the cultivating of the correct orientation and development of the soul overall. With respect to *sōphrosunē*, for example, it is possible to have a "well-tempered" relationship to the enacting of one's desires in general while still having bad desires. As Socrates says,

> Aren't [ordinary people] moderated by a sort of self-indulgence? . . . For since they're terrified of being robbed of some pleasures and yet desire them, they keep away from some through being mastered by others. And yet they call being ruled by pleasures self-indulgence. Nevertheless, as it turns out, they

master some pleasures only because they're mastered by other pleasures. (*Phaedo* 68e–69a)

The subsequent behavior of Charmides and Critias—their role in the regime of the Thirty Tyrants in particular—reveals that both have not reformed their souls such that they desire the good; they have, on the contrary, made a calculation, and reformed their souls such that they do not lose their access to their great (tyrannical) desires by pursuing lesser desires. They have, as Socrates says, "exchang[ed] pleasures for pleasures and pains for pains . . . as if they were coins" (*Phaedo* 69a). In other words, both have indeed succeeded in "persuading" their desires by their *logismos*—their calculation—but their calculation itself was fundamentally guided by the more basic persuasion of each of their souls by desire—the desire for wealth and power—rather than by the good as such.

In the *Phaedo*, as we saw in chapter 3, Socrates distinguishes between the cause and its conditions: "It's one thing to be genuinely the cause, and another to be that without which the cause wouldn't be a cause" (*Phaedo* 99b). What ultimately makes us good, healthy people—the cause—is our commitment to the good as such. The desire to be good, though, is not by itself sufficient to make us good; instead, we must first perfect many of our abilities so that we are able to be good: able to recognize what it takes and able to carry it out. Being truly good is inseparably (though not indistinguishably) being moderate, courageous, and wise—in this situation, we have "absolute" moderation, "absolute" courage, and so on, for this realization of these virtues is the defining instance of each.[36] Cultivating the independent "skill" of "relative" moderation is thus the condition of virtue in that it is only in the context made available by this relative virtue that a true commitment to the good as such is a possibility and thus only in this context that that cause can be a cause. As we see with the case of Critias, though, the relative virtues, though they are the perfection of isolated components of our ability as *logos*-beings, in fact work in the service of the bad when they are not oriented by a commitment to the good as such.[37] This point returns us to the discussion of the education of the philosopher, with which this chapter began.

III. Corruption

Flattery

As we saw, after having identified the true philosopher as having the comprehensive moral and cognitive development we have discussed (VI.490a),

Socrates points precisely to the fact that all the conditions that enable this good development—strong, native cognitive ability, supporting natural and social circumstances—are themselves all potential threats to this development. In general, all these "goods" offer us powers and pleasures of success that, like the sensual pleasure we considered in our discussion of *ēros*, tempt us to rest with them on their own rather than subordinating them to the deeper pursuit of the good. They are only relative goods, and we err precisely when we take them to be absolute goods, when we treat any of them as the good as such. In his discussion of the education of the philosopher, Socrates identifies a particular way in which we are vulnerable to making exactly this mistake.[38]

We noted above that it seems to be true by definition that the one who is logically best positioned to develop human excellence to the full would be one who has strong natural capacities and rich cultural resources.[39] This notable strength of such a one who is especially well-endowed to fulfill his *logos*-nature—to become truly virtuous—has the consequence, though, that this individual is quite (instrumentally) attractive to others. Socrates continues:

> Then I suppose kinsmen and fellow citizens will surely want to make use of him, when he is older, for their own affairs. . . . They will, therefore, lie at his feet begging and honoring him, taking possession of and flattering beforehand the power that is going to be his. (VI.494b–c)

As we have seen since the beginning, we depend on our participation in communities with other people, whether familial, social, or political. We are inherently vulnerable to others, in that we depend on their support, both materially and psychologically. This vulnerability, though, means that we are subject to their poor choices and bad intentions as much as to their wisdom and good will. As Socrates notes in this remark, those who are close to a developing individual will commonly be interested in how that individual can fit into their own vision of things: one sees the *potential*—"the power that is going to be his"—in the young person, and tries to draw that person to one's own camp, so to speak. The *Charmides*, again, dramatizes this well.

The young Charmides is marked out as especially "promising," as we say, in many areas, and this specific fact about him makes him interesting both to Critias and to Socrates. Socrates—a relative "outsider" in Charmides's life, but nonetheless a reasonably well-known "character" "from the neighborhood," so to speak—hopes to "turn" Charmides's attention to the good; Critias, a close relative and intimate companion, has adopted the role of mentor to Charmides and, as history reveals, clearly succeeded in drawing Charmides into his [Critias's] political affairs. The situation of Pheidippides in Aristophanes's *Clouds* is another clear example of a son whose father wishes to enlist him in his own schemes and who is also courted by Socrates for participation in his "thinkery." Within the Platonic dialogues, there are many other young men in analogous situations, such as Polus, Alcibiades, Lysis, and Glaucon, and, indeed, the very fact that Socrates was accused of "corrupting the youth" draws our attention to the prevalence of exactly the issue that Socrates identifies in the above quotation: the accusation of "corruption" makes it clear that Socrates is perceived as co-opting the powers of the youth to his own improper goals, and that the broader society in general has a vested interest of its own in the purposes to which those powers are turned. Indeed, in his opening discussion with Socrates in the *Protagoras*, Protagoras describes his own situation in a similar way:

> Your discretion [*promēthē*] on my behalf is appropriate, Socrates. Caution is in order for a foreigner who goes into the great cities and tries to persuade the best of the young men in them to abandon their associations with others, relatives and acquaintances, young and old alike, and to associate with him on the grounds that they will be improved by this association. Jealousy, hostility, and intrigue on a large scale are aroused by such activity. (*Protagoras* 316d–e)

We say that an individual "belongs to" a certain social group, and Protagoras's remark reminds us that that language captures well the sense of ownership that others typically feel toward that individual. The case of Charmides, then, and these various other cases all demonstrate that the surrounding social world into which a child grows is a charged environment in which different and conflicting interests are vying for the child's loyalty, trying, that is, to persuade the child to commit "the power that is going to be his" to their different causes.

In the above quotation from Book VI of the *Republic*, Socrates describes the particular form of behavior that is directed at the young man as "begging," "honoring," and "flattering." This, again, should be quite familiar, and we are especially accustomed to it in sexual situations: individuals with beautiful bodies are commonly the target of the sexual advances of many and, in the competition for their affection, they are typically bombarded with a heavy dose of praise, which is itself closely tied to a request for sexual gratification; the praise itself, though it may be honest, is more typically flattery—a praise rooted in the instrumental concerns of the one praising, rather than in any sincere effort to reflect accurately the nature of the one praised. Something analogous to that is operating in the more general efforts at winning the allegiance of the young: families, businesses, political parties, and religious organizations all regularly "recruit" their young "prospects," typically "selling" themselves as the best environment for enabling the individual to fulfill the young person's "promise."

By the time they are young men or young women, highly capable individuals especially will have long since had instilled in them a vision of their adult participation in the world.[40] As Socrates noted in Book II of the *Republic*, it is generally the case that there is a single thing that one "does" in one's life as a career (II.369d–370c), and before the time when young people enter adulthood their sense of what this thing will be has usually already developed a deep, habitual hold on their sense of self-interpretation. We noted in chapter 1 that sociologists speak of "narrow" socialization in traditional societies in which individuals typically grow up practicing that which will be their life-occupation, so much so that it never occurs to them that they might do something different. Even in our modern society, which encourages more experimentation and "choice," it remains the case that, by college age, individuals are quite strongly committed to a set of life-values and career expectations where the relative openness of going to college is itself a relatively uncommon choice. Further, even within the group who choose to attend college, the path of their subsequent study and development is largely already settled by the time of college entry. Thus, whether it is a matter of the explicit pursuit of the sort that Critias and Socrates direct toward Charmides or a matter of the implicit processes of socialization that typically characterize family life, it is generally the case that individuals with all levels of aptitude and resources will be thus "recruited" to various adult pursuits. It is in this general context that we can reflect on the situation of the individual who is specially gifted with ability and resources.

Socrates discusses the predictable effect of this "recruiting" behavior on the specially "promising" young man:

> What do you suppose . . . such a young man will do in such circumstances, especially if he chances to be from a big city, is rich and noble in it, and is, further, good-looking and tall? Won't he be overflowing with unbounded hope, believing he will be competent to mind the business of both Greeks and barbarians, and won't he, as a result, exalt himself to the heights, mindlessly full of pretensions and empty conceit? (VI.494c–d)

In the Platonic dialogues, we meet many young individuals who are clearly very capable and very accomplished generally: Phaedrus, Agathon, and Alcibiades in the *Symposium*, Polemarchus, Thrasymachus, Glaucon, and Adeimantus in the *Republic*, Charmides in the *Charmides*, Theaetetus in the *Theaetetus*, Polus in the *Gorgias*, Zeno in the *Parmenides*, and so on.[41] These individuals are characteristically smart, powerful, and attractive—promising and privileged—and thus are all good examples of the sort of people to whom one says, "You can do whatever you set your mind to." Each, in other words, is just the sort of individual who would have a strong chance of succeeding in the cognitive and behavioral studies that would allow the flourishing of his *logos*-nature in philosophy. In fact, though, by the time we meet these individuals, they are already significantly committed to different, specific paths, typically associated with the older, mentoring figures with whom they associate. Polemarchus belongs to the world of his father Cephalus, Charmides belongs to the world of Critias, Polus belongs to the world of Gorgias, Zeno belongs to the world of Parmenides, Theaetetus belongs to the world of Theodorus, and so on. In the comfortable context of this world to which each has been recruited, each is confident—often to the point of arrogance—both in his own abilities and in the validity of his endeavor, and is strongly loyal to his mentor. As we look on at these situations, some relations, such as those between Theaetetus and Theodorus, seem obviously healthier—more virtuous—and some, such as the relations between Gorgias and Polus, obviously more vicious. We have not, of course, witnessed the processes by which these individuals came to adopt these lives, but something like what Socrates describes in the quotation above seems apt. In each case, an older figure has won the loyalty of the younger figure by recognizing the potential of the young man and by encouraging the development of exactly those aspects of the young man's abilities that resonate with the goals and values of the older man; the more self-interested the older man, the more vicious the goals and the more arrogant the young acolyte. Individuals such as Alcibiades and Charmides seem to fit particularly well the description of the corruption of the philosophical soul that Socrates offers, for in their cases they have been precisely recruited to the pursuit of tyrannical power—the most promising youths recruited to the most vicious ends.

Misology

Within the large group of a society's young people, there will be those with high aspirations, and those aspirations will largely be the product of persuasion of those individuals by those surrounding them. And those with the greatest "endowments"—intelligence, strength, beauty, wealth, influence—will typically have been persuaded simultaneously to esteem themselves as "special"—a sense of superiority that is psychologically tied to their adherence to the people or projects who have won their loyalty. Inasmuch as these were the individuals with the greatest potential—the individuals most fit "by nature" for philosophy, for the commitment to the good as such—the lives of "relative" good to which they have committed themselves amount to a thwarting rather than a fulfillment of their natural potential. Inasmuch as these were the individuals with the greatest potential, it might also seem that these are still the individuals most suitable to "turning" to philosophy. In this context, though, Socrates talks about the weakness of the persuasive power of good teaching:

> Now, if someone were gently to approach the young man in this condition and tell him the truth—that he has not intelligence in him although he needs it, and that it's not to be acquired except by slaving for its acquisition—do you think it will be easy for him to hear through a wall of so many evils? (VI.494d)

As we already saw in chapter 3, it is a precisely a "turning" of the soul that philosophy requires, which is to say, the soul, already persuaded of one set of values, must be persuaded of another. The good, therefore, through the agency of someone like Socrates or some other who is practiced in the "art of turning around," must "speak" to the thwarted soul, which is to say, that soul must "hear" this persuasion. The very fact of its "prior commitment" to other values, though, inhibits this hearing.[42] Our studies so far of the ways in which the soul is persuaded allow us to understand this situation.

The interpretations of desire and "ego" to which one has been persuaded are not matters of reflective insight and are not matters of single occasions. As we have seen, *epithumia* and *thumos* are ways in which we have *already* been persuaded by the time our reflective calculation arrives on the scene, and they are ways of interpreting to which we have become *habituated*. What this entails is that, though our desires and our spirited feelings are matters of our taking account, they do not appear that way to us: on the contrary, they appear obvious and objective. Consequently, our calculations, by and large, *follow* these, our *pathē*: it is *epithumia* and *thumos* that supply us with the terms that we take as the starting point for our reflections on our situations. In our calculations, we reflect on *ta pragmata*, but the very way we experience our affairs already reflects the values of our desires and "ego." We can thus see here a twofold problem faced by the one who would change the orientation of his or her soul.

First, in such a situation, one has thus developed within oneself various structures and forces that actively work against one's "turning." Even as, for example, one wants to drink less alcohol or be less angry, one finds oneself repeatedly called to those exact behaviors by one's situation: it is not only one's reflective intellect that is addressed by *ta pragmata*, but also one's *epithumia* and *thumos*, and one is thus embroiled in a situation of self-conflict if the demands of reflective calculation are at odds with the established logic of one's desire and sense of ego. At the very least, then, "turning" is difficult, and involves a fundamental struggle.

Second, though, is a problem that is even more challenging than the simple struggle of conflicting forces in the soul. This second problem is that the ways that one has already been persuaded have persuasive, argumentative force themselves. If one is encouraged by another person or even by one's own moral reflection to be less angry, this voice of moral persuasion must actually *argue* with a voice within oneself that precisely affirms the propriety of such anger. In other words, it is typically not the case that one unequivocally grasps the correct theory and merely struggles with the resistance within one's behavior; instead, one's habits make *things seem* to call for exactly the behavior one habitually feels motivated to perform. In struggling with one's desires, for example, one must also struggle with the *theoretical* question, "Can something so pleasing really be bad?" or in struggling with one's sense of ego, for example, one must also struggle with the *theoretical* question, "Can it really be true that one should 'turn the other cheek'"? In addition to being existent forces of resistance to change within one's behavior, then, one's habitual ways of taking account—nonreflective ways that are embedded in one's immediate bodily response to situations—themselves also effectively "argue against" one's reflective reasoning. Pathologies of *ta pathē* thus "infect" our "reasoning" as well, transforming the conflict between reflection and the nonreflective into a conflict within reflection itself.

If we return, then, to Glaucon's situation of psychic conflict at the beginning of Book II of the *Republic*, we can now see more clearly the ambivalence of this "lived" uncertainty [*aporia*] that he faces. In the particular situation under consideration, some inarticulate feeling makes Glaucon distrust the reflective arguments he has heard from Thrasymachus and others. In fact, this *aporia* is good, because those arguments are flawed and Glaucon's habitual, behavioral predispositions are good. Those features that make this *aporia* good, though, are entirely contingent: it can just as easily be the case that one's distrust of argument is the inarticulate feeling of bad behavioral dispositions working against true insight.

This last stance—the inarticulate resistance to compelling argument because of bad habits of desire and ego—can be a merely occasional matter, such that one, otherwise "rational," is "irrationally" resistant to criticisms of specific aspects of one's behavior; it can also, though, be a more pervasive matter, namely, a distrust in principle of argument. The ability to be "spoken to" by argument—to be appealed to, and thus challenged, in our very nature as beings with *logos*—is precisely what is definitive of our humanity: it is why we can be educated, and it is that within us which affords the greatest potential for growth. And yet, precisely our susceptibility to argument, when handled poorly, can lead us to use our own agency—our ability to "think for ourselves"—to turn against this, the principle of our agency. It is precisely this latter "misology" that Socrates warns of in the *Phaedo*. "Let us be on guard," he says,

> so we don't undergo a certain experience [*pathos*]. . . . So that we don't become . . . haters of argument, as some become haters of human beings; for it's not possible . . . for anybody to experience a greater evil than hating arguments. . . . Hatred of human beings arises from artlessly [*aneu technēs*] trusting somebody to excess, and believing that human being to be in every way true and sound and trustworthy, and then a little later discovering that this person is wicked and untrustworthy—and then having this experience again with another. . . . [Arguments are similar in this respect]: when somebody trusts some argument to be true without the art [*technē*] of arguments, and then a little later the argument seems [*doxē*] to him to be false, as it sometimes is and sometimes isn't, and this happens again and again with one argument after another. . . . His condition would be a pitiable one if, when there was in fact some argument that was true and stable and capable of being detected, somebody—through his associating with the very sort of arguments that sometimes seem to be true and sometimes not—should not blame himself or his own artlessness but should end up in his distress being only too pleased to push the blame off himself and onto the argument. (*Phaedo* 89d–90d)

Our attitudes toward argument, that is, are rooted in matters of trust as are our attitudes toward people, and how we are initiated into these matters crucially shapes how we feel impinged on by the imperatives of argument: specifically, there is an "education" into bad argument—into sophistry— that precisely endorses the sorts of false reasoning that our vices encourage in us, an "education" that precisely results in the crippling of our defining relation to *logos* as such. This "education" into "misology"—this fundamental crippling of what is definitive of our humanity—has, it seems to me, two forms, one specialized and one popular.

The inability to appreciate argument [*logos*] according to its own norms, Socrates says, especially afflicts "those especially who've spent their days in debate-arguments [who] end up thinking they've become the wisest of men and that they alone have detected that there's nothing sound or stable—not in the realm of either practical matters or arguments" (*Phaedo* 90c–d). There are those, in other words, who "specialize" in the mishandling of argument; as we noted in our discussion of sophistry in chapter 3, this is the domain of intentional dishonesty but also, more perniciously because less self-consciously, this domain of argumentative miseducation is the sophistry of the "academics," as Augustine put it; that is, it is the skepticism that has always characterized the institutional practice of philosophy to a significant degree.[43] The cultivation of the skill of argument detached from substance is old—at least as old as the "teachers of rhetoric" from the generation before Socrates, and cultivated ever since in debating societies, law schools, philosophy departments, and so on. As we have seen, there is good reason to cultivate this skill in the abstract, but it is also crucial to recognize that argument in the abstract is not truth and that living as if the abstract conception of calculative reasoning were normative for experience is a vice. This belief in the inherently nonsubstantial character of reasoning—the idea that it is always possible to argue both sides of a case equally, for example—is also an attitude encouraged outside the specialized study of the schools, however, by many agencies other than formal logical and rhetorical training, and it is here that we can discern a second, and ultimately more serious, form of misology.

Just as the young are "recruited" to particular ways of life by the broad range of intimate influences that constitute "upbringing," so are they "taught"—by a broad range of intimate cultural influences that are not matters of formal education—to relate to their own *logos*-capacity as abstract and insubstantial. Behind our explicitly avowed views and our implicitly held prejudices lies the formative process of our informal education, and the analysis of the persuasive forces operative in this process allow us to recognize how there can be produced a more popular and more dangerous form of misology than that induced by the specialized studies of "the academy."

Music and Gymnastic

As infants, we are not moved by argumentation. Before we have learned to communicate in language, we must undergo a great deal of development, and thus in principle our inhabitation of the linguistic, rational perspective rests on a prelinguistic, prerational foundation. The *Laws* is especially rich in its study of this dimension of our experience and development. At the beginning of Book II, the Athenian Stranger makes this remark:

> I say that the first infantile sensation in children is the sensation of pleasure and pain, and that it is in these that virtue and vice first come into being in the soul. . . . Education, I say, is the virtue that first comes into being in children. Pleasure and liking, pain and hatred, become correctly arranged in the souls of those who are not yet able to reason [*mēpō dunamenōn logōi lambanein*], and then, when the souls do become capable of reasoning [*labontōn de ton logon*], these [*autē*] can in consonance with reason [*sumphōnēsōsi tōi logōi*] affirm that they have been correctly habituated in the appropriate habits. This consonance in its entirety is virtue. (*Laws* II.653a–b)[44]

The Athenian Stranger's analysis is quite insightful. For children, formative education is a matter of inculcation: it is the development of habits that in fact align the *pathē* with what is reason [*logos*]; however, that normative reason is not functioning in the children themselves, but comes, rather, from the ones responsible for directing this inculcation. Rather than engaging with the seriousness of reasoning, it is precisely through playing that this initial training of the feelings of pleasure and pain is enacted in a child's experience: it is in and by games, songs, and dances that the initial, formative education of the child is carried out. The Stranger continues:

> Education is the drawing and pulling of children toward the argument [*logon*] that is said to be correct by law. . . . To prevent the child's soul from becoming habituated to feeling delight and pain in a way opposed to the law . . . the things we call songs, but which are really incantations for souls [*epōdai tais psuchais*], have now come into being. These have as their serious goal the consonance we are speaking about. But since the souls of the young cannot sustain seriousness, these incantations are called "games" [*paidiai*] and "songs," and are treated as such. (*Laws* II.659d–e)

In playing games, singing, and dancing, the child channels the explosive energy of youth into organized forms:

> Every young thing . . . is incapable of remaining calm in body or in voice. . . . The other animals . . . lack perception of orders and disorders in motions (the orders which have received the names of "rhythm" and "harmony"); we, in

> contrast, have been given the aforementioned gods as fellow-dancers, and they have given us the pleasant perception of rhythm and harmony. Using this they move us, and lead us in choruses, joining us together with songs and dances. (*Laws* II.653d–654a)

It is the organized forms of their games, songs, and dances that are the presence of *logos* in the experience of children.

Through dance, we learn to move our bodies in an orderly and graceful fashion. Through song, we learn to realize and to appreciate coherence and beauty in what we sense and in how we express ourselves. Song and dance introduce us, at a bodily level and an affective level, to the basic phenomenon of "sense" in the rich sense of something encountered immediately that has intrinsic meaning or direction. In song and dance, we are initiated into the recognition that the immediate surface of our experience is pregnant with a deeper, beckoning reality—a reality to which we are naturally akin. Furthermore, song and dance—and games in general—are typically collaborative matters, which thus introduce us as well to the shared character of our existence: to our mutual dependence and to our intrinsic orientation to cooperation. The educational effects of these prerational forms of order are the focus of Socrates's conversation in Book III of the *Republic*.

In Book III of the *Republic*, Socrates identifies music [*hē mousikē*] and gymnastic [*hē gumnastikē*] as the primary structures of formative education. Like the Athenian Stranger in the *Laws*, Socrates here emphasizes that both of these activities, which might seem merely diversionary or entertaining, are actually fundamental to the healthy development of the soul (see II.410c). These prerational forms of behavior, however, educate by the habituation that comes through repetition, rather than by persuasive *argument*: "Imitations [*mimēseis*], if they are practiced continually from youth onwards, become established as habits and nature, in body and sounds and in thought" (III.395d). Thus, about music, he remarks,

> Isn't this why the rearing in music is most sovereign? Because rhythm and harmony most of all insinuate themselves into the inmost part of the soul and most vigorously lay hold of it in bringing grace with them; and they make a man graceful if he is correctly reared. (III.401d)

Inasmuch as it pertains to our basic sense of how we take pleasure in what we immediately sense, music encourages formative experiences of moderation: In song and dance, we take great pleasure, but we take pleasure in the rich depths of meaning with which the sounds we hear and the movements we feel are pregnant; it encourages us "to love in a moderate and musical way what's orderly and fine" (III.403a). And, roughly, as music is to our finding pleasure in what we encounter (i.e., *epithumia*), so gymnastic is to our sense of the primitive self-energy—energetic self-assertion or *thumos*—that we find rising within us:

> Won't the musical man hunt for a gymnastic by following these same tracks? ... He'll undergo these very exercises and labors looking less to strength than to the spirited part of his nature and for the purpose of arousing it, unlike the other kinds of contestants who treat diets and labors as means to force. (III.410b)

When we throw ourselves into gymnastic training, we cultivate that sense of raw energy and motivation that "stems from the spirited part of [our] nature, which, if rightly trained, would be courageous" (III.410d). The roots of *sōphrosunē* and *andreia*—moderation and courage—are thus laid in our formative experiences of play: in our games, songs, and dances.[45]

Just as music and gymnastic are educative, however, they can also be fundamentally miseducative. In the quotation above, Socrates remarked about rhythm and harmony that "they make a man graceful if he is correctly reared"; he continues, though, to note that, "if not, the opposite" (III.401d). Though habituation to beautiful music can encourage one to take pleasure in what is deep and subtle, habituation to more superficial forms of music can encourage one precisely to take pleasure in the most immediate and rough forms of sensual gratification. Similarly, about gymnastic, the quotation above is situated in the fuller context of Socrates's remarking thus: "The savage stems from the spirited part of their nature, which, if rightly trained, would be courageous; but, if raised to a higher pitch than it ought to have, would be likely to become cruel and harsh" (III.410d). There is thus a playful, sporting competitiveness that, when cultivated, encourages one to embrace challenge and opposition in throwing oneself into the pursuit of excellence in collaborative endeavors—courage. Sports can equally, however, be a site for cultivating a violent and vicious competitiveness linked intimately to an excessive and brittle sense of ego. Our forms of play—games, songs, and dances—are thus at the foundation of the formation of our characters: they are among the most basic forms of "persuasion" that we encounter. How they are embraced personally and culturally is thus quite significant for how the young are "recruited" and persuaded.

Socrates draws attention, in the *Crito*, to the ways in which the laws of one's society raise one in a way analogous to how one is raised by one's parents.[46] Dramatizing what the laws themselves would say, Socrates asks,

> Do you find anything to criticize in those of us who are concerned with marriage? ... Or in those of us concerned with the nurture of babies and the education that you too received? Were those assigned to that subject not right to instruct your father to educate you in the arts and in physical culture? ... And after you were born and nurtured and educated, could you, in the first place, deny that you are our offspring and servant, both you and your forefathers? ... We have given you birth, nurtured you, educated you, we have given you and all other citizens a share of all the good things we could. (*Crito* 50d–e, 51c–d)

By providing the parameters for shared action within a society, the laws implicitly inform our behavior and our development throughout all the aspects of our experience. Indeed, the laws of a culture regulate the behavior of adults; but, as Aristotle notes in Book II of the *Nicomachean Ethics*, the laws, like music and gymnastic in the experience of the child, more fundamentally are formative powers that train one's behavior and shape one's expectations even before one is in a position to make reflective judgments about these things (*Nicomachean Ethics* II.1.1103b3–4). These laws that are formative of our experience, however, are not just the explicitly legislated statutes or the principles inscribed in a formal constitution: the laws are also the traditions and customs handed down through generations—the "unwritten" laws of which Pericles speaks in his funeral oration recorded in Thucydides's *History of the Peloponnesian War* and for which Antigone is prepared to die in Sophocles's *Antigone*.[47] Whether in a society of honor, for example, or in a society of money, the very foundation of the society is the shared embrace, by a community, of the founding principles of social operation that precisely make it a society "of honor" or "of money," respectively. The laws, traditional and formal, that provide the matrix in which we grow into social participation, like music and gymnastic, persuade us of our fundamental commitments "beneath" and "before," so to speak, our explicit reflection on such matters.

These themes of the persuasive power of music and gymnastic and of the persuasive power of inherited custom and law are in turn united, for the customary values of a society are themselves powerfully and importantly passed down precisely through "music and gymnastic." In ancient Greece, the traditional epic poetry of Homer and Hesiod, the lyric poetry of Sappho or Pindar, and the tragedies of Aeschylus or Sophocles, for example, all served as transmitters of core social values as well as being immediately entertaining for their audiences. Athletic competitions, such as the Olympic games and the Nemean games, similarly were fundamental sites for the expressing and perpetuating of the values of aristocratic society, as well as being public entertainments.⁴⁸ When the Athenian Stranger, throughout Book II of the *Laws*, discusses how to establish songs and dances for the purpose of shaping the values of children and adults, he is not inventing a new theory of social control; on the contrary, he is drawing attention to precisely the ways in which human society has already developed some of its most powerful instruments and methods of formative persuasion.

Socrates in the *Republic* focuses on music and gymnastic in the city-state, and the Athenian Stranger in the *Laws* focuses on the games, songs, and dances in the city-state, but the cultural forces of persuasion that shape us at a prereflective level can be seen more broadly. In our contemporary culture, we surely can recognize in our televised professional sports and pervasive popular music a rhetorical force analogous to that identified by Socrates and the Athenian Stranger, but our culture has supplemented these media with a broader "entertainment industry," an advertising industry, and a public "news" industry that vastly extend the range and power of these persuasive forces. In trying to comprehend the "account-taking" of individuals, we must look behind the self-avowed reasons of individuals and beyond the explicit terms of formal law to the "grammar" and "vocabulary," so to speak, of these broader, culturally pervasive powers that, like ventriloquists, speak through the *epithumia* and *thumos* of those individuals. In these popular media, we see both the reflection of and the agency producing a cultural outlook that defines the basic parameters according to which the members of a society are persuaded to take account of *ta pragmata*: these media, in a non-*argumentative* way, habituate us to expectations about how we should desire, how we should relate to others, and what in general we should expect to be possible. It is, of course, conceivable that these media could contribute to the cultivation of the virtuous development of citizens; in our society at least, however, it is surely clear that their effect is typically quite the opposite. Indeed, resonating with Socrates's accusation that the general public is ultimately the greatest sophist (VI.492a–494a), our popular media seem generally to promote a pleasure-seeking and mercenary lifestyle that is also quite broadly anti-intellectual. Even without the theoretical focus of the sophistical "academy," these are strong cultural forces that cultivate a broad cultural attitude of "misology."⁴⁹

Socrates's discussion of musical and gymnastic education in Book III of the *Republic* focuses on the way that our formative, nonreflective engagement with these media "educates" us by forming the "patterns" [*paradeigmata*] within us that provide the framework for how we behaviorally and affectively take account of things.⁵⁰ In formal, deliberate education, it is these other forms of persuasion—that have already lodged themselves in the soul—with which and against which one is working. These forms of taking account have already persuaded us: they are already "locked in" at the unreflective levels of *epithumia* and *thumos*, and they have in turn established what we take to be the appropriate terms to which thinking itself must answer. In these contexts, it is precisely bad argumentation that seems most compelling, and good argumentation that seems most implausible. We are thus precisely returned by these reflections to the description of the one who returns to "the cave" that we quoted in chapter 3:

> If such a man were to come down again and sit in the same seat, on coming suddenly from the sun wouldn't his eyes get infected with darkness? . . . And if he once more had to compete with those perpetual prisoners in forming judgments about those shadows while his vision was still dim, before his eyes had recovered, and if the time needed for getting accustomed were not at all short, wouldn't he be the source of laughter, and wouldn't it be said of him that he went up and came back with his eyes corrupted, and that it's not even worth trying to go up? (VII.516e–517a)

As a whole, we are beings who "take account," who do not have a "nature" to guide us but instead must take our bearings from our own *logos*—from the culturally distilled version of making sense of things that is transmitted in and through our cultural institutions. As individuals, this means we are passive—vulnerable—in our formation to "reasons" that we are not yet capable of recognizing as such—the ways of taking account that are handed down to us by our parents and cultures—with the result that we are dependent on the intrinsic rationality of these culturally persuasive forces to teach us well how to recognize reason and how to be rational. Inasmuch, though, as these cultural forces do not reflect well the true nature of things, our ability to take account precisely makes us vulnerable, ultimately, to not being able to recognize a good account when we encounter it.

Conclusion

The distinctive character of our nature is that it requires education, and the distinctive character of education is that we must do it ourselves. In other words, we must take responsibility ourselves for our own development, but this, our self-education, is itself crucially shaped by our own limited perspective: the development of our *logos* depends on our *logos*, and thus our development is vulnerable to the weaknesses in our own perspective. Like the employment of *logos* in general, which we considered in chapter 3, there is thus a kind of insularity here—education is real, but, though it might appear to be a simple appeal to "reality," it is always an appeal to how beings with *logos* have made sense of things. This is true at both an individual level and a collective level.

This sense in which we are necessarily self-reliant does not entail, however, that we are strictly self-controlled, for being open to *logos* means being subject to persuasion. Persuasion affects us in our formation, prior to our developing the capacity to reflect and to analyze carefully, with the result that, by the time we can reflect effectively, we have already *been persuaded* of the basic terms of reflection, terms that are embedded in our sense of pleasure and our sense of ego. These persuasive forces that are now *internal* to the soul in turn make us vulnerable to rhetoric that implicitly appeals to these forces and also make us vulnerable to sophistry that explicitly relies on them.

The prejudicial dogmatism of perspective that is rooted in the formation of our *epithumia* and *thumos* is a consequence of our character as beings who need education in general; that is, *any* education—good or bad—will produce a habitual predisposition that guides our reflection in advance. This, indeed, is why true philosophical learning will always be a matter of self-critical "turning around." Within our development, then, there is always a strong motivation—a strong temptation—not to develop properly, but to treat as absolute the pedagogical goods that in fact are good only relative to the project of the commitment to the good as such. Thus music, gymnastic, or mathematics, each of which is an extremely valuable—indeed, a necessary—discipline if one is to develop fully, can each become a temptation: an "idol," as it were, that one "worships" rather than a "stepping stone" to the good. Even more serious, though, are those "pedagogical" forces, operative at both the cultural and the individual levels, that are not inherently good but that are, on the contrary, miseducative in principle. Individuals are subject to deceitful rhetoric that precisely encourages them to accept the already-fixed terms of their desires and ego and to resist the self-transformative demands of *logos*. Cultures, too, are subject to developing institutions and practices that serve to encourage and fortify these very same bad habits of soul. Because it is up to us, both individually and collectively, to take responsibility for our own education—precisely because we are beings with *logos*—it is thus very easy for us to produce situations in which our development is thwarted, where, indeed, our nature as beings with *logos* precisely results in our turning against *logos* itself.

Notes

1. Compare Socrates's remark to Hippocrates in the *Protagoras*: "If you are a knowledgeable customer, you can buy teachings safely from Protagoras or anyone else. But if you are not, please don't risk what is most dear to you on a roll of the dice, for there is a far greater risk in buying teachings than in buying food" (*Protagoras* 313e–314a).

2. On Socrates's argument against Thrasymachus, see *Being and Logos*, pp. 334–346, especially pp. 342–345.

3. On the dramatic relevance of Glaucon's question, see Sallis, *Being and Logos*, p. 347.

4. An analogous point is also made quite clearly in Book I of the *Republic*, when Polemarchus and Cleitophon comment on the logic of the exchange between Socrates and Thrasymachus, demonstrating that Thrasymachus's say-so is not sufficient to show an argument to be invalid (I.340a–c).

5. Baracchi interprets Glaucon's question as evidence of a philosophical orientation; see *On Myth, Life, and War in Plato's Republic*, p. 52. Brann, "The Music of the *Republic*," similarly treats Glaucon as a promising potential philosopher, noting in particular Xenophon's description in *Memorabilia* III.vi; see especially pp. 25–26. Sanday, "Philosophy as the Practice of Musical Inheritance," offers a provocative analysis of the implicit tensions involved in Glaucon's question. Dorter offers his analysis of Glaucon's character in *The Transformation of Plato's Republic*, pp. 55–56.

6. For a very precise interpretation of this remark by Socrates that is especially valuable because of its attention to the specificities of the language, see Benardete, *Socrates' Second Sailing*, p. 95.

7. Interpreters are often somewhat baffled by how precisely to define this dimension of experience, often either giving it an unsatisfactory interpretation as "emotion," as in the case, for example, of Irwin, *Plato's Moral Theory*, or simply accepting it as a "part" of the soul without giving it a philosophical justification, which is the case even with Sallis, who is otherwise quite systematic. Sallis, like many, says of *thumos* in *Being and Logos* that it "refers to the aggressive element in man, to the competitive and ambitious element, and to that which makes man feel indignant towards injustice" (p. 369); while these claims are surely true, they do not clarify why we should use such a notion to talk about our experience. As Gosling writes: "It is not at all obvious what Plato is trying to isolate with the term 'thymos,' and the problem has not been helped by a tendency to concentrate on a few prominent passages interesting largely for other reasons. The result is to suggest that he is trying to distinguish emotions from, say, intellect and desire, or to distinguish the will from intellect and affective parts of personality" (*Plato*, p. 71). I attempt here to show how this notion does indeed make experiential and philosophical sense. For interpreting the meaning of *thumos*, one of the most important texts is II.375a–b, where *thumos* is identified as that within us which will not accept defeat; in other words, it is both our most intimate experience of honoring and, hence, it is that within us which seeks victory; see also IV.440c for *thumos* as the sense of injustice. For an excellent and thorough analysis of the discussion of *thumos* that reaches conclusions very similar to my own, see Cooper, "Plato's Theory of Human Motivation," especially pp. 12–17; see also Fussi, "The Desire for Recognition," especially pp. 238–239, and Recco, *Athens Victorious*, chap. 2. Benardete, *Socrates' Second Sailing*, pp. 55–57, helpfully analyzes the notion of *thumos* in terms of the theme of not accepting defeat. Like Cooper, Benardete (pp. 55–56) and Recco (p. 54) emphasize that Plato is resuscitating an archaic usage of the term. See also Pangle's rich and provocative discussion of *thumos* in his

"Interpretive Essay" in his translation of the *Laws*, pp. 452–456, especially p. 453: "Beginning from the simple case of anger, we see in the first place that the drive to overcome and destroy is accompanied by a vivid sense of one's own affronted dignity.... In human beings, anger proves to be merely the crudest manifestation of pride, the passionate concern for one's individual rank."

8. Compare Aristotle, *Rhetoric* II.1.1378a31–32: "Anger may be defined as a desire accompanied by pain, for a conspicuous revenge for a conspicuous slight at the hands of men who have no call to slight oneself or one's friends." This is also why Adam Smith says, in *The Theory of the Moral Sentiments*, that we do not immediately sympathize with another's anger, namely, because we cannot see what motivates it—since it is not a "thing" but the relation to the other's sense of self that is the motivation.

9. Compare Aristotle, *Rhetoric* II.6.1383b14–19: "Shame may be defined as pain or disturbance in regard to bad things, whether past, present, or future, which seem likely to involve us in discredit.... We feel shame at such bad things as we think are disgraceful to ourselves or to those we care for."

10. *On the Soul* I.1.403a30; *Rhetoric* II.6.1384a24.

11. Liebert, "Pity and Disgust in Plato's *Republic*," challenges this interpretation of Leontius's motivation, arguing instead that he is conflicted by his desire to grieve for individuals who are not deserving of grief.

12. On the meaning of the term *duscherainō*, see Liebert, "Pity and Disgust in Plato's *Republic*," n. 30.

13. On anger as the source of courage, see the *Republic*, Book III: "The savage stems from the spirited part of their nature, which, if rightly trained, would be courageous; but, if raised to a higher pitch than it ought to have, would be likely to become cruel and harsh" (III.410d). Anger is the expression of *thumos* in that it is that savagery of self-assertion that comes from a sense of personal violation and the desire to respond by enacting revenge.

14. It is presumably this immediacy that leads Glaucon initially to propose that spirit is just desire (IV.439e).

15. Recall I.327c: Polemarchus asks, "Could you really persuade ... if we don't listen?" and, whereas Glaucon says, "There's no way," we never hear Socrates's answer. Sallis discusses the significance of Glaucon's answer in *Being and Logos*, pp. 321–322.

16. Socrates asks at IV.430e, "Isn't the phrase 'stronger than himself' ridiculous [*geloion*] though? For, of course, the one who's stronger than himself would also be weaker than himself and the weaker stronger. The same 'himself' is referred to in all of them." First, this is a (leading) question put to his interlocutors and not an assertion, and, second, though it notes the paradoxical—"laughable"—character of the language, it does not actually imply that the claim is false; his interlocutors (like many commentators on Plato) no doubt take this to be Socrates's view, but that is a poor handling of his words. Compare also the image of the spinning top at IV.436d–e. In general, the discussion of the "division of the soul" is a complex textual and conceptual matter. In particular, it seems clear here that Glaucon and Adeimantus either cause or allow to transpire various conceptual and argumentative errors in the conversation, and it is the job of the reader to be critically cognizant of this. For a precise reading of this text that is finely attuned to both the conceptual and the conversational matters, see Recco, *Athens Victorious*, chap. 1, which ultimately comes to conclusions comparable to my own; on the image of the spinning top, see in particular pp. 21–24. See also Sallis, *Being and Logos*, pp. 368–371, on the textual and conceptual difficulty of the conversation about the division of the soul. Dorter, *The Transformation*

of Plato's Republic, argues that the discussion of the division of the soul is exemplary of a defining characteristic of the *Republic* that important distinctions are initially handled in an overly rigid way that is subsequently refined throughout the discourse: "What the doctrine of the tripartite soul is meant to show is that the self can be divided against itself and that the ways it can be divided can be classed conveniently into three broad categories, but this tripartite division turns out to be anything but definitive" (p. 119); see pp. 2 and 369 for this overall theme and pp. 113–123 for a detailed discussion of the division of the soul specifically. Roochnik, *Beautiful City*, has an approach that is very similar to Dorter's on this issue and, indeed, on interpreting the book overall; see especially pp. 18–30 for the argument that it is necessarily one and the same individual who *is* all the "parts" of the soul. Achtenberg, *Essential Vulnerabilities*, has a related critique of how the tripartite soul is presented in Book IV; see pp. 57–59, 152–54, and 180. Benardete, in *Socrates' Second Sailing*, writes, "If [Socrates] is successful, no one can ever use either 'I' or 'soul' unequivocally in any sentence about his thinking or desiring" (p. 94); on pp. 94–102 he gives a particularly careful discussion of the text. Brann discusses the division of the soul in "The Music of the *Republic*," pp. 40–44.

17. Compare Aristotle, *Nicomachean Ethics*, Book I, chap. 13. Aristotle here notes that, as animals with *logos*, we have aspects of our being that are not themselves *logos*. Some of those *alogon* aspects—our vital functions, such as digestion or growing—are not subject to direct influence by our intelligence, by our *logos*; others, such as our appetites [*to d' epithumētikon kai holōs orektikon*], though not matters of *logos* as such, are "persuadable by" *logos* [*peitharchei tōi logōi*] (*Nicomachean Ethics* I.13.1102a32–33, 1102b11–12, 1102b13–26, 1102b28–31). It is precisely these *alogon* aspects of ourselves that we have been reflecting on in our discussions of desire [*epithumia*] and spirit [*thumos*]. Aristotle's point is that bringing our nature as "animals with *logos*" to a state of flourishing is a twofold task: it requires the cultivation of our *logos* as such—the cultivation of our capacities for self-conscious intelligence—and it requires the transformation of our *alogon* appetites into a state that harmonizes with the demands of *logos* (*Nicomachean Ethics* I.13.1103a3–5). The former—intellectual virtue or excellence of thinking [*aretē hē dianoētikē*]—comes about, as Aristotle notes in Book II, chap. 1 of the *Nicomachean Ethics*, through teaching in the familiar sense; the latter—moral virtue or excellence of character [*aretē hē ēthikē*]—comes about through the development of good habits (*Nicomachean Ethics* II.1.1103a14–18).

18. *Nicomachean Ethics* I.13.1102b26.

19. Whereas in Book III of the *Republic*, piety is prominently included in the discussion of virtue, as are liberality and magnificence, which are also included in the list of the philosopher's virtues in Book VI, in Book IV the discussion of virtue focuses only on courage, moderation, wisdom, and justice. My own analysis will focus on wisdom, courage, and moderation, the three virtues that pertain directly to each of what I shall argue are the three distinct forms of motivation in the soul.

20. See, for example, IV.441e: "Isn't it proper for the calculating part to rule, since it is wise and has forethought about all the soul?" Recco has a careful analysis of the ways in which the analysis in the *Republic* goes astray by confusing wisdom with the rule of *logismos*; see *Athens Victorious*, pp. 56–66. Sallis addresses the definition of *wisdom* in *Being and Logos*, pp. 363, 367, and 370. That the words *sophia* and *phronēsis* are both used as if they mean the same thing appears to be the case by a comparison of IV.427e and IV.433b, where each is used as the name for the fourth virtue, along with courage, moderation, and justice (and, indeed,

at one point *epistēmē* also seems to be equated with these terms); the language of Book IV goes back and forth between *sophia* and *phronēsis*, though *sophia* has more frequent use.

21. See IV.440c on *thumos* as the sense of injustice.
22. In "Personality as Equilibrium," I have discussed the thresholds that are definitive of our emotional life.
23. See II.375a–b on *thumos* as that within us that will not accept defeat.
24. See Kirk, "Initiation, Extraction, and Transformation," for a parallel discussion of the characters of Theaetetus and Charmides.
25. Aristotle, *Nicomachean Ethics* III.6.1151a24–30.
26. Compare Xenophon, *Apology of Socrates to the Jury* 29.
27. Compare *Laws* II on the different songs appropriate to children and adults.
28. Compare the analysis of the judge at *Laws* I.627e–628a. I have discussed this passage in "Education in Plato's *Laws*."
29. North, *Sophrosyne*, is a classical study of the range of meaning of this term in Greek culture and history.
30. The theme of redirecting, rather than suppressing, desire is discussed by Sallis in *Being and Logos*, p. 398. See also pp. 380–382, where Sallis discusses the complex relation of *ērōs*, *philia*, and *epithumia*. In general, Sallis identifies the ambiguous place of desire throughout the text.
31. An absence long enough that Chaerophon can say of Charmides, "You probably know him . . . but he was not yet grown up when you went away," to which Socrates replies, "Good heavens, of course I know him . . . because he was worth noticing even when he was a child. By now I suppose he must be pretty well grown up" (*Charmides* 154a-b).
32. Critias's introduction is at *Charmides* 157d; Charmides's initial response to Socrates's questions is *Charmides* 158c–d.
33. I have discussed this passage from the *Laws* in "Education in Plato's *Laws*."
34. *Aidōs* is a prominent theme in many Platonic dialogues, including especially the *Protagoras* and the *Laws*. The familiar sense here of "modesty" falls far short of the depth of meaning this term can hold, but that deeper analysis is beyond the scope of this study.
35. Thrasymachus behaves in a comparable way in Book I of the *Republic*; see I.336b.
36. On the theme of the unity of the virtues in the *Republic*, see Dorter, *The Transformation of Plato's Republic*, pp. 126–128.
37. On this theme, see David Sachs, "A Fallacy in Plato's Republic." Sachs argues that the virtues as independently defined are compatible with injustice. See Kirk, "Self-Knowledge and Ignorance in Plato's *Charmides*," for an insightful discussion of Critias's problematic relationship to *sōphrosunē*.
38. Sallis discusses the corruption of the philosopher in *Being and Logos*, pp. 399–400, especially considering this theme in relationship to Glaucon and his role in the *Republic*.
39. That it is in fact often those who are not "the best" who are best suited to developing philosophically is made clear in Hegel's analysis of the slave in *Phenomenology of Spirit*, or by Freire's *Pedagogy of the Oppressed*; these are the ones who often have the *empeiria* with the real demands of human life.
40. Compare Achtenberg, *Essential Vulnerabilities*, pp. 48, 49: "In our early education, what we think are true are simply reflections of the views of others—authoritative others who make sure that their views are influential in our milieu, that their artifacts cast shadows placed so that we will see them from our limited position in our limited cave. . . . The first

stage [of achieving freedom] is turning around and seeing that the views I think are mine are instead reflections of the authoritative views of others in our cave."

41. Indeed, Xenophon's description in *Memorabilia* III.6 suggests that this quotation might be a description of Glaucon himself.

42. Compare Benardete, *Socrates' Second Sailing*, p. 152: "It is both a necessity for philosophy to become Socratic and an accident that it ever become so; just as it is a necessity for human happiness to be found only in philosophy and an accident that there ever be philosophy."

43. See VII.537e–539d on the dangers that come from being exposed too early to sophistic modes of refutation.

44. I have removed the word "passions" from Pangle's translation—the Greek says only "these."

45. On education in music and gymnastic, see Recco, *Athen Victorious*, p. 59; on the relation of "dialectic" (philosophy) to music and gymnastic, see pp. 221–222; consistently with the claims made by Recco, Brann, "The Music of the *Republic*," p. 32, argues that Socrates's philosophy is music. See Sallis, *Being and Logos*, pp. 360–361, on education in music, and p. 374 on the notion that gymnastic is for the soul.

46. I have discussed the implications of Socrates's argument about the laws in the *Crito* in "The (Childish) Nature of the Soul in Plato's *Apology*."

47. Thucydides, *History of the Peloponnesian War* II.37; Sophocles, *Antigone* lines 499–508. See *Laws*, III.679e–680a, for the difference between laws before and after writing.

48. Kurke, *The Traffic in Praise*, pp. 3–4: "Athletic games in general were the province of the aristocracy.... *Aretē* is ... very much a competitive virtue and a virtue of the aristocracy.... Indeed, the great Panhellenic games were, to quote one scholar, 'a conspicuous arena for demonstrations of the superiority of the ruling class.'"

49. Brann, "The Music of the *Republic*," discusses this on p. 44: "There follows a series of images that show that the greatest of all sophists, the Many, is in fact the greatest corrupter of natures, who corrupts the best most deeply; this Public Sophist is like a great brute that the little private sophists know how to propitiate (492a–493d)." Benardete, *Socrates' Second Sailing*, discusses this on p. 150.

50. See, for example, III.409c. Compare IV.424b–d.

CONCLUSION

Ancient Greece underwent a cultural revolution in the centuries immediately preceding the writing of the Platonic dialogues. This revolution was effectively the performative recognition of our *logos*-character at a cultural level, a recognition that is reflected in the emergence of a culture in which the separation of substance and surface—the distinctive character of *logos* itself—is definitive of the functioning of that culture. This is a culture, in other words, of writing, money, democracy, and philosophy. The *Republic*, I have argued, is a careful analysis of this revolution as a distinctively human reality, revealing why these developments are simultaneously inherently fulfilling and inherently corruptive of our nature.

We are beings with *logos*. This gives us possibilities that we do not recognize anywhere else in the natural world: it gives us, uniquely, the possibility—and the necessity—of being self-responsible. More broadly, it is the capacity to take account, which results in the capacity to know, the capacity to learn, the capacity for politics, and more. Central to all of these possibilities is a core ability: the ability to abstract, that is, to hold apart "in *logos*" what cannot be held apart in reality. This is our ability to hold ourselves back from things in a stance of reflection, and it is our ability to analyze those things, to differentiate within them part from whole and property from substance. This power to abstract, however, also makes it possible for us to engage with something superficially: to address its surface without regard to its substance. This "abstractive" power of *logos* is what allows us to have a history—to develop our world on the basis of the accomplishments of our forebears; it also means, however, that our reality is essentially inherited, that is, we live on the basis of the accomplishments of others without being able immediately to recognize the nature of this debt. In our study of the *Republic*, we have seen the complex implications of both the positive side and the negative side of *logos* worked out in relationship to three main (and highly interrelated) themes: politics, knowledge, and psychological development.

As we saw in chapter 1, it is by virtue of our *logos* that we are political beings. Because we take account of things, we collectively give an account to ourselves of how we should live, and we hold ourselves accountable to this. Government, though, can take many forms, formal and informal, and, as we saw in chapter 2, what is most decisive here is that to which a society—a government—primarily holds itself accountable: what is its highest value. Through our analysis of the forms of government, we have seen that it is democracy that essentially fulfills the immanent trajectory of politics, in that democracy is the form of government that (correctly) recognizes our account-taking as what is most definitive of us. It is only the democratic form of government that can do justice to our nature as beings with *logos*—can give us "what we are due"—introducing the situation in which it is truly possible for us to be self-responsible, self-governing. By thus uniting government and governed, guardians and guarded, democracy might seem to obviate the problem identified by Socrates, Glaucon, and Adeimantus: that a government detached from those whom it governs is itself a permanent threat to the governed. In fact, though, the requirement that "philosophy and political power come together in one" is no less true of democratic self-government than it is of alienated forms of government: unless the ordinary citizenry, the *demos*, are themselves wise, the democratic society is its own worst enemy, opening itself to the worst forms of exploitation. Indeed, it is precisely the characteristic anti-intellectual populism that is the obvious (but false) rhetoric of democracy that leads to the self-undermining of democracy. Democracy is the regime in which we can engage freely with our own free character: the regime that acknowledges that it is up to us to take account. But this very regime, in which we cut ourselves loose fully from nature, is the one in which we are then most vulnerable, for there is nothing in this regime that is paternalistically set up as a fixed surrogate for nature to "take care" of us. In this regime, what we are vulnerable to is our own nature: humans vulnerable to humans.[1] Democratic politics requires knowledge—expertise, good judgment, philosophy—and thus democratic politics is the regime in which we can use our human powers to fulfill our human needs. But it is also the regime that is inherently vulnerable to exploitation by sophistry; indeed, the trial and execution of Socrates are a mark of just how profoundly Athens failed as a democracy.[2] This regime that opens up our fullest potential is thus also the regime that makes us most vulnerable to misology and tyranny, themselves established through the rhetoric and sophistry made viable in democracy. That and how knowledge is possible was our theme in chapter 3, and that and how the sophistical manipulation of the human soul is possible was our theme in chapter 4.

The capacity to take account is what makes knowledge possible. As we saw in chapter 1, it is our *logos*-capacity that allows us to recognize the first principles of things, and thus learn about the *logos* of reality itself. This same capacity, though, allows us to absorb the principle without the experience it explains, thus allowing us to imagine that we know when in fact we do not. These powers that facilitate learning also make it the case that learning is never guaranteed. We become vulnerable to the temptations of superficiality. In part, this reliance on abstraction is what allows education to exist, for it means we can take in the principles of things without having to devote our lives to the laborious empirical practice that gives rise to the recognition of those principles. On the other hand, it means we are always more and more dependent, in the knowledge we inherit, on empirical work we have not ourselves done, and this makes our state of knowledge fragile—and one in which we are easily convinced of our own knowledge when what we have is mere superficiality. To "own up" to the responsibilities of knowledge, as we saw in chapter 3, requires our "turning around" and recognizing the very nature of our *logos*-capacity, a turn that is inseparable from a wholesale bodily, affective, and cognitive commitment to the good as such. Not surprisingly, we often fall short of this commitment, as we studied especially in chapter 4.

Because knowledge is not just a cognitive matter, but a matter of the whole soul, education is not simply a matter of learning the abstract principles of things, but is instead the careful development of all aspects of our soul toward an honest taking account of things—which ultimately means toward a commitment to the good as such. But this very fact that our taking account is not just a matter of reflective cognition implies that many dimensions of our taking account are not ones we ourselves avow: not ones of which we take account. Our very nature, then, is to find ourselves, by the time we engage in reflective cognition, already having taken account, already persuaded about the nature of things. *Logos* has made its way into our souls "behind" and "beneath" our *logos*, as it were, and our experience is thus always a matter of some form of nonintegration, of self-conflict. These ways in which we have already been persuaded about the *logos* of things—these ways that define our experiences of pleasure and ego, *epithumia* and *thumos*—are either the resources or the obstacles with which our subsequent account-taking must deal, depending on whether we have developed good habits or bad habits, respectively. If our habits are good, our prereflective, bodily, and affective predilections will themselves be stepping stones for our turning around and grasping ever more deeply the reality they engage; if our habits are bad, those predilections will instead be the constant temptation to accept surface over substance, a temptation that is particularly ripe for championing the very sophistical "*logos*" that denies *logos*, and in turn produces individuals and a society that are particularly ripe for exploitation by tyranny.

Because our *logos*-character makes us inherently self-responsible, it also makes us vulnerable to our own failures of education. The ability to separate surface from substance, itself the capacity that makes education possible, is also the source of our temptation to corruption. Our investigation of *logos* has thus allowed us to see why it propels us essentially into both politics and knowledge and why, through the possibility of abstraction, it simultaneously makes us exist permanently in a situation of essential risk and responsibility. There is no solution to this except the better development of our *logos*.[3]

Notes

1. Compare *Laws* IX.853c: "We are human beings legislating for human beings."
2. One could construe the whole of the *Republic* as a condemnation of what Athens did to Socrates. See Brann, "The Music of the *Republic*," p. 18, on the degeneration of the real democracy; see Baracchi, *On Myth, Life, and War*, p. 40, on the *Republic* as a reflection on the generation of the city in the context of its actual degeneration.
3. For the idea that the institutions of democracy are ultimately institutions of education, see Recco, *Athens Victorious*, p. 230.

BIBLIOGRAPHY

Achtenberg, Deborah. *Cognition and Value in Aristotle's Ethics: Promise of Enrichment, Threat of Destruction.* Albany: State University of New York Press, 2002.
———. *Essential Vulnerabilities: Plato and Levinas on Relations to the Other.* Evanston, IL: Northwestern University Press, 2014.
Agamben, Giorgio. *State of Exception.* Translated by Kevin Attell. Chicago: University of Chicago Press, 2005.
Althusser, Louis. "Idéologie et appareils idéologiques d'État (Notes pour une recherche)." *La Pensée* 151 (1970).
Annas, Julia. *An Introduction to Plato's Republic.* Oxford: Clarendon, 1981.
———. "Classical Greek Philosophy." In *The Oxford History of Greece and the Hellenistic World*, edited by John Boardman, Jasper Griffin, and Oswyn Murray, 277–305. Oxford: Oxford University Press, 1991.
Anthony, David W. *The Horse, the Wheel and Language: How Bronze-Age Riders from the Eurasian Steppes Shaped the Modern World.* Princeton, NJ: Princeton University Press, 2007.
Aquinas, Thomas. *On Truth.* Indianapolis: Hackett, 1994.
Aristophanes. *Clouds.* In *Four Texts on Socrates.* Rev. ed. Translated and edited by Thomas G. West and Grace Starry West, 115–176. Ithaca, NY: Cornell University Press, 1998.
Aristotle. *Analytica Priora et Posteriora.* Oxford Classical Texts. Edited by W. D. Ross. Oxford: Clarendon, 1964.
———. *The Complete Works of Aristotle.* 2 vols. Edited by Jonathan Barnes. Princeton, NJ: Princeton University Press, 1984.
———. *Ethica Nicomachea.* Oxford Classical Texts. Edited by L. Bywater. Oxford: Clarendon, 1920.
———. *Metaphysica.* Oxford Classical Texts. Edited by W. Jaeger. Oxford: Clarendon, 1957.
———. *Nicomachean Ethics.* Translated by Robert C. Bartlett and Susan D. Collins. Chicago: University of Chicago Press, 2011.
———. *Politica.* Edited by W. D. Ross. Oxford: Clarendon, 1957.
Arnett, Jeffrey Jensen. "Broad and Narrow Socialization: The Family in the Context of a Cultural Theory." *Journal of Marriage and the Family* 57, no. 3 (1995): 617–628.
Augustine. *Against the Academicians and The Teacher.* Translated by Peter King. Indianapolis: Hackett, 1995.
Aygün, Ömer, "An *Apology* in the Cave Light." In Fagan and Russon, *Reexamining Socrates in the Apology*, 250–270.
———. *The Middle Included: Logos in Aristotle.* Evanston, IL: Northwestern University Press, 2017.
Bailey, Jesse I. *Logos and Psyche in the Phaedo.* Lanham, MD: Lexington Books, 2018.
Baracchi, Claudia. *Of Myth, Life, and War in Plato's Republic.* Bloomington: Indiana University Press, 2002.

———. "The 'Inconceivable Happiness' of 'Men and Women': Visions of Another World in Plato's *Apology of Socrates*." In Fagan and Russon, *Reexamining Socrates in the Apology*, 273–290.

Barnes, Jonathan. "An Aristotelian Way with Scepticism." In *Aristotle Today: Essays on Aristotle's Ideal of Science*, edited by Mohan Matthen, 51–76. Edmonton: Academic Printing and Publishing, 1987.

Benardete, Seth. *Socrates' Second Sailing: On Plato's Republic*. Chicago: University of Chicago Press, 1989.

Bernabé, Alberto. "What Is a Katábasis? The Descent into the Netherworld in Greece and the Ancient Near East." *Les Études Classiques* 83 (2015): 15–34.

Bett, Richard. "Language, Gods, and Virtue: A Discussion of Robert Mayhew, *Prodicus the Sophist*." *Oxford Studies in Ancient Philosophy* 44 (2013): 279–311.

Bourdieu, Pierre. *Distinction: A Social Critique of the Judgment of Taste*. Translated by Richard Nice. Cambridge, MA: Harvard University Press, 1984.

Brann, Eva. "The Music of the *Republic*." *The St. John's Review* 39 (1989–90): 1–103.

Burger, Ronna. *The Phaedo: A Platonic Labyrinth*. New Haven, CT: Yale University Press, 1984.

Carson, Anne. *Eros the Bittersweet*. Princeton, NJ: Princeton University Press, 1986.

———. "How Not to Read a Poem: Unmixing Simonides from Protagoras." *Classical Philology* 87, no. 2 (1992): 110–130.

Cooper, John M. "Plato's Theory of Human Motivation." *History of Philosophy Quarterly* 1, no. 1 (1984): 3–21.

Corey, David D. *The Sophists in Plato's Dialogues*. Albany: State University of New York Press, 2015.

Corrigan, Kevin, and Elena Glazov-Corrigan. *Plato's Dialectic at Play: Argument, Structure, and Myth in the Symposium*. University Park: Pennsylvania State University Press, 2004.

Darwin, Charles. *On the Origin of Species: By Means of Natural Selection*. Dover Thrift Edition. Mineola, NY: Dover Publications, 2006.

Davis, Mike. *City of Quartz: Excavating the Future in Los Angeles*. New York: Verso, 1990.

Demosthenes. *Orationes XXVII–XL*. Greek text with English translation by A. T. Murray (Loeb Classical Library). Cambridge, MA: Harvard University Press, 1939.

Derrida, Jacques. "Plato's Pharmacy." In *Dissemination*. Translated by Barbara Johnson. Chicago: University of Chicago Press, 1981.

———. *Rogues: Two Essays on Reason*. Translated by Pascale-Anne Brault and Michael Naas. Stanford, CA: Stanford University Press, 2005.

Dewey, John. *Art as Experience*. London: TarcherPerigee, 2005.

———. *Democracy and Education: An Introduction to the Philosophy of Education*. New York: Macmillan, 1916.

Diamond, Eli. *Mortal Imitations of Divine Life: The Nature of the Soul in Aristotle's De Anima*. Evanston, IL: Northwestern University Press, 2015.

Dobson, John F. *The Greek Orators*. London: Methuen, 1919.

Dorter, Kenneth. *The Transformation of Plato's Republic*. Lanham MD: Lexington Books, 2006.

Duplouy, Alain. "The So-Called Solonian Property Classes: Citizenship in Archaic Athens." *Annales Histoire Sciences Sociales* 69, no. 3 (2014): 409–439.

Ehrenberg, Victor. *From Solon to Socrates: Greek History and Civilization between the 6th and 5th Centuries BC*. 2nd ed. New York: Routledge, 1990.

Fagan, Patricia. "'He Saw the Cities and He Knew the Minds of Many Men': Landscape and Character in the *Odyssey* and the *Laws*." In Recco and Sanday, *Plato's Laws: Force and Truth in Politics*, 105–117.
———. "Philosophical History and the Roman Empire." In *Hegel and the Tradition: Essays in Honour of H. S. Harris*, edited by Michael Baur and John Russon, 17–39. Toronto: University of Toronto Press, 1997.
———. *Plato and Tradition: The Poetic and Cultural Context of Philosophy*. Evanston, IL: Northwestern University Press, 2013.
———, and John Russon, eds. *Reexamining Socrates in the Apology*. Evanston, IL: Northwestern University Press, 2009.
French, A. "The Economic Background to Solon's Reforms." *The Classical Quarterly* 6, no. 1/2 (1956): 11–25.
Fornara, Charles W., and Loren J. Samons II. *Athens from Cleisthenes to Pericles*. Berkeley: University of California Press, 1991.
Freydberg, Bernard. "'Oracles and Dreams' Commanding Socrates: Reflections on *Apology* 33c." In Fagan and Russon, *Reexamining Socrates in the Apology*, 5–15.
———. *Philosophy and Comedy: Aristophanes, Logos, and Eros*. Bloomington: Indiana University Press, 2008.
———. *The Play of the Platonic Dialogues*. New York: Peter Lang, 1997.
———. "Retracing Homer and Aristophanes in the Platonic Text." In Russon and Sallis, *Retracing the Platonic Text*, 99–112.
Freire, Paolo. *Pedagogy of the Oppressed*. New York: Continuum, 1993.
Fussi, Alessandra. *Retorica e Potere. Una lettura del Gorgia il Platone*. Pisa: Edizioni ETS, 2006.
———. "The Desire for Recognition in Plato's *Symposium*." *Arethusa* 41, no. 2 (2008): 237–262.
———. "Why Is the *Gorgias* So Bitter?" *Philosophy and Rhetoric* 33, no. 1 (2000): 39–58.
Garner, John V. *The Emerging Good in Plato's Philebus*. Evanston, IL: Northwestern University Press, 2017.
Gifford, Mark. "Dramatic Dialectic in *Republic* Book I." In *Oxford Studies in Ancient Philosophy*. Vol. 20, edited by David Sedley, 53–106. Oxford: Oxford University Press, 2001.
Goldhill, Simon. "The Great Dionysia and Civic Ideology." *Journal of Hellenic Studies* 107 (1987): 58–76.
Gonzalez, Francisco J. "Caring and Conversing About Virtue Every Day: Human Piety and Goodness in Plato's *Apology*." In Fagan and Russon, *Reexamining Socrates in the Apology*, 117–167.
Gordon, Jill. *Plato's Erotic World: From Cosmic Origins to Human Death*. Cambridge, UK: Cambridge University Press, 2012.
Gosling, J. C. B. *Plato*. New York: Routledge & Kegan Paul, 1973.
Gregory, George. "Verbs of Seeing in Plato's Republic." Unpublished manuscript.
Guthrie, W. K. C. *A History of Greek Philosophy*. Vol. 3, *The Fifth Century Enlightenment*. Cambridge, UK: Cambridge University Press, 1969.
Halperin, David. "Platonic *Erôs* and What Men Call Love." *Ancient Philosophy* 5 (1985): 161–204.
Havelock, Eric A. *A Preface to Plato*. Cambridge, MA: Belknap, 1982.
Hegel, G. W. F. *Encyclopaedia of the Philosophical Sciences*. Vol. 3, *Philosophy of Mind*. Translated by A. V. Miller. Oxford: Clarendon Press, 1970.

———. *The Letters*. Translated by Clark Butler and Christiane Seiler. Bloomington: Indiana University Press, 1985.
———. *Phenomenology of Spirit*. Translated by A. V. Miller. Oxford: Oxford University Press, 1977.
Herington, Jon. *Poetry into Drama: Early Tragedy and the Greek Poetic Tradition*. Berkeley: University of California Press, 1985.
Herodotus. *The Histories*. Translated by Aubrey de Selincourt. Harmondsworth, UK: Penguin, 1996.
Homer. *Iliad*. Translated by Richmond Lattimore. Chicago: University of Chicago Press, 1961.
———. *Odyssey*. Translated by Richmond Lattimore. New York: Harper Perennial, 2007.
Howland, Jacob. "Re-Reading Plato: The Problem of Platonic Chronology." *Phoenix* 45, no. 3 (1991): 189–214.
Hume, David. *A Treatise of Human Nature*. Edited by L. A. Selby-Bigge. Oxford: Clarendon, 1968.
Husserl, Edmund. *Ideas Pertaining to a Pure Phenomenology and Phenomenological Psychology*. First Book. Translated by Fred Kersten. Dordrecht, The Netherlands: Kluwer Academic Publishers, 1983.
Hyland, Drew A. *Finitude and Transcendence in the Platonic Dialogues*. Albany: State University of New York Press, 1995.
Ibn Khaldûn. *The Muqaddimah: An Introduction to History*. Translated by Franz Rosenthal. Abridged by N. J. Dawood. Princeton, NJ: Princeton University Press, 1967.
Ibn Sīnā. *The "Metaphysica" of Avicenna (Ibn Sīnā)*. Edited by Parviz Morewedge. New York: Routledge, 2015.
Ingham, Geoffrey. *The Nature of Money*. Cambridge, UK: Polity, 2004.
Ionescu, Cristina. *On the Good Life: Thinking through the Intermediaries in Plato's Philebus*. Albany: State University of New York Press, 2019.
Irwin, Terence. *Plato's Moral Theory: The Early and Middle Dialogues*. Oxford: Clarendon Press, 1977.
Ivković, Sanja Kutnajak. "To Serve and Collect: Measuring Police Corruption." *Journal of Criminal Law and Criminology* 93 (2003): 593–650.
Jaklic, Emily. "But Socrates, What Is It That You Do? Education and the Discourse of Plato's Socrates." PhD diss., University of Guelph, 2013.
Kagan, Donald, and Gregory Viggiano, eds. *Men of Bronze: Hoplite Warfare in Ancient Greece*. Princeton, NJ: Princeton University Press, 2013.
Kelder, Jorrit. "A Great King at Mycenae: An Argument for the *Wanax* as Great King and the *Lawagetas* as Vassal Ruler." *Palamedes* 3 (2008): 49–74.
———. "Ahhiyawa and the World of the Great Kings. A Re-evaluation of Mycenean Political Structures," *Talanta* 44 (2012): 41–52.
———. "A Thousand Black Ships: Maritime Trade, Diplomatic Relations, and the Rise of Mycenae." In *Empires of the Sea: Maritime Power Networks in World History*, edited by R. Strootman, F. van den Eijnde, and R. van Wijk, 39–51. Leiden: Brill, 2019.
Kirk, Gregory. "Initiation, Extraction, and Transformation: What It Takes to Answer Socrates's Question." *Idealistic Studies* 45, no. 1 (2015): 103–123.
———. *The Pedagogy of Wisdom: An Interpretation of Plato's Theaetetus*. Evanston, IL: Northwestern University Press, 2015.
———. "Self-Knowledge and Ignorance in Plato's *Charmides*." *Ancient Philosophy* 36, no. 2 (2016): 303–320.

Kirkland, Sean D. *The Ontology of Socratic Questioning in Plato's Early Dialogues*. Albany: State University of New York Press, 2012.
Klein, Jakob. *A Commentary on Plato's Meno*. Chicago: University of Chicago Press, 1989.
Kurke, Leslie. *Coins, Bodies, Games, and Gold: The Politics of Meaning in Archaic Greece*. Princeton, NJ: Princeton University Press, 1999.
———. *The Traffic in Praise: Pindar and the Poetics of Social Economy*. Ithaca, NY: Cornell University Press, 1991.
Lacey, W. K. *The Family in Classical Greece*. Ithaca, NY: Cornell University Press, 1968.
Lambert, Laurence. *How Philosophy Became Socratic*. Chicago: University of Chicago Press, 2010.
Lane, Melissa. "Socrates and Plato: An Introduction." In *The Cambridge History of Greek and Roman Political Thought*, edited by Christopher Rowe and Malcolm Schofield, 155–163. Cambridge, UK: Cambridge University Press, 2000.
Leão, Delfim F., and Peter J. Rhodes. *The Laws of Solon: A New Edition with Introduction, Translation, and Commentary*. London: I. B. Tauris, 2016.
Liebert, Rana Saadi. "Pity and Disgust in Plato's *Republic*: The Case of Leontius." *Classical Philosophy* 108, no. 3 (2013): 179–201.
Livy. *The Early History of Rome: Books I–V*. Translated by Aubrey de Selincourt. Repr. ed. Harmondsworth, UK: Penguin, 2002.
Lysias. *Collected Works* (Loeb Classical Library, no. 244). Translated by W. R. M. Lamb. Cambridge, MA: Harvard University Press, 1930.
Macaré, Joe, Maya Schenwar, and Alana Yu-Ian Price. *Who Do You Serve, Who Do You Protect? Police Violence and Resistance in the United States*. Chicago: Haymarket Books, 2016.
McCoy, Marina Berzins. *Image and Argument in Plato's Republic*. Albany: State University of New York Press, 2020.
———. *Plato on the Rhetoric of Philosophers and Sophists*. Cambridge, UK: Cambridge University Press, 2008.
McGlew, James F. *Tyranny and Political Culture in Ancient Greece*. Ithaca, NY: Cornell University Press, 1993.
Meiksins Wood, Ellen. *Peasant-Citizen and Slave: The Foundations of Athenian Democracy*. London: Verso, 1988.
Merleau-Ponty, Maurice. *Phenomenology of Perception*. Translated by Colin Smith. London: Routledge, 1961.
Metcalf, Robert. *Philosophy as Agōn: A Study of Plato's Gorgias and Related Texts*. Evanston, IL: Northwestern University Press, 2018.
Middleton, Guy D. *The Collapse of Palatial Society in LBA Greece and the Postpalatial Period* (BAR International Series). Oxford: British Archaeological Reports, 2010.
Mintz, Avi I. "'*Chalepa Ta Kala*,' 'Fine Things Are Difficult': Socrates' Insights into the Psychology of Teaching and Learning." *Studies in Philosophy and Education* 29 (2010): 287–299.
Moore, J. M., trans. *Aristotle and Xenophon on Democracy and Oligarchy*. Berkeley: University of California Press, 2010.
Morris, Ian. *Burial and Ancient Society: The Rise of the Greek City-State*. Cambridge, UK: Cambridge University Press, 1987.
———. *Death-Ritual and Social Structure in Classical Antiquity*. Cambridge, UK: Cambridge University Press, 1992.

---. "Equality and the Origins of Greek Democracy." In Robinson, *Ancient Greek Democracy: Readings and Sources*, 45–73.
Morrow, Glenn. *Plato's Cretan City: A Historical Interpretation of the Laws*. Princeton, NJ: Princeton University Press, 1960.
Munn, Mark. "*Erōs* and the *Laws* in Historical Context." In Recco and Sanday, *Plato's Laws: Force and Truth in Politics*, 31–47.
---. *The Mother of the Gods, Athens, and the Tyranny of Asia: A Study of Sovereignty in Ancient Religion*. Berkeley: University of California Press, 2006.
---. *The School of History: Athens in the Age of Socrates*. Berkeley: University of California Press, 2000.
Nagy, Gregory. *The Best of the Achaeans: The Concept of the Hero in Archaic Greek Poetry*. Baltimore: Johns Hopkins University Press, 1979.
---. *Pindar's Homer: The Lyric Possession of an Epic Past*. Baltimore: Johns Hopkins University Press, 1990.
Nails, Debra. "The Dramatic Date of Plato's Republic." *The Classical Journal* 93, no. 4 (1998): 383–396.
---. *The People of Plato: A Prosopography of Plato and Other Socratics*. Indianapolis: Hackett, 2002.
Newell, Waller. *Tyranny: A New Interpretation*. Cambridge, UK: Cambridge University Press, 2014.
Nicholson, Graeme. "The Discourses of the Phaedrus." In Russon and Sallis, *Retracing the Platonic Text*, 19–31.
Nietzsche, Friedrich. *Beyond Good and Evil*. Translated by R. J. Hollingdale. Harmondsworth, UK: Penguin, 1993.
---. *The Genealogy of Morals: A Polemic*. Translated by Douglas Smith. Oxford: Oxford University Press, 2008.
North, Helen. *Sophrosyne: Self-Knowledge and Self-Restraint in Greek Literature*. Ithaca, NY: Cornell University Press, 1966.
Noutsopoulos, Thomas. "The Role of Money in Plato's *Republic*, Book I: A Materialistic Approach." *Historical Materialism* 23, no. 2 (2015): 131–156.
Ober, Josiah. *Mass and Elite in Democratic Athens: Rhetoric, Ideology, and the Power of the People*. Princeton, NJ: Princeton University Press, 1989.
Osborne, Robin. "The Economics and Politics of Slavery at Athens." In Robinson, *Ancient Greek Democracy: Readings and Sources*, 265–281.
Oyama, Susan. "The Lure of Immateriality in Accounts of Development and Evolution." In *Mattering: Feminism, Science, and Materialism*, edited by Victoria Pitts-Taylor, 91–103. New York: New York University Press, 2016.
Planeaux, Christopher. "The Date of Bendis' Entry into Attica." *Classical Journal* 96, no. 2 (2000–2001): 165–92.
Plato. *Complete Works*. Edited by John M. Cooper. Indianapolis: Hackett, 1997.
---. *The Laws of Plato*. Translated by Thomas L. Pangle. Chicago: University of Chicago Press, 1988.
---. *Opera*. Edited by J. Burnet. 5 vols. Oxford: Clarendon, 1900–1907.
---. *Phaedo*. Translated by Eva Brann, Peter Kalkavage, and Eric Salem. Newburyport, MA: Focus Philosophical Library, 1998.
---. *Phaedrus*. Translated by Stephen Scully. Newburyport, MA: Focus Philosophical Library, 2003.

———. *The Republic of Plato*. Edited by James Adam. 2 vols. Cambridge, UK: Cambridge University Press, 1926–1929.
———. *The Republic of Plato*. Translated by Allan Bloom. New York: HarperCollins, 1991.
Popper, Karl. *The Open Society and Its Enemies*. Vol. 1, *The Spell of Plato*. London: George Routledge, 1945.
Raaflaub, Kurt A. Foreword to *Aristotle and Xenophon on Democracy and Oligarchy*. Translated by J. M. Moore, 3–7.
———. "Homer and the Beginning of Political Thought in Greece." In Robinson, *Ancient Greek Democracy: Readings and Sources*, 28–40.
———. "Homer to Solon. The Rise of the 'Polis.' The Written Sources." In *Polis: An Introduction to the Ancient Greek City-State*, edited by Mogens Herman Hansen, 41–105. Copenhagen: Royal Danish Society of Sciences and Letters, 1993.
Rabinoff, Eve. *Perception in Aristotle's Ethics*. Evanston, IL: Northwestern University Press, 2018.
Recco, Gregory. *Athens Victorious: Democracy in Plato's Republic*. Lanham MD: Rowman and Littlefield, 2008.
———, and Eric Sanday, eds. *Plato's Laws: Force and Truth in Politics*. Bloomington: Indiana University Press, 2013.
Reid, Heather. "Performing Virtue: Athletics and Mimesis in Platonic Education." In *Politics and Performance in Western Greece: Essays on the Hellenic Heritage of Sicily and Southern Italy*, edited by Heather L. Reid, Davide Tanasi, and Susi Kimbell, 260–271. Syracuse, NY: Parnassos Press, 2017.
Robinson, Eric W. *Ancient Greek Democracy: Readings and Sources*. Malden, MA: Blackwell, 2004.
———. *Democracy Beyond Athens: Popular Government in the Greek Classical Age*. Cambridge, UK: Cambridge University Press, 2011.
———. *The First Democracies: Early Popular Government Outside Athens*. Stuttgart: Franz Steiner Verlag, 1997.
Roochnik, David. *Beautiful City: The Dialectical Character of Plato's 'Republic.'* Ithaca, NY: Cornell University Press, 2003.
Rothleder, Dianne. *Fraught Decisions in Plato and Shakespeare*. Lanham, MD: Rowman and Littlefield, 2020.
Russon, John. "Aristotle's Animative Epistemology." *Idealistic Studies* 25, no. 3 (1995): 241–253.
———. "Education in Plato's *Laws*." In Recco and Sanday, *Plato's Laws: Force and Truth in Politics*, 60–74.
———. "Emotional Subjects: Mood and Articulation in Hegel's *Philosophy of Mind*." *International Philosophical Quarterly* 49, no. 1 (2009): 41–52.
———. "*Eros* and Education: Plato's Transformative Epistemology." *Laval Théologique et Philosophique* 56, no. 1 (2000): 113–125.
———. "*Erōs* and *Eris*: Love and Strife in Ancient Greek Thought and Culture." In *A Companion to Ancient Philosophy*, edited by Sean Kirkland and Eric Sanday, 83–95. Evanston, IL: Northwestern University Press, 2018.
———. "Expressing Dwelling: Dewey and Hegel on Art as Cultural Self-Articulation." *Contemporary Pragmatism* 12, no. 1 (2015): 38–58.
———. "Hermeneutics and Plato's *'Ion.'*" *Clio* 24, no. 4 (1995): 399–418.
———. "Just Reading: The Nature of the Platonic Text." In Russon and Sallis, *Retracing the Platonic Text*, ix–xix.

———. "Personality as Equilibrium: Fragility and Plasticity in (Inter-)Personal Identity." *Phenomenology and the Cognitive Sciences* 16 (2017): 623–635.
———. "Plato's Republic." YouTube. https://www.youtube.com/playlist?list=PLZyk__e49-Cv86nHOUeQWzoKI8U9VkWni.
———. "Self-Consciousness and the Tradition in Aristotle's Psychology." *Laval Théologique et Philosophique* 52, no. 3 (1996): 777–803.
———. *Sites of Exposure: Art, Politics, and the Nature of Experience.* Bloomington: Indiana University Press, 2017.
———. "The (Childish) Nature of the Soul in Plato's *Apology*." In Fagan and Russon, *Re-examining Socrates in the Apology*, 191–205.
———. "The Elements of Everyday Life: Three Lessons from Ancient Greece." *Philosophy in the Contemporary World* 13, no. 2 (2006): 84–90.
———. "To Account for the Appearances: Phenomenology and Existential Change in Aristotle and Plato." *Journal of the British Society for Phenomenology* 52 (2021): 155–68.
———. "We Sense That They Strive: How to Read (the Theory of the Forms)." In Russon and Sallis, *Retracing the Platonic Text*, 70–84.
———. "Why Sexuality Matters." In *Desire, Love, and Identity: Philosophy of Sex and Love*, edited by Gary Foster, 38–48. Toronto: Oxford University Press, 2017.
———, and Patricia Fagan. "Introduction: Socrates Examined." In Fagan and Russon, *Reexamining Socrates in the Apology*, xiii–xxiv.
———, and John Sallis, eds. *Retracing the Platonic Text.* Evanston, IL: Northwestern University Press, 2000.
Sachs, David. "A Fallacy in Plato's Republic." *Philosophical Review* 72, no. 2 (1963): 141–158.
Sallis, John. *Being and Logos: Reading the Platonic Dialogues.* 3rd ed. Bloomington: Indiana University Press, 1996.
Sanday, Eric. "Philosophy as the Practice of Musical Inheritance: Book II of Plato's *Republic*." *Epoché* 11, no. 2 (2007): 305–317.
Schaps, David M. *The Invention of Coinage and the Monetization of Ancient Greece.* Ann Arbor: University of Michigan Press, 2003.
Seaford, Richard. *Money and the Early Greek Mind: Homer, Philosophy, Tragedy.* Cambridge, UK: Cambridge University Press, 2004.
———. *Reciprocity and Ritual: Homer and Tragedy in the Developing City-State.* Oxford: Clarendon Press, 1994.
Schevill, Ferdinand. *Medieval and Renaissance Florence.* 2 vols. New York: Harper & Row, 1961.
Schmidt, Dennis J. *On Germans and Other Greeks: Tragedy and Ethical Life.* Bloomington: Indiana University Press, 2001.
Smith, Adam. *The Theory of the Moral Sentiments.* Glasgow: Liberty Classics, 1982.
———. *The Wealth of Nations.* New York: Modern Library, 1984.
Sophocles. *Antigone.* Translated by Richmond Lattimore. In *Greek Tragedies*, vol. 1. Edited by David Grene. Chicago: University of Chicago Press, 1992.
Sparshott, Francis. "An Argument for Thrasymachus." *Apeiron* 21, no. 1 (1988): 55–68.
———. "Socrates and Thrasymachus." *Monist* 50, no. 3 (1966): 421–459.
———. *Taking Life Seriously: A Study of the Argument of the Nicomachean Ethics.* Toronto: University of Toronto Press, 1994.
Stanton, G. R. *Athenian Politics c. 800–500 BC: A Sourcebook.* New York: Routledge, 1990.

Taylor, C. C. W., and Mi-Kyoung Lee. "The Sophists." In *The Stanford Encyclopedia of Philosophy* (Fall 2020 Edition), edited by Edward N. Zalta. https://plato.stanford.edu/archives/fall2020/entries/sophists/.
Thomas, Carol G., and Craig Conant. *Citadel to City-State: The Transformation of Greece, 1200–700 B.C.E.* Bloomington: Indiana University Press, 1999.
Thucydides. *History of the Peloponnesian War.* Translated by Rex Warner. Harmondsworth, UK: Penguin, 1974.
Townsend, Mary. *The Woman Question in Plato's Republic.* Lanham MD: Lexington Books, 2019.
Transparency International. *Global Corruption Barometer.* Berlin: Transparency International, 2017.
Von Reden, Sitta. *Money in Classical Antiquity.* Cambridge, UK: Cambridge University Press, 2010.
Wallace, R. W. "The Sophists in Athens." In *Democracy, Empire, and the Arts in Fifth-Century Athens*, edited by Deborah Boedeker and Kurt Raaflaub, 203–222. Cambridge, MA: Harvard University Press, 1998.
Walsh, John. "The Dramatic Dates of Plato's *Protagoras* and the Lesson of *Arete*." *Classical Quarterly* 34, no. 1 (1984): 101–106.
Walsh, W. H. "Plato and the Philosophy of History: History and Theory in the *Republic*." *History and Theory* 2, no. 1 (1962): 3–16.
Wilson, Robert A., ed. *Species: New Interdisciplinary Essays.* Cambridge, MA: MIT Press, 1999.
Woodiwiss, Michael. *Organized Crime and American Power: A History.* Toronto: University of Toronto Press, 2001.
Xenophon. *Memorabilia.* Translated by Amy L. Bonnette. Ithaca, NY: Cornell University Press, 1994.
———. "*Politeia* of the Spartans." In *Aristotle and Xenophon on Democracy and Oligarchy*, translated by J. M. Moore.
———. *The Shorter Socratic Writings: "Apology of Socrates to the Jury," "Oeconomicus," and "Symposium,"* edited by Robert C. Bartlett. Ithaca, NY: Cornell University Press, 1996.
Zuckert, Catherine. *Plato's Philosophers: The Coherence of the Dialogues.* Chicago: University of Chicago Press, 2012.
———. "On the Implications of Human Mortality: Legislation, Education, and Philosophy in Book 9 of Plato's *Laws*." In Recco and Sanday, *Plato's Laws: Force and Truth in Politics*, 169–188.

INDEX OF SUBJECTS

Adeimantus, 9, 28, 33, 55, 172
Alcibiades, 160, 170, 172
Anytus, 160
Apology, 32, 44–45, 98–102, 135, 146, 160
Aristophanes, 97–98
Aristotle: on anger and shame, 152; being qua being, 107; on Cleisthenes, 85; cognition of first principles, 104; eternity of species, 119; human as animal with *logos*, 6, 35; on money, 49; nature of *polis*, 35, 65; on persuading the *pathē*, 157; relation of law and virtue, 180; relation of *technē* and *empeiria*, 37–38, 42, 44; on Solon's historical context, 80; virtue of *megaloprepeia*, 68
Athens: Aristophanes's critique of, 97–98; emergence of democracy in, 80–81; and death of Socrates, 190; and Solon, 71–74, 80
Augustine, 5, 176

Bacchylides, 68
beauty, 120–29
being, 104, 112–14, 128, 131, 135, 155

Callicles, 160
cave (image), 106, 182
Cephalus, 48–49, 172
Charmides, 101, 105, 165–68, 169–70, 172
Charmides, 160, 165–68, 169–70, 171, 172
Cleisthenes, 80, 85
Clouds, 97–98, 101–2, 135, 146, 170
courage: defined, 159–60; equated with virtue, 65, 67; and gymnastic, 179
Crete, 66–67
Critias, 165–68, 170, 171
Crito, 32, 160, 179–80

debt: in *Clouds*, 98; and *logos*, 56–57; in gift economy, 74; in money-economy, 74, 76–77; often unacknowledged, 37; unacknowledged in money, 50–51; unacknowledged in sophistry, 135–37; unacknowledged in technology, 47
democracy: ambiguity of, 85; central study of, 79–85; defined, 81–82; emergence of, 2; emergence in Athens, 80–81; and ideal of knowledge, 95; and *logos*, 16, 82, 85, 86, 190; relation to guardians, 31, 82; virtue and justice possible in, 83
desire (*epithumia*), 151–52, 157, 161–64, 173–74, 179, 181–82. See also *Erōs*
dialogue: as form of Plato's writing, 4, 7–10; and nature of rationality, 5, 10
Dianoia, 115, 118, 154
Diotima, 99, 124–28
divided line (image), 16, 117–19, 130
division of labor, 28, 29, 75–76
division of soul, 149–155

education: ambivalence of, 43–44; cave as image of, 104; and change of desire, 161; into distinction of nature and artifice, 25; and *erōs*, 124–27; as human need, 42, 156; and learning how, 145; music and gymnastic in, 177–82; personally transformative nature of, 106–7; of the philosopher, 146–47, 169–72, 173; relies on *logoi*, 42–44, 54–55, 148; and virtue, 155–56, 177–79
Eidē, 103, 109–12, 116–17, 119–20, 121–22, 130
Empeiria: defined, 37–38; as "earning," 50; forgotten in culture, 43, 47; with respect to *psuchē*, 105
epinician poetry, 67–68
equality, 108–9
erōs, 123–28
Euthydemus, 133–34, 136

freedom, 30, 31, 33, 81–84, 152

gift economy, 64, 68, 72–73, 78
Glaucon, 148–50, 170, 172, 174–75
good: compared to mathematics, 120–22; in democracy, 81; desire to be good, 168; focal study of, 129–34; goal of human life, 16; in Homeric society, 64, 65; as immanent norm, 40, 131; inherent vs. instrumental, 68; and *logos*, 82–83, 99–100; in money-economy, 77; orients the Divided Line, 115; in the *Phaedo*, 129–131; relation to honor, 83
Gorgias, 37–38, 42, 97, 172
Gorgias, 96–97, 136, 172
guardians: problem of, 32–33, 36, 65, 77, 190; role of, 30; and Sparta, 67
gymnastic, 178–82

Heraclitus, 3
Hesiod, 3–4
history (of Greece): Bronze Age society, 64; class warfare in, 79–80; cultural revolution in, 1–2, 14, 189; emergence of money-economy, 48–49; emergence of *polis*, 27, 65–66; portrayal in *Laws*, 52–53; Solon and emergence of democracy in Athens, 71–74, 80–81
Homer: and Bronze Age society, 63–64; *epos* contrasted with *epinikia*, 68; and heroic code, 64–65; Homeric society as timocracy, 64–65, 68; theme of debt in, 74
honor: ambivalence of, 65–67, 68–69; and debt, 74; as motive force, 83; relation to good, 83; and social self-interpretation, 62; society of, 63–70

inheritance: and capacity for knowing, 137; contrasted with earning, 49–50; historical, 79; and *logos*, 56; in technology, 47

justice: central theme of *Republic*, 1; and debt, 74; in democracy, 81, 83, 85; Glaucon's conflict about, 148–49; in Homeric society, 64–65; justice and law, 55–56; and the problem of the guardians, 34; in Protagoras's speech, 7

knowledge: as analyzed with the Divided Line, 103–34; intrinsic connection to democracy, 95; personally and socially ambivalent, 95; *technē* as basic form of, 37

Laches, 100
law: and justice, 55–56; and the *polis*, 52–53; and virtue, 180; written vs. unwritten, 180
Laws, 52–53, 65, 162, 165, 177–78, 181
logismos, 118, 153, 154, 157, 158, 160, 164, 168, 174
logos: as ability to be persuaded, 147–48; as ability to take account, 6, 99, 102; central focus of this study, 5, 14–15, 26; as concrete rationality, 5; definitive of human condition, 7, 82, 99, 145, 156, 189, 192; and democracy, 82, 85, 86; an existential matter, 134–35; and the good, 133–34; in *Protagoras*, 6–7; range of meanings of, 5–6; and recognition of being, 114; and separation of surface from substance, 36, 42–43, 47, 52, 56–57, 82, 103, 123–24, 158, 189; and Socrates's practice, 100–1
Lycurgus, 65–66
Lysis, 41

mathematics, 108–9, 119–20, 128
megaloprepeia, 68
mimēsis, 6, 9, 128
misology, 175–76
moderation, 164–68, 178–79
money: central study of, 44–51; defined, 48–49; and democracy, 16; emergence of money-economy in Greece, 2, 14, 70–71; impact of, 54–56; intersection of *polis* and *technē*, 26; money-economy, 48, 72–73
music, 177–82

nature: ambivalent relation to humanity, 26, 147, 156–57; vs. artifice, 25
nous, 40, 115, 118

oikos: in Homeric society, 64; vs. money, 55–56; vs. *polis*, 52–53
"Old Oligarch," 67
oligarchy: ambivalence of, 71–72; central study of, 70–79; defined, 71; Socrates's critique of, 72, 75, 76–79

Parmenides, 3–4, 13, 172
Paul (Saint), 153–54
Peisistratus, 84–85

persuasion: and beauty, 123; central study of, 147–56; in music and gymnastic, 18; and philosophy, 5
Phaedo, 40, 43, 104–5, 107–10, 113, 116–19, 120–21, 129–31, 136, 167–68, 175–76
Phaedrus, 43, 100–1, 123–28
philosophy: as fulfillment of human life, 16; institutionalized form as sophistry, 5, 137; intimate relation to sophistry, 97, 102, 134–35; nature of, 3–5; orientation to the good, 16; vs. poetry, 4–5; requires education, 145
Pindar, 68
Plato: character of authorship, 4, 9, 11; Fagan as exemplary of method for reading, 13; originator of philosophy as we know it, 3–4; prejudices about, 2
Polemarchus, 39–40, 49, 74, 172
polis: ambiguous usage of term, 28; as anti-aristocratic environment, 68; central study of, 27–37; emergence of, 2; emerges from need, 28; fully developed form, 56; and impartiality, 53; and law, 52–53; like and unlike nature, 29–30, 33, 35–37; vs. *oikos*, 52–53, 65; topic of Books II and VIII of *Republic*, 26, 28; volatile character in democracy, 83–85
Protagoras, 5–6, 42, 67–68, 84, 97, 136, 137, 170
Protagoras, 5–6, 42, 96–97, 136, 170

recollection (*anamnēsis*), 108–9, 145
Republic: date of, 8; emergence of *polis* as context of, 2, 14, 95; emergence of *polis* as framing issue, 26; justice and human nature as topic of, 1; justice as defining question, 27; method for interpreting, 8–12; reflection on the distinctive realities of the human environment, 26; structure of, 7–11
rhetoric: of aristocratic institutions, 68; as deceitful, 4–5; intrinsic to philosophy, 5; in relation to music and gymnastic, 180–81; and *technē*, 37; and tyrannical populism, 85, 190

sex. See *Erōs*
shadows, 115–17
Simonides, 39–40, 67–68

Solon, 71–74, 80
Sophist, 136
sophistry: confuses relative and absolute, 16; dishonest about debt, 135–37; forms of, 134–37; intimate relation to philosophy, 97, 102, 134–35; permanent threat, 16–17; and "the public," 181
sophists: historical reality of, 96–97; philosophy opposed to, 4
soul (*psuchē*): capacity to grasp being, 104, 114, 117, 119; "division of," 17; and the good, 129; as inner life, 105; pregnancy in soul, 126–27; "separation of soul from body," 104–5
Sparta, 64, 66, 68–70
spirit (*thumos*), 32, 152–54, 157, 159–60, 164, 173–74, 179, 181–82
Symposium, 99, 124–28, 160, 172

technē: abuse of, 46–47; as care, 39–41, 45–46; central study of, 37–44; defined, 38; ontologically analogous to *polis*, 26; value of, 53–54
Theaetetus, 136, 172
Theaetetus, 160, 172
Thrasymachus, 34, 36, 38–39, 45–46, 148–49, 160–172
Thucydides, 3, 42, 51
timocracy: ambivalence of, 68; central study of, 63–70; defined, 64; and Homeric society, 64–65, 68; and Sparta and Crete, 66–67, 68
turning around (*periagōgē*): and education, 107, 119; in relation to the good, 133; in relation to mathematics and beauty, 120–29; psychological obstacles to, 173–74
tyranny: permanent threat, 16–17; pursuit of, 168, 172; relation to democracy, 84–85
Tyrtaeus, 67

virtue: athletic, 68; central study of, 156–68; and play, 177–79; relative vs. absolute, 158–59, 160–61, 163–64, 168; and upbringing, 177

wisdom: in the *Apology*, 98–99; in democracy, 82–84; virtue of, 158–59
writing, 42, 51–54

Xenophon, 66–67, 69

INDEX OF PASSAGES

I.327a, 7
I.327b, 8
I.327c, 185n15
I.330a–b, 50
I.330b–c, 50, 137
I.330c, 71
I.331b–c, 74
I.331e, 39, 74
I.332c–334b, 59n31, 59n36
I.332c, 40
I.335b, 40
I.336b–354c, 148
I.336b, 187n35
I.340a–c, 184n4
I.340e, 38
I.341c, 39, 48
I.342b, 39
I.342e, 38
I.343a–b, 45
I.343b, 40
I.345b–347a, 40
I.352d–353e, 40
I.354a, 8

II.357a–b, 148
II.357b–d, 88n20
II.358c–d, 149
II.365a–367a, 73n4
II.368c, 141n26
II.368e, 141n26
II.369b–372d, 28
II.369b–c, 28
II.369b, 28
II.369c, 28–29, 55
II.369d–370e, 29
II.369d–370c, 171
II.369d, 45
II.369e, 55
II.370a–c, 75–76
II.370a, 90n43

II.370c, 29
II.370e–373d, 29
II.370e–371b, 54
II.371d–e, 56
II.371e–372a, 55
II.372c–d, 29
II.372d–375d, 28
II.372e–373a, 56
II.372e, 28, 29, 73n3
II.373d–375d, 29
II.374a, 32
II.374b–c, 31
II.374c–e, 31
II.374e, 32
II.375a–b, 32, 184n7, 187n23
II.375b–d, 32
II.376d–IV.427c, 28

III.389a, 57n4
III.394b–398b, 9
III.394d, 9
III.395b, 30, 33
III.395d, 178
III.398a–b, 9
III.401d, 178
III.402d–403c, 143n50
III.403a, 143n50, 178–79
III.406e, 90n43
III.409c, 188n50
III.410b, 179
III.410d, 185n13
III.412c–414b, 30

IV.419a, 33
IV.424b–d, 188n50
IV.427c, 57n4
IV.427e, 186n20
IV.428b, 158
IV.430b, 159
IV.430e, 163, 185n16

IV.431a, 154
IV.432d, 141n26
IV.433a–d, 90n43
IV.433b, 186n20
IV.434c, 90n43
IV.434e, 141n26
IV.435c, 17
IV.436d–e, 185n16
IV.437b–c, 151
IV.439e–440b, 153
IV.439e, 185n14
IV.440c, 184 n. 7, 187n21
IV.441e, 186n20

V.458d, 57n3
V.462a–e, 78
V.462c–d, 154
V.473d, 34
V.474d–475a, 125
V.475e–476d, 110–11
V.476a, 111
V.477c–d, 112
V.477c, 112

VI.485b–487a, 146
VI.490a–c, 146
VI.490a, 146, 168
VI.490c, 146
VI.491b–c, 146–47
VI.492a–494a, 181
VI.494b–c, 169
VI.494c–d, 171
VI.494d, 173
VI.497d, 17
VI.504c, 108
VI.505d–e, 129
VI.507d–e, 132
VI.508b–c, 132
VI.509b, 132
VI.509d–511e, 115
VI.509d–510a, 115
VI.509d, 119, 141n28

VI.510a, 116
VI.510d–e, 108
VI.510d, 120

VII.514a–d, 106
VII.514a, 106
VII.515d–e, 107
VII.516c–d, 106
VII.516e–517a, 182
VII.518c–d, 106, 142n39
VII.522e–523a, 119
VII.523a–c, 142n43
VII.533d, 115
VII.533e–534a, 115
VII.537e–539d, 188n43

VIII.544c, 80, 87n12
VIII.545c, 67
VIII.547c, 69
VIII.547d, 69
VIII.548a–b, 70
VIII.550c–d, 70
VIII.550d, 70
VIII.551a, 62
VIII.551b, 71
VIII.551c, 72
VIII.551d, 75, 77, 79
VIII.552a, 75, 76
VIII.553c–d, 77
VIII.555b–c, 76–77
VIII.555c, 57
VIII.555d–556a, 76–77
VIII.557a–b, 81
VIII.557a, 81
VIII.558d–559c, 57n3
VIII.560a, 80
VIII.562b, 81, 82
VIII.562c, 82
VIII.563b–d, 91n53
VIII.586a–d, 9

X.607b, 18n3

JOHN RUSSON is Professor of Philosophy at the University of Guelph and Director of the Toronto Summer Seminar in Philosophy. He is author of *Sites of Exposure: Art, Politics, and the Nature of Experience* and *Infinite Phenomenology: The Lessons of Hegel's Science of Experience*. He also has many accessible lectures on philosophy available on YouTube (https://www.youtube.com/channel/UCKxB8T8BQl6Ib3eOKaOlA5g).

www.ingramcontent.com/pod-product-compliance
Lightning Source LLC
Chambersburg PA
CBHW030622230426
43661CB00053B/2103